WORD PAINTING

REVISED EDITION

WORD REVISED EDITION
PAINTING

THE FINE ART OF
WRITING DESCRIPTIVELY

REBECCA McCLANAHAN

WD

WRITER'S DIGEST
BOOKS

WritersDigest.*com*
Cincinnati, Ohio

For more resources for writers, visit www.writersdigest.com.

18 17 16 15 14   5 4 3 2 1

Distributed in Canada by Fraser Direct
100 Armstrong Avenue
Georgetown, Ontario, Canada L7G 5S4
Tel: (905) 877-4411

Distributed in the U.K. and Europe by F+W Media International
Brunel House, Newton Abbot, Devon, TQ12 4PU, England
Tel: (+44) 1626-323200, Fax: (+44) 1626-323319
E-mail: postmaster@davidandcharles.co.uk

Distributed in Australia by Capricorn Link
P.O. Box 704, Windsor, NSW 2756 Australia
Tel: (02) 4577-3555

ISBN-13: 978-1-59963-868-3

Edited by Rachel Randall
Designed by Claudean Wheeler
Cover photo by fottoo/Fotolia.com
Production coordinated by Debbie Thomas
Cover painting by Edouard Manet (1832–1883), "Claude Monet and His Wife in the Floating Studio." Neue Pinakothek, Munich, Germany.

a content + ecommerce company

Contents

Introduction 1

CHAPTER ONE:
What Is Description? 4

CHAPTER TWO:
The Eye of the Beholder 13

CHAPTER THREE:
From Eye to Word: The Description 38

CHAPTER FOUR:
The Nose and Mouth and Hand and Ear of the Beholder 66

CHAPTER FIVE:
Figuratively Speaking: A "Perception of Resemblances" 91

CHAPTER SIX:
Bringing Characters to Life Through Description 123

CHAPTER SEVEN:
The Eye of the Teller: How Point of View Affects Description 152

CHAPTER EIGHT:
The Story Takes Its Place: Descriptions of Setting 188

CHAPTER NINE:
Plot and Pace: How Description Shapes the Narrative Line 212

CHAPTER TEN:
The Big Picture 235

End Notes, Toward a Beginning 259
Index 261

For my father,
who showed me the holiness of detail,

and my mother,
whose all-accepting eye takes in the big picture

ABOUT THE AUTHOR

Rebecca McClanahan has published ten books—of poetry, essays, writing in-struction, and memoir—most recently *The Tribal Knot: A Memoir of Family, Community, and a Century of Change*. Her work has appeared in *Best Amer-ican Essays*, *Best American Poetry*, *The Georgia Review*, *The Kenyon Review*, *The Gettysburg Review*, *The Sun*, and numerous anthologies. McClanahan's awards include the Wood Prize from *Poetry*, a Pushcart Prize in fiction, the Carter Prize for the Essay, the Glasgow Award in nonfiction, literary fellow-ships from the New York Foundation for the Arts and the North Carolina Arts Council, and a Governor's Award for Excellence in Education. She cur-rently lives in Charlotte, North Carolina, and teaches in the MFA programs of Rainier Writing Workshop and Queens University.

Introduction

In 1998, when the editors of Writer's Digest Books approached me about writing a book on description, I responded the way I respond to all new challenges: *Yes. No. Well, I'll think about it. Yes* is the child in me, taking my seat on the roller coaster that will whiplash me into the tunnel, up the rickety mountain, and around the next exhilarating loop. *No* is the adult, walking away from the ticket booth: What if the car derails? Does my insurance cover roller coasters? I suspect that most writers hear both these voices, often simultaneously, each time they put pen to paper. And I suspect that every book is a duet of opposing voices attempting some semblance of harmony.

Finally, *I'll think about it* won out. When I thought about it, I realized I was being offered the chance to combine three of my primary passions: writing, reading, and teaching. How could I refuse?

As a writer, I know the daily struggle of describing the world around me and the world that dwells only in my head; my recycling bin holds evidence of the struggle. I also know the occasional click of the lock, the satisfaction of words slipping into place, and those few unspoiled seconds when the images in the developing tray coalesce. Yes, there's the barn in all its rotting splendor. There's the lumpy boy slicking back his cowlick and approaching the long-legged girl.

As a reader, I know which descriptions move me to laughter, terror, or unwept tears. I can point to those I wish I had written. *Wait*, I say, running alongside you with a book in my hand. *Listen to this one. You've got to hear this!*

And as a teacher, I am privileged to share with students what I've learned about description from writers I admire and what I continue to learn through my own writing process.

Since *Word Painting* grew from these three passions, the book combines direct instruction with personal reflections on the reading and writing process. I set forth basic guidelines for effective description and suggest specific writing exercises. (Some exercises are embedded within the text; others appear at the end of each chapter.) Along the way, I point out some of my favorite passages from novels, stories, poems, and nonfiction works, suggesting ways to use these passages as models for our writing. Occasionally I take you behind the scenes of my own ongoing journey to write effective descriptions.

The book is organized around three main concepts: *eye, word,* and *story.* After establishing what we mean by *description* and summarizing its basic elements, I move directly into a discussion of the writer as the beholding eye. Like painters, writers are the receptors of sensations from the real world and the world of the imagination, and effective description demands that we sharpen our instruments of perception. So in the first few chapters, I suggest practical ways to train our attention on the real world and engage the eye of imagination.

As I move from *eye* to *word,* I consider how to render our subjects clearly, accurately, and imaginatively. Although engaging the senses is an important component of word painting, it takes us only so far; we must also describe those sensory details in a fresh way, by avoiding clichés and employing action-based description and effective figures of speech. Fresh description also requires attention to the musical qualities of language. The *word* sections of the book deal with shaping descriptions that are accurate, sensory, imaginative, and musical.

Finally, moving from *eye* and *word* into *story*, I explore how description contributes to the larger story, poem, or nonfiction piece. How do we select the revealing detail, spatially organize our descriptions, and weave description into the narrative arc? How do we use description to develop believable characters and settings, establish point of view, modulate tension, and move the plot along? How can description reveal our work's theme and suggest the prevailing tone, mood, or feeling? These are the concerns that dominate the *story* sections of the book.

Fifteen years have passed since *Word Painting* was first published in 1999, and I am grateful to the editors of Writer's Digest Books for the opportunity to revise and expand the book for this second edition, which includes many additional passages of instruction and literary examples along with twenty-five new writing exercises. I am grateful to every writer whose descriptions have challenged me to see the world in new ways, and to every writing teacher who encouraged me—and even those who did not. I am grateful also to the thousands of students with whom I have worked, the five-year-olds and the eighty-five-year-olds, the beginners and the experts, and most of all, the continuers. And to readers like you, who, with every page you turn in this book, complete the painting I've begun.

CHAPTER ONE

What Is Description?

If I were fully conscious of my surroundings at this moment, I would describe the light through the window, the way it searches out the apples in the glass bowl, buffing them to an unnatural sheen. I bought them for their fragrance, not their freshness, so even if you were to close your eyes, you'd know you were in the presence of apples. You would smell the heavy softening, the sweet rotting where apple ends and cider begins.

Or I would tell you how the sofa cushion feels beneath my bare neck—rough and scratchy, a bit lumpy. A few minutes ago, before I lay down, I pounded the cushion with my fist to loosen the foam stuffing, and now it's fighting back. If I were noticing such things right now, I might even describe the pinprick tingling in my toes (a result of my feet being slung over the sofa back) and the stupefying sensation of willing the toes to move, as if they belonged to a stranger.

If you were sitting in the chair beside me, you'd probably notice the sounds filling the open window—the pneumatic wheeze as a bus rounds the corner, a jay's raspy squawk, the rhythmic *clackclackclack* of a roller skate counting each sidewalk seam. You might look in my direction, start to speak, then, noticing the open book in my hands, think better of it. Think better of stirring a reader from the world of her book. I might bolt, like anyone shaken too suddenly from a dream.

The place I've entered is what John Gardner, in his classic book *The Art of Fiction*, calls the fictional dream. Because the writer has done her job, the world of the book I am reading has become, for the moment at least, more real than the world at my elbow. Books this good should carry a warning: *Your quiche might burn, your child might escape his playpen, the morning glory vine might strangle your roses, and you'll never know.*

As a reader, my job is not to worry how the writer accomplishes her task. My job is to turn the pages, to enter the dream and remain there until someone, or something, wakes me. Most often that something is the work that awaits me at my desk. The words I've not yet written lure me, like silver trout flashing their fins. If only I could net them. If only I could create the kind of dream a reader would willingly enter.

Fiction writers aren't the only ones who create this dream. Poets do it, too, and essayists and memoirists and biographers and travel writers and nature writers and journalists and letter writers and diarists. Even, at times, business writers and those who draft advertising copy—once I nearly drowned in a catalog description of a blue gauze dress.

What lures me into these writers' worlds is, in part, the power of their descriptions. This is no small gift, no mere ornamental flourish. Description is not, as one of my students once called it, "all that flowery stuff." Or, if description *is* the flowering, it is also the root and stem of effective writing. Although literary works vary widely, almost all writers employ description and can benefit from increasing their descriptive powers.

The afternoon sun has moved. Now it stripes the wall rather than the shiny apples. My toes have stopped tingling. I close the book, grab an apple from the bowl, and walk across the living room, down the fourteen smoothly varnished steps that lead into my study. I'm fully awake now. No longer a reader adrift in the fictional dream, I've washed ashore, stunned and reeling. I blink my eyes. Yes, it's all coming back now. The oak desk, the ink-splotched blotter, the window, the empty page. My ballpoint is cocked and loaded. I pick it up and begin.

THE BASICS OF DESCRIPTION

What do we mean by *description*? Perhaps no word is more commonly used in discussions of reading and writing. As writers, we struggle over *descriptive* passages. As readers, we close the cover on books that fail to accurately *describe* our world or the world of the imagination. As teachers or editors, we write in the margin "I can't visualize the character. Can you *describe* him?" or "I'm just not situated in the barber shop. Maybe if you *described* it more clearly …" But what do we really mean? What are we asking for?

In the fields of science, linguistics, grammar, and mathematics, description concerns itself with the study of things *as they exist*, with bringing forth the attributes of subjects rather than simply explaining or labeling them. In literature, description refers to the language used to bring these attributes to the reader's mind. Description is an attempt to present as directly as possible the qualities of a person, place, object, or event. When we describe, we make sense impressions, attempting through language to represent reality. Description is, in effect, *word painting*.

Description, of course, is only one of the four traditional discourse modes; exposition, argumentation, and narration are the other legs on which literary work stands. Exposition supplies background information, argumentation presents reasons and evidence, and narration supplies the storyline, leaving description to paint the word pictures.

These are helpful concepts in theory. The problem is, no literary work exists *in theory*. It lives and breathes only *in practice*, as it unfolds on the page. In the real world of writing, description cannot be totally separated from exposition, argumentation, and narration. Sometimes description supplies information. Sometimes it moves the plot along. Sometimes it convinces and persuades. Although a theorist may assert that exposition, argumentation, narration, and description are discrete elements, a practicing writer knows that they are often inextricably linked, working together to shape the poem, story, or nonfiction piece.

Given the complex relationships among the literary modes, perhaps the best way to fully define description is by considering what it is *not*.

- Description is not, as we've already pointed out, "all that flowery stuff." It isn't an embellishment, something we stitch to the top of our writing to make it more presentable.
- Description isn't optional. The success of fiction, and most poetry and nonfiction, depends in part on description's image-making power.
- Description doesn't always mean detailing how something *looks*. (One of the best descriptions I've ever read was written by a blind child.) Evocative and memorable description is rooted not only in visual detail but also in the smells, tastes, textures, and sounds of our world.
- Description doesn't begin on the page. It begins in the eye and ear and mouth and nose and hand of the beholder. Careful and imaginative observation may well be the most essential task of any writer.
- Description is not a way to hide from the truth. The world isn't always pretty, and describing our world honestly sometimes requires facing difficult, even ugly, subjects.
- Writing descriptively doesn't always mean writing gracefully. Description won't necessarily make our writing more refined, polished, or poetic. Some descriptions demand uneven syntax and plainspoken, blunt prose. Jagged, even. Fragments, too: Slice of chin. Buzz saw.
- Description doesn't always require a bigger vocabulary. In terms of word painting, *house* is probably a better choice than *domicile*, a *horse* is easier to visualize than an *equine mammal*, and *red blood* is brighter than *the sanguine flow of bodily fluids*.
- Writing descriptively doesn't necessitate writing *more*. Description isn't a steroid, something to make our language bigger and stronger, nor is it an additive promising more miles to the literary gallon. Sometimes writing descriptively means writing *less*. Our 300-word description of the wedding cake in chapter four might need to lose 200 words; it may need to disappear altogether.

- Description rarely stands alone. Most description exists as part of a larger work of poetry or prose, seamlessly intertwined with other literary elements. Description isn't something we simply insert, block style, into passages of narration, argumentation, or exposition. Yes, sometimes we write *passages* of description. But *passage* suggests a channel, a movement from one place to another; it implies that we're going somewhere. That *somewhere* is the story, nonfiction work, or poem.

WHAT MAKES DESCRIPTION EFFECTIVE?

For as long as writers and speakers have been shaping discourse, they have debated the question of what makes for good description. In Book III of *Rhetoric*, penned more than two thousand years ago, Aristotle discusses several techniques for calling forth the qualities of an object or a scene. Although his suggestions are aimed primarily at orators of persuasive rhetoric, they apply to writers as well. Aristotle's treatise is not an exhaustive one, nor should it be swallowed whole, like a pill, in an attempt to cure our descriptive ills. But it does provide a starting point for identifying the qualities of descriptive writing while also suggesting ways to expand our repertoire of techniques.

First, good description is **carefully worded**. When our aim is conciseness, says Aristotle, naming a subject directly and precisely is the most effective route. It follows that we must know the correct terms for the objects, people, places, and events we describe. Although description begins with an accurate naming of our subject, it also requires a precise naming. We must select the word that will call forth the particular image, emotion, or attitude our story requires. To accomplish this, we must use language that, to quote Aristotle, is "appropriate in sound and in sense." Good description extends beyond accuracy and precision to include the musical qualities of language. The sounds of our words and the cadences of our sentences must reinforce the content of our description.

Second, good description is **sensory**, making the audience or reader, as Aristotle suggests, "see things." Good description, like most powerful things in the world—a salty kiss, a dancer's leap, the fine brown hairs on a lover's arms—accomplishes more than we are consciously aware of. We may not notice its power until our blood begins to simmer or cool, the Windsor knot in our stomach tightens, our breathing shifts to quick, hard pants. These responses are due, in part, to description's root in the physical world. Good description almost always employs specific, concrete detail so the reader can "see" what is being described or experience it through one of the other four senses.

These sense impressions are enhanced, explains Aristotle, by "using expressions that represent things as in a state of activity," our third test for description. It is not enough simply to engage the senses. We must also represent the literary dream through word pictures—and, wherever possible, these should be *moving* **pictures**. (Moving pictures are especially important in fiction, where a descriptive passage must push the plot along or nudge a character from here to there.) Good description can create the illusion of movement and vitality, bringing even a static object to life.

Fourth, good description often employs metaphor or other **figurative language**. Although we usually think of metaphor and simile in terms of poetry, Aristotle argues that the use of figurative language is at least as important in prose, since prose writers have fewer of the poet's other tools available to them—rhyme, meter, and established poetic forms. Description that employs figurative language, he says, can lend "metaphorical life to lifeless objects."

However, description might contain all of these elements and still not be effective. Description is judged not only for its intrinsic value but also for how it **serves the larger story, poem, or nonfiction piece**. A 500-word description of a deserted barn might ruin the suspense of one story yet supply a breathtaking climax for another. A description employing metaphor might be the perfect choice in one poem while destroying the clarity of another. If we isolate a passage of description, we might conclude that it is, say, lyrical or dramatic or physically revolting or sexually stimulating. But we cannot conclude that it is *effective* until we see how it affects the total piece of writing.

These guidelines are intended merely as starting places for expanding the ways we think about descriptive writing, not as rules to follow blindly. If we confine ourselves to a few tried-and-true rules for description, our writing will never break free from mediocrity, never create the kind of literature that, to paraphrase Emily Dickinson, can blow the top of a reader's head off. And if we think of description only as a tool to accomplish some literary task, we cut ourselves off from all the other ways description can serve us, our readers, and the work itself.

THE REWARDS OF DESCRIPTION

In exchange for your careful attention to its needs, description provides many rewards.

- Descriptive passages create the illusion of reality, inviting the reader to unpack his bags and settle in for a spell. They provide verisimilitude, what John Gardner calls the "proofs" that support and sustain your fictional (or nonfictional) dream.
- Description composed of sensory detail penetrates layers of consciousness, engaging your reader emotionally as well as intellectually.
- Carefully selected descriptive details can establish characters and settings quickly and efficiently.
- As a framing device, description establishes the narrator's, or character's, point of view. Shifts in the description frame (or eye) can signal shifts in point of view or a significant change in the character.
- Well-placed descriptive passages can move your story along, shape the narrative line, and unfold the plot.
- Descriptive passages can act as gear shifts that change the pace of the narrative—speeding it up or slowing it down—thus increasing tension.

- Description can serve as a transitional device, a way to link scenes, travel through time and space, further an argument, or signal shifts in narrative stance.
- Description can serve as a unifying thematic device, suggesting the idea or feeling that lives beneath the storyline.
- Description can provide the palette for gradations in mood and tone. Dip your brush in one description and the sky darkens; in another, and the sun breaks through.
- The language of your descriptions, its rhythms and sounds, can provide the equivalent of a musical score that plays beneath your story, nonfiction work, or poem.

AN INVITATION

The dictionary on my desk suggests three definitions for *describe*.

> To transmit a mental image or impression
> To trace or draw the figure of; to outline
> To give a verbal account of; to tell about in detail

Considering each definition in turn, we can map our journey to more descriptive writing. "Mental image or impression" suggests *seeing*. "Outline" or "figure" suggests a representation, the image made *word*. "Account" or "telling" suggests a *story* to be transmitted.

To discover and describe images, we must engage our senses. Simply put, we must look, listen, taste, smell, and touch the real world or the world of the imagination. We must also find the words that will represent this world, or, as often happens during the writing process, allow the words to find us. Finally, we must consider how our descriptions shape the larger world of the story, poem, or nonfiction work.

By suggesting this three-part model, I'm not implying that creating descriptions is a simple, three-step procedure. The creative process is rarely linear. It loops back upon itself like a snake devouring its own tail. For some writers the story or idea comes first; as the telling progresses, descriptions emerge. For other writers a physical, sensory detail is the starting point. Still others, particularly poets, find within the words themselves—the sounds and rhythms and shapes—the route into description. The order in which these processes occur is not important. What *is* important is that somewhere along the way we give full attention to each of these matters: eye, word, and story.

CHAPTER TWO

The Eye of the Beholder

While giving birth to her second child, my sister contracted a bacterial infection that blinded her. At the time, we didn't know the blindness would be temporary. The family wept, we walked the halls of Intensive Care, we muttered the strange dialect people mutter at such times—half curse, half prayer. We made promises we'd never be able to keep. I offered up (to God, the universe, or anyone who might be listening) my own eyes in exchange for my sister's. After all, she was a photographer; her vision was more essential than mine. I was a writer. What did I need with eyes?

When my sister finally woke to light, she could not stop staring—at the hospital bed, the ceiling, her new son, the back of her own hand. "Bring me my camera," she said. That was many years ago. Today her walls are filled with photographs she has taken since her son's birth. She claims that the world is brighter than it used to be, the outlines more defined.

Amazing grace, it appears, is bestowed not on the perpetually sighted but on those who, to paraphrase the familiar hymn, once were blind but now can see. Just as youth is wasted on the young, eyes are wasted on those of us who see. Or think we see. The problem with vision is that we take it for granted. We get used to seeing our same old world in the same old way; marriages end every day because of this. On those evenings when I need to fall in love with my life again, I step out the door, down the front steps, and past the iron gate that surrounds our townhouse. For emphasis, I slam the gate and listen for the clang that reverberates, traveling down each iron post.

I'm outside my life now, a visitor at the gate. I close my eyes long enough to erase the accustomed scene the Dorothy in me has yawned away. Then I take a deep breath, open my eyes, and we're not in Kansas anymore. The lights are on (all things become more beautiful when lit from within) and a man stands at the second-floor window, holding a cat in his arms. *What a handsome man*, I think. *Wouldn't it be nice to live in that house, with that husband?*

Description begins in the beholder's eye, and it requires *attention*. If we look closely enough at something and stay in that moment long enough, we may be granted new eyes. Or ears. On his album *Noel*, Paul Stookey (of Peter, Paul and Mary fame) discusses his process of writing songs: "Sometimes," he says, "if you sit in one place long enough, you get used. You become the instrument for what it is that wants to be said."

Gee, you might be thinking. *If it's that easy, I should have finished a dozen novels by now.* And I'd nod right along with you, wondering why the hundreds of hours I've recently logged on the sofa haven't translated into a new book of poems.

Merely lounging on the sofa, of course, does not equate with attention. An attendant is one who is present at an event, one who waits expectantly. *Attention* is a servant's word; it requires work, concentration, and patience for the task. Most of us simply don't stay in one place long enough to be used. A few years ago I heard a radio interview with a scientist, a comet hunter who admitted that he had logged a total of nine hundred hours at the eyepiece before he saw his first comet. His advice to novice hunters?

1. Stay at the eyepiece and keep looking.
2. Watch the sky every day.
3. Study as many established comets as you can so you'll recognize one when it appears.
4. Be patient. The do-or-die approach rarely works.

The comet hunter's advice could easily apply to those of us attempting to write more descriptively. In order to describe—the world at our elbow or the one that dwells within our imagination—we must first stay at the eyepiece. Depending on your writing process and style, the eyepiece could be the physical world or it could be the world of the inner eye, the world of dreams and illusions. Or you might be a writer for whom the words themselves—their sounds, rhythms, and shapes—focus the world of the story or poem. No matter what eyepiece you use, put your writer's eye to it as often as possible, waiting for the forms to emerge, to change patterns and reconfigure themselves.

In the meantime, read the best literature you can find, particularly literature rich in detail, so that you'll be able to recognize an effective description when one appears in your work. I say *when*, not *if*, for the comet *will* appear. The universe is stacked in favor of possibility. If we are patient enough, if we don't force the process but rather remain open to discovery, one day, probably when we least expect it, a comet will show itself. We'll know it by its earthborn dust, its solid head, and the fiery tail that ignites the sky in front of our eyes.

THE NAKED EYE

Good description begins with observation. The most common things can yield startling surprises when we give our attention to them. Look at what Audre Lorde does with two ordinary household objects: the mortar and pestle her mother used for grinding spices.

> The mortar was of a foreign fragrant wood, too dark for cherry and too red for walnut. To my child eyes, the outside was carved in an intricate and most enticing manner. There were rounded plums and oval indeterminate fruit, some long and fluted like a banana, others ovular and end-swollen like a ripe alligator pear. In between these were smaller rounded shapes like cherries, lying in batches against and around each other …
>
> The pestle was long and tapering, fashioned from the same mysterious rose-deep wood, and fitted into the hand almost casually, familiarly. The actual shape reminded me of a summer crook-necked squash uncurled

and slightly twisted. ... Long use and years of impact and grinding with-in the bowl's worn hollow had softened the very surface of the wooden pestle, until a thin layer of split fibers coated the rounded end like a layer of velvet. A layer of the same velvety mashed wood lined the bottom in-side the sloping bowl. —from *Zami: A New Spelling of My Name*

To train your naked eye to see more intently, try this exercise in observation. Choose an ordinary object in your home. It might be something you use every day—a comb, a blanket, a salad bowl. Or it might be an object that's been around forever but is seldom used—your mother's wedding pearls, a hammer hanging on a Peg-Board, the avocado-green fondue pot from your first marriage.

Set a timer for ten minutes, and don't move until the time is up. During these ten minutes, your only job is to study the object. Stare at it. Notice every detail—its color, its shape, each part that contributes to the whole. If a memory floats to the surface, something you associate with the object, bring yourself back to your physical examination of the object. You might wish to pick it up, turn it around or upside down. Notice its heft, its texture. How does it feel in your hand, against your face? How does it smell?

When the timer goes off, begin writing a description of the object. Use sensory details the reader will be able to imagine: colors, shapes, smells, tex-tures. Concrete nouns will anchor your description. Use only those adjectives that call forth the qualities of the object; avoid adjectives that label or explain. Words like *lovely, old, wonderful, noteworthy,* or *remarkable* are explanatory labels; they do not suggest sense impressions. Adjectives like *bug-eyed, curly, bumpy, frayed, or moss-covered,* on the other hand, are descriptive. Although Lorde's description above contains some labeling adjectives (*intricate, entic-ing*) most of her details are sensory and concrete, allowing us to experience the mortar and pestle as physical objects rather than as disembodied ideas.

After you've described the object's qualities in concrete, sensory terms, you may wish to explore qualities only your *imaginative* eye can see. During your ten minutes of observation, did your mind wander? Did the object remind you of something else? Did you recall a memory associated with the object? Meditation often takes us into reverie, memory, digression, and even dream-like states. As John Berger notes in *Ways of Seeing,* "We never look at just one thing; we are always looking at the relation between things and ourselves."

The object of our attention doesn't have to be large or, on the surface, important. The smallest key can open a door into a large, sumptuous room. I think of Barbara Mallonee's essay "Semi-Colon," a paean for what is often considered the lowliest of punctuation marks. I think of G.K. Chesterton's "A Piece of Chalk," in which a seemingly mundane occurrence—the speaker's inability to locate a piece of white chalk—grows into an exploration of, among other things, religious morality, mercy, the souls of cows, the nature of art, and the landscape of Southern England. And who has written more eloquently about the first crisp days of autumn than A.A. Milne in his rhapsodic meditation on a stalk of celery in "A Word for Autumn"?

The tiniest thing can yield wonders when we give it our careful attention; indeed, it may be the quality of smallness itself that invites our keenest focus as writers and as readers. Decades have passed, but I still remember my first encounter with Virginia Woolf's essay "The Death of the Moth." Reading her words, my own breath quickened as I fixated on the moth "fluttering from side to side of his square of the window-pane." Had a St. Bernard trotted past the window of my mind at this moment, I doubt that his presence would have registered, so intent was I on the miniature scene playing out before my eyes. I would never look at a moth in the same way again, and to this day I continue to be astonished by Woolf's astonishment: "It was as if someone had taken a tiny bead of pure life and … had set it dancing and zigzagging to show us the true nature of life."

The naked eye provides us with sensory, concrete experiences. The imaginative eye opens up other worlds.

THE EYE OF IMAGINATION

"Sometimes the soul takes pictures of things it has wished for but never seen," wrote the poet Anne Sexton. Like the soul in Sexton's quote, the imaginative eye can photograph things we've never seen, and these imagined pictures are as important to the writer as the actual pictures that register with the naked eye. We might fill hundreds of notebooks with precise, accurate, realistic depictions of objects, people, and events without once writing an effective description. Effective description occurs only when the naked eye merges with the imaginative eye. As Eudora Welty phrased it, "[F]iction's whole world is human nature. … But the imagination is the only thing that can find out anything about it and the only way you can see."

But how, exactly, does the imagination teach us to see? Like *description*, *imagination* is a term tossed around casually in literary circles. We accept imagination's existence the way we accept air into our lungs, with little thought of its molecular structure. According to my junior high school English teacher, imagination was what my writing lacked. She preferred "creative" writers like Joel Aspinall, the boy who sat in front of me and stared out the window a lot. Joel wrote stories about three-eyed aliens sprouting from daisy petals and jabbering a kind of truncated Pig Latin. My poem about my mother repotting a geranium was returned to me with a pale check mark and the teacher's suggestion that I beef up my description with more adjectives and similes, or, better yet, read one of Joel's stories to get my creative juices stirring.

Although this experience did not stop me from writing poems, it did stop me from showing them to English teachers. Imagination, it appeared, consisted of making things up, which apparently didn't include writing about the things of my everyday world—the things I saw, heard, touched, smelled, and tasted. I concluded that I'd never be a creative writer; I'd just write poems instead. I liked the way I felt when I wrote, the places my mind traveled. When I wrote about my mother repotting the geranium, I could almost smell the rich, moist compost and feel the grainy dirt in my hand. After several lines I began to see my mother brushing back a strand of her thick black hair with the edge of the trowel, though I'd never actually seen her do this. Or had I? It was hard to remember every detail. It was October, after all, when I wrote the poem, and she'd repotted the geranium the previous July.

It would be many years before I understood that I'd been writing imaginatively all along. Although I hadn't set out to invent anything, to make something appear out of thin air like a magician's dove, I was nevertheless writing from the eye of the imagination. I was doing what the poet Stanley Plumly discusses in his essay "Words on Birdsong": "Poets cannot make things up. Poets make things *from*—from memory; from matter that cannot be changed, only transformed; from the rock of fact that may disappear ... but cannot be made, out of hand, to evaporate." These are comforting words to those of us who fear we lack imagination because we're unable to "make things up."

One of the reasons I dislike the label "creative nonfiction" (I prefer "literary nonfiction" or Gay Talese's "the literature of reality") is because it often prompts a discussion of whether it is permissible for nonfiction writers to "make things up," ignoring the myriad other ways nonfiction writers can approach their subjects with imagination. Nonfiction writers are free to speculate, to wonder, to employ what Fern Kupfer—in her essay "Everything But the Truth?"—names "the gift of perhaps," without inventing or distorting factual information. For instance, in her essay "Moon Snail," Barbara Hurd does not tell us that she painted an image of the moon snail; rather she speculates on how she *might* paint the moon snail, moving through three possibilities: still life painting to diptych and finally to triptych. In a similar way, S.L. Wisenberg, in "Margot's Diary," does not pretend to know what the diary of Margot Frank contained. Unlike her sister Anne's diary, Margot's was lost, so we can only imagine what she might have written. And that is exactly what Wisenberg does in her essay, using the "gift of perhaps" to compose Margot's thoughts, the words she probably did not write but might have. Without misleading the reader or reporting untruths, Wisenberg nevertheless engages the eye of imagination. This eye is known by many aliases, among them *the mind's eye, the child's eye, the dream eye, the eye of memory, the eye in the back of your head.*

THE EYE OF MEMORY

"Any writer has more to thank memory for than most anything," Eudora Welty once told an interviewer. She wasn't referring to instant recall; memory is more than merely recalling information. A writer whose mind is stuffed with random, meticulously recalled details may have trouble selecting which details to use. If you have a mind like a sieve, be grateful. A sieve filters, strains, and selects; although much falls through the meshwork, the essential elements remain.

Welty also wasn't referring to memory in terms of writing about the past. What we remember can just as well be used in writing about the present or the future. We store up the sights, smells, textures, and sounds of our lives and draw upon those experiences as we write. Writing isn't about transcribing the raw material of past experience. (Is such an act even possible?) Writing is an act of transforming that raw material into a new shape.

Life continually provides us with raw material for our writing. Henry James calls this material—the fact, event, or memory that is given to us—the "donnée." But the donnée is only one component in the making of a story, a poem, or an essay. More important is how we organize and describe the raw material, how we marry experience to imagination. This may require letting go of what we've been given. We may need to release fact for fact's sake in exchange for fact for art's sake.

One way to depart from the donnée is to take an event from your life—your first home run, the birth of your child, the death of your father—and loan the entire experience to a fictional character. If you really want to engage the imaginative eye, loan the memory to a character very different from you. If you're a redhead, make the character a brunette; if you're a tall, shy man, give your experience to a short, vivacious woman. Hand over the event, no strings attached, and see what your character does with it. Describe the event from your character's point of view, perhaps even in his own words. Don't worry about losing the emotional impact of the event. If the event was emotionally moving for you, chances are the emotion will transfer to your character.

Another way to reshape the donnée is to take two events, years apart, and place them in the same story or poem to see how they interact. For instance, describe a childhood scene between one of your characters—let's call her Ellen—and her mother. Maybe the mother is brushing Ellen's hair before a mirror or pulling a splinter from Ellen's thumb. Stop the description before it's completed and insert a description of another scene between Ellen and her mother, a scene many years removed from her childhood. Maybe the two are shopping for a wedding gown, or Ellen is visiting her mother in the nursing home after the mother's stroke. The interaction between the two events will force you to describe the scenes in new ways. In the interplay between the two moments, your imaginative eye will take over, navigating the space between the two experiences.

Another way to engage your imaginative eye is to describe two or more versions of the same event—say, your sister's version and your husband's—and place them in the same piece. I used this method in the opening of "The Tale," an essay about the day my grandmother amputated a dying dog's leg in an attempt to save him.

> There were as many versions of the tale as there were tellers. Grandma's neighbor, Mrs. Sisson, made it autumn. She said she was walking back from the milking barn when she saw a black horse leaping a bale of rolled hay with my grandmother on his back, clinging to his mane. Uncle Leland remembered it as April, the last gray patches of snow melting by the mailbox. Great Aunt Bessie, Grandma's sister, recited it reverently as if it were a Bible story, focusing on the wound itself, the miracle of the quick healing ... .

Describing each character's memory of the event allowed me to engage my imaginative eye. Once I relinquished my allegiance to the bare facts, which varied from teller to teller, I was able to find the larger emotional truth beneath the event.

This does not mean that I lied about the facts. As I mentioned earlier, the creative part of nonfiction lies not in making things up but rather in engaging our imaginative eye by selecting significant details, combining and recombining information, and reshaping experience. Artful arrangement of information was one of the cornerstones of the new journalism of Tom Wolfe and Truman Capote, and remains an important component of nonfiction writing. Facts, information, and real-life events do not have to be presented dryly, like encyclopedia entries. They can emerge wrapped in the skin of story or shaped like prayers, lists, recipes, letters, confessionals, dialogues, or diaries. When the eye of the imagination is engaged, it illuminates the artful possibilities hidden within actual events. From the hard rock of fact, stone by stone, the writer builds a castle.

Engaging the imaginative eye is hard work, especially when we find ourselves trapped within one version of an event, one way of describing the world. Sometimes we don't want the imaginative eye to intrude on our memories. But intrude it must, if anything new is to be born. One of our duties as writers is to become surprised, to land in a different place from where we'd planned to arrive—a more difficult, provocative place. If we wish to engage the eye of memory, we must be willing to transform, reshape, even discard the donnée for the sake of the work.

THE GROWING EYE, THE THIRD EYE, INSIGHT

In 1988 scientists recorded the first sighting of what they termed "deep light," a mysterious light that emanated from the ocean floor. The existence of this light, which was too faint to be perceived by the human eye and could be accessed only through the use of a special camera, seemed to suggest that undersea objects produced their own radiance independent of the sun.

Had the poet and priest Gerard Manley Hopkins been alive at the time, he would not have been surprised by the discovery. Hopkins, like many other artists and mystics, believed that nature's expressive forms are molded by spiritual power, and he spent much of his life articulating the belief that each object in nature contains what he named "inscape." Inscape can be explained—and I am simplifying Hopkins's concept here—as the shape within the shape, a kind of glowing from within. This radiance emanates from even the most common forms and is visible only to the eye of the imagination.

Sister Wendy Beckett, the nun who wrote *The Story of Painting*, a book based on the PBS series she hosted during the 1990s, spent twenty-seven years in chosen seclusion, practicing silence and prayer several hours a day. Much of this time was devoted to simply *viewing* art, usually postcard reproductions she kept in her room. *Viewing*, however, does not begin to describe Sister Wendy's process, which she calls "quiet attention" or "looking with awe and wonder." She says that if she looks long enough and hard enough at a painting—even one that she doesn't like at all—it begins to take on a life of its own, and she is able to see why it's considered a great work of art. I presume that what she's seeing with her imaginative eye is something akin to Hopkins's "inscape."

Hopkins called this eye the "growing eye" because it expands as it learns to participate emotionally and spiritually with the object itself. When we engage not only the naked eye but the growing eye as well, we begin to see the extraordinary within the ordinary. Our eye begins to grow. If this discussion of the growing eye sounds a bit suspect, like a UFO sighting by some New Ager who's been grazing too long on tofu, let's consider how the growing eye affects a writer's descriptions. Here, Annie Dillard describes the first moments of waking in a house on Puget Sound.

> I wake in a god. I wake in arms holding my quilt, holding me as best they can inside my quilt. ...
>
> I open my eyes. The god lifts from the water. His head fills the bay. He is Puget Sound, the Pacific; his breast rises from pastures; his fingers are firs; islands slide wet down his shoulders. Islands slip blue from his

shoulders and glide over the water, the empty, lighted water like a stage.
—from *Holy the Firm*

Dillard's is a rapturous description, infused with spiritual awe. When she looks at the Pacific, she sees the Pacific, yes. But she sees more than the Pacific. Because she is looking with wonder, expectantly, the view expands to fill her growing eye. Puget Sound moves out of the realm of common sense and into the realm of the imagination. It's as if the writer is shining a flashlight from the inside of her subject, illuminating its inner workings.

In ancient myth, soothsayers, prophets, and other clairvoyants were called *seers*, although many of them, like Tiresias of Greek legend, were blind. Because their eyes were not distracted by external reality, so the theory goes, their inner eye could see more clearly into the heart and mind of the universe. The quest for internal vision continued with those mystics, saints, and monks who practiced—and still practice—mortification of the senses. Through disciplines such as surrender, silence, darkness, fasting, and meditation, they seek to "empty" their senses. Once, for a period of six months, Gerard Manley Hopkins refused to use his eyes. External reality, it seemed, only clouded the inner eye, his *insight*.

Few of us would go so far as Hopkins did, but there are less radical ways to shut out the world of appearances. Practicing fifteen minutes of meditation a day, directly before you write, can do wonders for your inner eye. Try it and see. Find a quiet place, close your eyes (or focus on a still object), and breathe slowly and deeply from your diaphragm rather than your chest. Pay attention to your breathing, to its regular and sustained rhythm. Clear your mind of distractions, focusing only on the experience of the moment—your breathing, the silence.

If you find that your mind is wandering, take note of the distraction but do not dwell on it. You might want to try a technique used by hypnotists and Lamaze instructors: Stare at a focal point until the distraction is removed. Or repeat a mantra or chant to bring yourself back to the present moment. Books such as Ira Progoff's *The White Robed Monk* contain entrance meditations you can speak aloud or listen to on recordings as a way of focusing attention on what you are about to write.

Another focusing activity is the "third eye" exercise I learned from Kenneth Koch's *Wishes, Lies, and Dreams*. At first I used the exercise only with children in my poetry-in-the-schools work, but I discovered that the third eye concept works equally well for adults. Imagine that you have a third eye in the middle of your head, an eye that sees only what your other two eyes cannot see. Your third eye can see into any dimension of time and space, penetrating unseen mysteries. It possesses unlimited power. Well, almost unlimited. Remember, it can't see what the naked eye sees. The only way to engage your third eye is to refuse to use images perceived through the naked eye.

Sometimes the best way to describe our world is with our eyes closed. Daily life clouds our sight and our insight, especially when we spend time before televisions and various computer devices, where the visual world is frantic and fragmented, breaking into images lasting only seconds. Overwhelmed by visual stimuli, we can take in no more. The world has become a blur, each color and shape vying for our attention. Our naked eye becomes so filled that our inner eye refuses to see.

Fortunately, eyes come equipped with lids. We can lower them like shades when we've seen enough.

THE ALL-ACCEPTING EYE

There are other reasons for pulling the shades over our eyes. Anyone who looks long, hard, and honestly at the world will see things he'd rather not see: children bald from chemotherapy, mothers stuffing fetuses down laundry chutes, refugees drinking raw sewage in order to be admitted into the camp's infirmary. What we do with these images will define, in part, our creative vision. In one of his letters collected in *Letters on Cézanne*, the poet Rainer Maria Rilke reminds us that "even something horrible, something that seems no more than disgusting, *is*, and shares the truth of its being with everything else that exists." What this means for the creative artist, in Rilke's words, is that he is not "permitted to turn his back on anything: a single refusal, and he is cast out of the state of grace and becomes sinful all the way through." Writers like Rilke seem incapable of ignoring the world's horrors; to deny them would be tantamount to artistic death.

For other writers, however, the unspeakable remains unspoken. Rather than confront the ugliness, they push it out of their mind's eye, training their attention only on what appears, on the surface, to be beautiful. Although this may seem the path of least artistic resistance, it probably isn't. Objects of unquestioned beauty can be as difficult to absorb, and to describe, as objects of ugliness or horror. Like the effect of a ravishing woman on a shy man, an overly beautiful sight might render a writer literally speechless. Vincent van Gogh, in a letter to his brother, wrote that one particular olive grove was "too beautiful for us to dare to paint it or to be able to imagine it." Of course, being van Gogh, he did dare, at least fifteen times, though none of the olive tree paintings ever satisfied him.

Another problem with unquestioned beauty is that it can quickly become boring. Although a flawless, seemingly perfect subject might catch our eye momentarily, it is the flawed subject we are most likely to remember. Flaws reveal what my grandmother used to call "character," something she promised I would get someday, a quality more important and lasting than beauty. I inherited little of my grandmother's beauty and, thus far, even less of her inimitable character. But I'm still hopeful.

In the meantime, I enjoy a well-placed crack in a piece of pottery, an ink-smudged letter, the errant cowlick in my nephew's hair. "What is always provocative in a work of art," wrote E.M. Forster in *Aspects of the Novel*, is "roughness of texture." As readers, he says, we long for descriptions "full of dents and grooves and lumps and spikes which draw from us little cries of approval and disapproval. When they have past, the roughness is forgotten, they become as smooth as the moon."

How can we write descriptions that are "rough in texture" yet "smooth as the moon"? The first step, as I said earlier, is to really *look* at your subject. Look with your naked eye and your inner eye. Most important, look with an all-accepting eye. Accept every part of the subject, removing convention-al labels—*lovely, gross, sweet, inspiring, depressing*—commonly associated with the image. Try not to view the subject as you've been taught to view it. Look long enough and hard enough, and you're bound to find the "dents and grooves and lumps and spikes."

One of the biggest challenges we face as writers is describing something that almost everyone agrees is beautiful—a sunset, a rose, a new baby, the ocean—without resorting to cliché. Although we want to write descriptions that are evocative and memorable, we end up filling our pages with phras-es like "velvety petals" or "sparkling waves." When this happens to me, it's usually because I've proceeded, as my uncle used to say, "bass-ackwards." Rather than beginning with the thing itself, I've begun with a label, or with a judgment or conclusion, and then merely provided details that support my conclusion.

Let's say I want to describe a vase of tulips. My first thought is *beautiful, springlike, fresh.* Already I've jumped to conclusions, providing labels before I've taken the time to consider my subject, the tulips themselves. My descrip-tion is bound to fail. It will be no more than a series of clichéd, forgettable details concocted to support my judgment about the tulips.

But if I look before I leap, bringing forth the qualities of the tulips rather than merely labeling or explaining them, I might discover a more memora-ble description, like Richard Selzer's description of a vase of tulips delivered to a seriously ill man.

> They are the largest tulips of his life. A closer examination would have revealed that the long stems had been impaled on a bed of spikes and wired such that the distant hydrocephalic blossoms would respond to the least current of air. Placed on the window ledge, the evil heads are in a constant state of motion, nodding or shaking as if to vote yea or nay in

the matter of his fate. At night the shadows of these flowers are magnified and thrown upon the wall—seven bald witches lunging for his thoughts. ...

There they are! On the wall! Sheeted by the moon, those caricatures of tulips, hunchbacked, swollen. —from *Raising the Dead: A Doctor's Encounter with His Own Mortality*

Another challenge we face is describing something commonly thought of as ugly, imperfect, or disgusting. Again, we're likely to jump to conclusions. Rather than considering our subject firsthand and describing what we observe, we label it. Because we've already established, for instance, that slugs are disgusting, we go on to describe them as "slimy" creatures that leave "gooey trails." Cliché upon cliché.

But when we engage our all-accepting eye, when we look beyond surface prejudices and preconceptions into the actual nature of our subject, clichés disappear. In her poem "The Connoisseuse of Slugs," Sharon Olds transforms her subject with descriptive phrases like "naked jelly of those gold bodies,/ translucent strangers glistening among the/stones" and "glimmering umber horns/rising like telescopes." Her description forces us to see an old subject in a new way. We no longer have to choose between ugliness and beauty; they have realigned themselves, each side illuminating the other. When we engage our all-accepting eye, we discover the flaws that make surface beauty interesting as well as the arresting details that redeem a seemingly ugly image.

THE GLIDING EYE

The year is 1873, and we're standing on the banks of the Seine. A small, flat-bottomed boat cruises past. On its deck is a three-legged easel. The bearded man holding the paintbrush is Claude Monet, who will soon come to be known as the father of impressionism. He works each day in this studio boat, floating down the river while the scenery passes by him, through him. Unfortunately, we can't see the scene through Monet's eyes. For one thing, we're standing on the bank, while he is moving. For another, we don't spend each day of our lives concentrating on the scene before us. And finally, we are not Monet, the "Raphael of Water" whom Cézanne once described as "only an eye. But my God, what an eye."

Monet's artistic vision, coupled with a seemingly unquenchable passion for light, led him to create works that captured the most fleeting and fluid moments in nature. Realistic description was not Monet's goal. He was not struggling to reproduce reality but to coax a new reality out of the world his eyes saw. As one critic put it, Monet was "gliding with the light" rather than trying to conquer it. Monet not only chose to paint the most unstable of subjects—it is impossible to "capture" moving water—but he chose, at least part of the time, to paint his subject while he was in motion.

When we think of paying attention, we usually think of sitting still, of clearing our eyes and ears of distractions and concentrating on the object or scene before us. But sometimes the best way to be still—to still your mind and focus on your subject—is to get moving. Physical activity is good not only for your muscles and joints but for your mind as well. Before you write, take a long walk, swim, lift weights, jog, dance, or take a spin on your bike. Focusing on your body can free your mind to embark on its own journey. You may even find that the physical rhythms of the activity suggest the rhythms of sentences or poetry lines. This happened to me on the rowing machine; the even, repetitious strokes, coupled with the whooshing sound of the machine, led me to write a meditation on the heart, its iambic lub and dub.

If you hate exercise, take a tip from Monet and float down a river. Or take a long train ride, or set off on a road trip. As a child, I watched the world rush past the back window of our family's station wagon, and traveling long distances still turns my mind to reverie. The car is my floating studio, though the view passes more quickly than Monet's view and is more tightly framed. Of course you can't write while you're driving, but your gliding eye can record moving pictures you can later translate into descriptions that invite the reader along for the ride. Each time I read Reg Saner's essay "Late July, 4:40 A.M.," I ride shotgun in his pickup truck, feeling "the adrenaline rush of early hour highway euphoria." As the essay roars forward, "billboards loom, growing in size like imperatives: THREE MILES FROM THE LARGEST PRAIRIE DOG IN THE WORLD." We are in motion, writer and reader together, while "[d]iesel cab after cab, all chrome-glint and smoke, rushes toward and past like an explosion." Do you feel it, too, the adrenaline rush of his words? Saner's descriptions are effective because he has engaged his gliding eye, setting himself in motion while the world rushes by.

THE CHILD'S EYE

For almost fifteen years as poet-in-residence for a large metropolitan school district, I worked side by side with children, encouraging them to read and write poems. Their writing never ceased to surprise me.

> I have fierce, perfect muscles that you can see far away. I used to have a perfect mouth, till I lied.

> My parents got divorced and my dad got me.

> What's quieter than the rain Wednesday morning? Silence is the quietest thing that people break.

> Sometimes I feel kinda only.

Lines like these appeared every day, written by children of all ages, races, and economic and achievement levels. Later, when they read the children's poems, adults shook their heads. "What happens to us along the way?" they lamented. "I used to be creative, too. Where did it go? Why can't I write lines like that? Kids!" they said, lifting their palms as if in surrender.

Although I, too, was impressed with the children's poems, I have trouble believing that imagination is a gift bestowed freely in childhood only to be snatched away at adulthood. What about all those artists who continue their creative work well into old age? "Man's maturity," wrote Nietzsche, is "to regain the seriousness that he had as a child at play." This concept—of creativity as an artistic seriousness that still contains a highly concentrated playfulness—is quite different from the notion of buttoned-down seriousness we often associate with the creative process.

Watching the children's faces as they wrote, I tried to guess what was happening within their minds. Some children smiled to themselves, their expressions ranging from devilish to thoughtful to serene. Some laughed aloud, as if enjoying a private joke. Many scowled in concentration. A few cried unabashedly, tears dripping down onto the page. Yet no matter how different the expressions on their faces, the quality of intense encounter was the same; each child was fully engaged in the task at hand.

Another thing I noticed as the children wrote was how often they changed their viewing perspectives. A child rarely looks at his world straight on. He lies flat on his back in the middle of a field, or peeks out from a hiding place, or climbs a tree and watches the scene from above. I used to spy from a crack in the haymow floor as my grandfather milked the cows. From my vantage point, I could see only the cows' smooth, brown backs, their square, white-speckled heads, and the swishing ropes of their tails. They had no feet, or so my eyes told me. These cows were dream creatures, and I imagined them floating in midair, listlessly presenting their full udders to my grandfather's hands.

Suppertime brought no end to dreaming. Like most children, I was fond of partially obstructed views, and while the grown-ups weren't looking—which seemed to be most of the time—I crawled under the oak table to witness the drama of legs and feet. My grandfather often wore galoshes over his shoes; my aunt, in open-toed red pumps, crossed one leg over the other and swung it in my direction; my grandmother, who wore her stockings rolled below her knees, used her right foot as punctuation, stomping it adamantly to make a point.

Later in the evening, as my mother ironed a tablecloth for Sunday's upcoming dinner, I'd sit beneath the ironing board and let the white damask cover me like a cloud. Children love small spaces—tents, closets, and department store clothing racks. These spaces provide a crowded security while also encouraging subterfuge. While hidden, a child can spy on the outside world without giving himself away, thus gaining an advantage over those whose secrets are now open to his view. He squeezes down into the smallest space possible, lies as still as he can, and holds his breath.

The moment does not last, of course, for a child at play is a child in motion. Soon he's spinning in dizzy circles, then stopping on a dime, gravity tipping him drunkenly towards earth as heaven swirls over him. Or he's on a swing, pumping his legs toward that highest branch. He throws back his head, and the green world, broken by shards of sky, shatters into a thousand pieces. Who knows? Once grown, this same child might buy a studio boat, set up an easel, and begin to describe the floating world.

Regaining the seriousness of play. Changing our viewing perspective. Hiding in small spaces and looking out. Setting ourselves in motion in order to watch the world swirl by. These are but a few of the ways we can regain the child's eye we thought was surely lost.

THE DREAM EYE

Every night as you sleep, the dream eye sets about to destroy your world—the world of logic, literal meaning, lockstep order, and cause and effect. It dismantles daylight visions, razes buildings, ravishes the landscape in preparation for paving what Sigmund Freud called "the royal road to the unconscious." *You're at the altar, dressed in a white bridal gown and rubber hip boots, blowing "I Do" through a snorkel. Your father floats by, blinking his eyes, but they're not eyes. They're clear blue bowls where tiny minnows dart.*

In bed, dreaming the wedding dream, you toss, flail, cry out in fear or exaltation. The bug of REM crawls beneath your eyelids. Then slowly, quietly, the dream eye begins its repair work, paving the road, raising the scaffolding, pouring the foundation. By the time you wake, dry-mouthed and woozy, the house is built, your old furniture rearranged, a few symbolic pictures framed. In some strange, inexplicable way, the pictures make sense. Not the kind of sense a news report makes, or an algebraic equation. The pictures make *dream* sense. Like art, dreams do not necessarily *mean* anything—that is, their significance cannot be separated out. The pictures are not asking to be understood and explained; they want only to be looked at with care and attention.

Our culture doesn't put much stock in dreams, at least not the kind we have while we're asleep. Usually when we talk about dreams, it's in terms of daylight wishes, goals to attain, jobs to secure, hopes for our children's futures—things that we assume are within our control. Nighttime dreams are beyond our control. Perhaps that's why we discount their power to shape and reshape our lives. Many of us claim not to dream at all; others claim not to remember dreams.

And even those of us who say we value dreams often try to tame them, to analyze them, to make them *mean* something that our conscious, logical brains can use. We buy dream dictionaries that reduce our nighttime paintings to the sum of their parts: white, altar, blue, fishes, snorkel. We labor to find a lesson or moral: "The dream must be telling me not to marry Josh" or "Gee, maybe we shouldn't have an outdoor wedding, since it's obviously going to rain." Rather than give our attention to the dream itself, its shapes and textures and colors and emotions, we bypass its art, looking for logical answers. This is the equivalent of glancing at the *Mona Lisa*, then turning to our companion and saying, "Leonardo's saying that we should keep our secrets; it makes us more mysterious." Yes, dreams mean something, just as paintings do. But their meaning cannot be extracted like a motto for a bumper sticker.

When we stop trying to figure out our dreams and stop trying to apply our conscious minds to the pictures our unconscious minds are painting, we may begin to feel the power of their images. And we may begin to see those images emerge in our writing. The process can be as simple as keeping paper and pen on your bedside table and then, when you wake from a dream, recording everything you remember—the feelings, shapes, physical details, dialogue—without trying to decipher meaning.

When recording dreams in my notebook, I use the present tense; it makes the scenes more immediate, bringing them more vividly to my mind's eye.

The present-tense verbs act as guides, leading me by the hand through the dream. The present tense is also helpful because it suggests *presenting* rather than explaining. It's as if I'm back in the dream and the scenes are emerging before my eyes as I watch. To use the past tense would suggest that the images have already been distilled, that they have acquired the weight of meaning and logic. I don't need dreams weighted with meaning and logic any more than I need didactic art. I need dreams that penetrate beneath my consciousness, that reveal the world of the imagination in all its strange and beautiful guises.

Once you get into the habit of recording your dreams, of replaying them directly onto a pad of paper or in a dream journal, you'll probably find that you remember more of your dreams, and that you remember them in more vivid detail. After several months you'll have quite a collection of surreal images. If you reread them, you may see certain images repeating themselves. You may even see a pattern emerging. Beyond giving you information about your obsessions, fears, and desires, these images can also provide entries into new poems or stories. (The underwater dream, by the way, was *my* dream, and the image of my father's eyes was the triggering image for what became an essay focusing on my father's uneasy relationship with water.)

Dream images can also help solve writing problems. They can provide insight into your characters or suggest a different plot direction for the story you're working on. This does not mean that you can simply retell a dream, detail by detail, and call it a story. Blow-by-blow descriptions of dreams are interesting only to the teller. If you don't believe this, try recounting last night's dream to your co-worker while you wait in line at the copy machine, and watch his eyes glaze over. Suddenly he glances at his watch, remembers a meeting he needs to attend, and is out of there—and just when you were getting to the good part, too. Although dreams can pave the way to a story, they are not the story itself. Images seen through the dream eye must be tested the way any image is tested by a prudent writer: by how it serves the larger work.

EXERCISES

1. Follow the example of poets A.R. Ammons and Jorie Graham: Take up painting or sketching as a way of keeping your vision new. Or follow the example of journalist Frye Gaillard, who claims to have a bad "visual memory." When he visits a research site or interviews a subject, he takes detailed notes on what he sees, later expanding the notes into sensory descriptions.

2. Change your visual point of view. Stare at the same scene from several different focal points—lying flat on your back and looking up, peering through a peephole, looking down from a mountain, airplane, or diving board. Or frame an ordinary scene in new ways. Look through a window. Roll a sheet of paper into a tube and study the scene through a new lens. Distort a realistic view by looking through prisms, kaleidoscopes, or 3-D glasses. Then describe the scene through the lens of each eyepiece. For literary examples, read Theodore Roethke's "Child on Top of a Greenhouse," William Carlos Williams's "Nantucket," or James Wright's "Lying in a Hammock at William Duffy's Farm in Pine Island, Minnesota."

3. Listen to Paul Simon's "Fifty Ways to Leave Your Lover." Substitute *donnée* for *lover* and see how many ways there are to leave your story, to get beyond fact for fact's sake. ("Just drop off the key, Lee, and get yourself free.")

4. Make a list of images that you find ugly, even disgusting, in objects, nature, people, and yourself. Your list might include an amputee's stump, wrinkles, a smoggy sky, cockroaches, stretch marks, a charred corpse, varicose veins, maggots, obscene graffiti, rubble from a bombed building. Then choose one image from the list and write a description that redeems that image, removing it from the realm of ugliness and disgust.

5. Study a "beautiful" object until you discover an interesting flaw. Record the details you see, giving the ugly and the beautiful qualities equal weight.

6. Keep a dream journal in which you record not only nighttime dreams but also twilight imagery, daybreak reverie, and simple old-fashioned daydreams. Once a month, look through your entries, circling arresting images.

Use one of these images in an opening line to a story, a poem, or an essay. Or loan the dream to one of the characters in your story.

7. Change the way you record images. Try writing on adding machine tape, restaurant napkins, or index cards. Or use unlined paper that encourages you to mix drawing with writing, to sketch characters or maps, and to write without the boundaries of margins or lines. Write in the dark with a lighted pen, or on a chalkboard, or with colored pencils. If the thought of filling a blank sheet of paper with description terrifies you, reduce the terror. Fold the paper in half, then in half again, and again. Your terror has now been reduced eightfold. Write one sensory detail on the folded section, then unfold the paper, adding a detail to each section until the empty page is filled.

8. To engage your imaginative eye, change an ordinary or habitual act by adding a new dimension to it. For instance, eat the same flavor of ice cream in three different ways in three different settings: straight from the carton while sitting in a bubble bath, out of a crystal goblet while sitting in a tree or under one, with your bare hands while shut up in a dark closet. Then write a description of each experience.

9. Wear headphones or earbuds while you walk the same blocks three times, varying the style of music each time. For one trip, a Strauss waltz; for another, heavy metal; for another, blues guitar. Notice how the same scene changes depending on the music. Recently, while walking past the retirement home in my neighborhood, I was listening to Grieg's "Wand of Youth." Suddenly the women in the window of the exercise room weren't old women in leotards and sweatpants, straining to lift their arms above their heads. They were pastel petals, ballerinas of the folding chair, their sinuous tendrils reaching. (I went straight back to my desk and recorded what I had seen.)

10. Reread one of your old descriptions. Circle adjectives that merely label or explain, and replace them with descriptive adjectives that evoke concrete, sensory qualities.

11. Choose an object from your past (or your culture's past) that has been lost to time. That is, although it may still be physically present in the world, it

has lost its former glory, its original reason for being (for instance, a fallout shelter, a 3-D View-Master, a wind-up clock, or a desert canvas water bag). Write about the object, beginning with physical description and moving on to other connections: cultural or historical context, personal memories, thematic issues. You might even imagine the object's redemption or reincarnation, showing how it might live on in another form.

12. Employing your imaginative eye while incorporating Fern Kupfer's notion of "the gift of perhaps," describe an event or scene that may not have happened but that you can imagine, in detail, might have happened.

13. After studying a photograph, describe it as precisely as possible, using concrete and specific detail to show what your naked eye sees. Then engage your imaginative eye. Employ negative space, describing what you can't see. What might lie outside the borders of the image? Who do you imagine took the photo? Who or what is missing from the scene? What happened right before the photograph was snapped, or right after? Speculate, interrogate, place the image side by side with other images. Do whatever it takes to move the description to a deeper level. For literary examples, study Judith Kitchen's brief essays based on photographs: "Young Woman On Fence" and "On the Farm."

CHAPTER THREE

From Eye to Word: The Description

Marvelous Truth, confront us
at every turn,
in every guise, iron ball,
egg, dark horse, shadow,
cloud
of breath on the air ...
—**DENISE LEVERTOV**, FROM "MATINS"

You've opened your eyes and stayed at the eyepiece, giving your attention to the world around you. You've engaged the eye of your imagination. And you've spent time reading the best literature you can find, poems and stories and nonfiction rich in detail. You're eager to write a stunning description. Where do you begin?

Start with what's in front of your eyes. Description is word painting, and many painters begin with the subject before their eyes: a person, place, event, or object. Georgia O'Keeffe collected objects such as bleached bones, skulls, feathers, shells, and stones. She called them her "treasures," and they filled her studio and her canvases. When she left New Mexico to return east, she crated a barrel of bones to accompany her. Later the contents of the barrel provided the raw material for the first of her famous cow skull paintings; the background was provided by the blue pajamas of a friend's young son.

As you describe your subject, think of yourself as a painter of still life. You are painting a stationary subject, revealing its qualities as it remains in a fixed state. (Later we'll move on to action-based description.) Chapter two included Audre Lorde's description of a mortar and pestle, followed by an exercise in observation and description. If you haven't yet written a description of a common object, write one now, following the suggestions in chapter two. Be sure to use specific nouns and only those adjectives that describe; avoid modifiers that label or explain.

When we write a description of a static subject—a pine tree, a deserted house, a rusted plow—we are in effect freezing the scene for ourselves and for the reader. A frozen scene allows us to focus on our subject's permanent, fixed qualities. When an object or a scene holds still, it gives us time to observe every detail. One way to focus on details is to describe the various parts that make up the whole. A tangerine, for instance, consists of rind, juice, seeds, fruit, pulp, grainy membranes, stem, blossoms, and leaves. Describing each of these parts will force you to notice details you might otherwise overlook, what Chekhov called the "little particulars." Later you may decide you've included too many particulars. If so, you can always remove some of them or group them in a different way.

In description, the organization of details is as important as the details themselves. If you toss all the details at the reader without providing a pattern, he'll have trouble visualizing your word painting. So once you've described the details of your subject, you must order them. There are many ways to organize a description of a static subject: spatially, temporally, or in terms of certain innate qualities.

In describing the tangerine, for instance, you might group the details by the quality of texture, how various parts of the tangerine feel on your tongue or in your hand. You could also organize the details in relation to a process that occurs over time—as the tangerine is peeled and eaten, for example, or as it evolves from seed to fully mature fruit. You might organize your description spatially, beginning at the inside of the tangerine and proceeding out, or from the outside in, ordering each detail to fit a visual schematic. (When you describe a larger static subject such as a room or a forest, the same principles apply; the only difference is the size of your canvas. In chapter eight I'll describe specific methods for organizing descriptions of place.)

Jim Crace uses spatial ordering in the opening to his novel *The Gift of Stones*. Notice how your mind's eye travels the landscape of the description, beginning with the top of the father's arm and ending in the scar at the center of the stump.

> My father's right arm ended not in a hand but, at the elbow, in a bony swelling. Think of a pollard tree in silhouette. That was my father's stump. Its skin was drawn tight across the bone and tucked frowning into the hole left by the missing lower joint. The indented scar was like those made in the ice by boys with stones—a small uneven puncture, wet with brackish puss.

Regardless of how distasteful his subject might be, it's hard to discount the power of Crace's description. He manages not only to include specific, concrete details and order those details effectively, but also to bring the description to life, proving that the description of a fixed, static subject needn't *feel* static. Good descriptions, you'll recall, follow Aristotle's dictum of revealing things "in a state of activity," and the best writers know how to make even stationary objects pulse with life. Later in this chapter we'll discuss how active, vivid prose can animate even the most static scene. For now, simply note Crace's strong verbs ("drawn," "tucked") and his use of figurative language ("pollard tree," "ice scars") that, taken together, lend "metaphorical life to lifeless objects."

Once you've painted a still life—that is, written a description of a subject in a fixed, permanent state—describing a subject in motion should come easy. You don't have to infuse it with life; you need only follow its movement with your mind's eye and describe what you see. The same principles that apply to describing a static object apply to action-based description. Begin by looking closely with your naked eye or the eye of your imagination. Visualize the scene. Break the subject or scene into its various parts, and then order the parts for a smoothly flowing description.

A good place to start is to describe someone at work or play, performing a task involving several discrete steps. The details order themselves, since they occur chronologically. The following description from Jane Brox's essay "Bread" details the actions of a baker preparing loaves of Syrian bread.

> Flour swirled in a slant of light and lined the creases of the baker's neck, salting his hair. He doused the work table with flour and kneaded the dough until it felt soft as an ear lobe, then cut pieces off the mass and balanced them on the enamel scale. He flattened the pieces with the palm of his hand to make thin disks, which he slipped into the oven. In the intense heat of the fires the loaves puffed up, hollow in the center. Once out of the ovens they collapsed as they cooled, and he wrapped the bread in towels or muslin to keep it soft enough to fold around an olive or fresh cheese or a slice of cooked lamb.

If you were to underline each action the baker performs, you'd see that each phrase centers on an active verb. The baker douses, kneads, cuts, balances, flattens, slips, wraps, and folds—eight strong verbs, eight steps in the process. Reading the description, we can visualize each movement, yet Brox's description is more than a series of chronological steps. The whole scene is alive with movement. Flour swirls around the baker's head, landing in the creases of his neck. Hollow-centered loaves puff up, then collapse. And through sensory details—in this case, details focused on the sense of touch—Brox takes us into the center of the baker's experience. We feel the dough in our hands, "soft as an ear lobe," and the heat emanating from the oven.

More basic even than Brox's strong verbs and sensory detail is her use of concrete, specific nouns. By naming the items of the baker's world accurately and precisely, providing what Aristotle called "the proper and special name of a thing," she invites us into the literary dream: flour, dough, enamel scale, disk, oven towels, muslin, olive, fresh cheese, slice of lamb. Each noun anchors us, keeping us firmly planted in the world being described.

THE PROPER AND SPECIAL NAME OF A THING

It makes sense that Aristotle begins his discussion of description with the importance of the individual word. Naming is universally regarded as one of the first acts, if not *the* first act, of creation. In the Genesis account, God *said* let there be, and there was. The world sprang to life through the power of the word. Until *light* was spoken, the earth was formless, a void. But once light and its fraternal twin, darkness, were named, the world of possibility opened up. And the evening and the morning were the first poem.

Naming is so basic to the writing process, so intricately woven into every effective description, that we often overlook its importance. Yet without this first act, without a precise, significant, and musical naming, no description can be attempted, no work of literature born.

But creating a literary work is not the same as creating the world, and we must forgive ourselves in advance for not being God. No matter how long we study a lake or our grandfather's handsaw or our husband's mustache, and no matter how hard we labor to bring forth a precise, significant, and musical description of what we see, we will not be able to re-create reality. Nor to capture it. "I know I cannot paint a flower," wrote Georgia O'Keeffe, "but maybe in terms of paint color I can convey to you my experience of the flower or the experience that makes the flower of significance to me at that particular time."

Unlike visual artists, we have no brushes, no clay, no glazes, no many-colored palettes to aid us in describing our world. And unlike performing artists, we have no keyboard, no trombone, no toe shoes, no tutu, no midair leap with which to stun our audience and ourselves. What we have is the alphabet, that small but loyal band of vowels and consonants.

Since the word is our only tool, we cannot afford to be imprecise, to say *knife* when we mean *scalpel*; fictional blood might be shed. Nor can we afford to squander five letters on saying it was a *green* tablecloth if green has nothing to do with the scene we are trying to portray. *Green*, although it is an accurate naming, will not serve in this case. And what is *ripple* doing in the middle of a poem about the weight of loneliness? *Ripple* weighs close to nothing. It tiptoes across the ear. It is a bad choice.

An Accurate Naming

The first test of naming is accuracy. Part of a writer's job is to learn the exact names of things and to have more than a passing acquaintance with them. When we read an essay by Richard Selzer, we trust that he is naming the surgical instruments correctly. In the same way, we trust Annie Dillard to know the difference between a beetle and a scorpion, and to describe their exoskeletons precisely. And when poet Mary Oliver writes "long-billed curlew," we must be assured she does not mean "great horned owl." Although the reader may not know the exact name for everything in a piece of writing, she nevertheless expects the writer to know.

Every world has its own vocabulary, even those worlds that might seem simple or mundane, and precise naming takes us deeper into the world being described. You probably cannot write a convincing story about a hair salon, for instance, without knowing the difference between a tint and a dye, or between a root touch-up and a highlight. It might also help to know how long each procedure takes and how much it costs. If you're writing a story from the point of view of a high school biology teacher, you may need to know not only what your students are wearing but also how to properly prepare a slide and dissect a fetal pig, and how to fill out a midterm grade report.

Finding out the names and histories of things and how they work sometimes requires outside research. Essayists, journalists, and other nonfiction writers know the importance of accurate naming, and their work often reflects their research. In her essay "The McKenzie River," Kathleen Dean Moore provides the precise names of plants she encounters along the river trail—wild ginger, vanilla leaf, twisted stalk, and monkey flower among them—and even includes details about her process of researching the name of a particular fern. As the essay progresses, we learn that Moore's father was a taxonomist, a fact that Moore expands upon: "Taxonomy, from the Greek word *nomos*, a rational principle, *taxare*, to rate, to place a value on, to assess, to call to account." This close attention to naming is essential to her essay not only because it serves to characterize her taxonomist father and his relationship with her but also because it reinforces the larger theme of the essay: the philosophical and spiritual power of naming our world.

Research is an important component of fiction and poetry as well as nonfiction. In the midst of revising a short story about a girl who helps deliver a calf, I realized I knew almost nothing about the subject. I spent the next two days in the library and the following day at a local farm interviewing a farmer. The best way to learn would have been to deliver a calf with my own hands, but it was winter and I had a deadline.

Before I sent the final version to my editor, I asked the farmer to read the description of the delivery. Other than an error in my use of the term *freemartin*, which I set about to correct, my description met the farmer's standards. "Yes ma'am," he said, "that's just how it is, you got it right. That's exactly how a calf is born, cord and all." (A freemartin, for those who are wondering, is the female twin of a bull calf. I've been waiting three sentences to tell you. Aristotle was right—what a joy to find "the proper and special name of a thing.")

A Significant Naming

Precision extends beyond mere accuracy. Although there might be several correct names for something, according to Aristotle, "[O]ne word may come closer than another to the thing described ... set it more distinctly before our eyes." For example, if you are describing a girl's white face, *milky*, *bloodless*, and *alabaster* all pass the correctness test; all refer to whiteness. Yet each word brings forth a different visual image. While milky skin calls out to be touched, *bloodless* connotes a sickly, perhaps deathly countenance. And *alabaster*, though it might look good on a statue, suggests an unearthly quality.

Although all three girls have white skin, they are definitely three different girls. The one with alabaster skin belongs on a pedestal; the one with bloodless skin, in an ambulance. And the girl with skin of milky white? Well yes, go ahead. Reach out and touch her.

My favorite descriptions of color appear in *Letters on Cézanne*, in which Rainer Marie Rilke describes not only his responses to the paintings of Cézanne and other artists but also his firsthand encounters with objects and landscapes during his visits to Paris and Prague. Of van Gogh's *Night Café*, Rilke notes "its artificial wakefulness in wine red, lamp yellow, and utterly shallow green," and, in Cézanne's work, a "glandular activity within the intensity of colors." But Rilke reserves his most original, passionate descriptions for variations on the color blue: "blue dove-gray," "waxy blue," "juicy blue," "densely quilted blue," "ancient Egyptian shadow blue," and many others, including my favorite, "listening blue," a blue that "listens to" the bright primary reds and yellows. When ordinary names—Prussian blue, cobalt, azure, peacock blue—are insufficient to describe his ardent experience with these colors, Rilke invents new names, thus taking us more directly into his experience and helping us see our world in a new way.

Word choice, then, refers not only to correctness but also to precision of image. In his essay "The Inheritance of Tools," Scott Russell Sanders chooses the perfect verb to describe the sound of his mother's voice when she calls to break the news of his father's death: "the long distance wires whittling her voice until it seemed too thin to bear the weight of what she had to say. ..." Why is "whittling" the perfect choice? Because it suggests the tools and actions of carpentry, an avocation Sanders describes sharing with his father; the word also reinforces the scene that opens the essay—Sanders accidentally banging his thumb with a hammer that had belonged to his father. Finally, "whittling" supports the deeper subject of the essay—the skills, behaviors, and techniques passed down through generations—and evokes feelings of loss and diminishment.

As writers, we must go beyond selecting the correct name for something. We must also select the word or phrase that calls forth the significant image, attitude, and emotion our story requires.

A Musical Naming

Finally, our naming must be musically precise. That is, the sounds of our words must reinforce their meanings. To return to an earlier example, *ripple* is probably not the best word to use in a poem describing the weight of loneliness. Not only does the word *mean* something slight, almost insignificant, it *sounds* slight. The short *i* is a bantamweight vowel, the lightest, most childlike sound in our language. Furthermore, the word's consonants slide easily into one another like liquid evaporating into mist. As softly as it began, the word ends. Not with a bang but with a whimper.

A more weighty choice would be a word like *stone* or *root* or *nobody*. Is there a vowel more heavy or sad than the long *o*? It hollows out the mouth, intones the deepest sorrow. In "The Philosophy of Composition," Poe discusses his choice of *nevermore* as the refrain in "The Raven." He wanted a word that was "sonorous and susceptible of protracted emphasis," which led him inevitably to the long *o*, "the most sonorous vowel."

It isn't merely the long vowel that makes *stone* and *root* weigh more than *ripple*. Because *stone* and *root* are one-syllable words, we feel their individual heft as we place them on the page or as we read them. And their ending sounds make a strong final impression. The *t* of *root* supplies an abrupt ending, closing down completely, while the *n* of *stone* remains before our eyes and deep in our throats, providing weight and texture to reinforce the word's heaviness.

When we consider the concept of "a musical naming," it's important to remember that not all music is melodic, harmonious, pleasing to listen to, or even, to some listeners, recognizable *as* music. Some music is atonal; some hurts our ears. As I mentioned in chapter one, writing descriptively doesn't always mean writing gracefully; some descriptions require uneven syntax, jagged prose, and sounds that some readers may not name "musical." For instance, to travel the road of Reg Saner's essay "Late July, 4:40 A.M.," the reader's ears require the "damp splat of fur-bearing roadkill" and the "bulk and chuff of each mastodon eighteen-wheeler," phrases that might not ordinarily be considered "musical" but that are, to quote Aristotle, "appropriate in sound and sense."

Later I'll discuss in more detail how the sounds and rhythms of individual words, phrases, and sentences affect our descriptions. For now, it's enough to remember that effective description requires not only an accurate and appropriate naming but a musical naming as well.

The Back-Door Technique

Sometimes the best way to name an object, a person, or a scene is by what it is *not*. After reading "Sonnet 130," we don't know what the eyes of Shakespeare's mistress look like, only that they "are nothing like the sun." Likewise, in her cheeks, there are no roses, and in her voice, no music. From a list of what she is not, the reader fashions his own mental picture.

Some scholars have categorized this sonnet as anti-Petrarchan, meaning that it purposely eschews the attributes an Elizabethan sonneteer might commonly assign to his beloved. But Shakespeare's poem goes beyond rebellion against established literary conventions. His technique of negation, describing his mistress in terms of what she is not, also allows him to avoid clichés (rosy cheeks, a musical voice) while leaving room for the reader to supply his own image of the beloved.

The technique of description by negation works well when the object being described is viewed as ideal—a mistress, a beautiful scene, a lofty idea. For these subjects, a direct approach would likely yield sentimentality or cliché. Arguably the most famous piece of writing employing the back-door technique is found in the New Testament, in the thirteenth chapter of the first letter to the Corinthians, often referred to as "the love chapter." Is there any subject that invites more sentimentality or cliché? Yet in his description of love (or "charity"), the author is able to avoid these traps, in part by listing the qualities love does *not* contain.

… charity envieth not; charity vaunteth not itself, is not puffed up …

Doth not behave itself unseemly, seeketh not her own, is not easily pro-
voked, thinketh no evil. Rejoiceth not in iniquity …

Describing by negation also opens up physical spaces that would otherwise
be closed to characters, narrators, and readers. Norman Maclean, in *Young
Men and Fire*, details a scene that would be impossible for someone to witness and still live to tell about. In the following passage, he describes the last
few minutes of several firefighters' lives.

It is really not possible to see the center of a blowup because the smoke
only occasionally lifts, and when it does all that can be seen are pieces,
pieces of death flying around looking for you—burning cones, branches
circling on wings, a log in flight without a propeller …

The back-door technique provides entry not only into physical landscapes but
psychic landscapes as well. Describing something in terms of what you don't
see, hear, or know reinforces a feeling of emotional distance. In "The Secret
Sharer," Joseph Conrad reveals, by way of negation, the aloneness the young
captain experiences before the ship embarks.

At that moment I was alone on her decks. There was not a sound in her—
and around us nothing moved, nothing lived, not a canoe on the water,
not a bird in the air, not a cloud in the sky.

You can also employ the back-door technique to create ironic or comic touches.

The new secretary squeaked by his desk in crepe-soled oxfords. Marilyn
Monroe, she wasn't.

Or to introduce a fantastic or surreal setting.

What she saw in her dream bore no resemblance to her earthly, day-lit
home. Gone was the sturdy pin oak, the brick columns, the white fence
stretching to the end of the driveway …

The back-door technique can also build suspense, demonstrating the confusion or disorientation of the viewer.

> Up in the sky, it's a bird, it's a plane, it's …

When the back-door technique is sustained, as in Ivan Turgenev's "The Tryst," it also builds rhetorical suspense. Here's Turgenev's description by negation of a birch grove in early autumn when the leaves first begin to fall.

> It was not the cheerful, laughing rustle of springtime, not the soft whispering, not the long conversation of summer, not the cold and timid stammering of late autumn, but a barely audible, dreamy chatter.

The repetition of "it was not" slows down the revelation—a kind of verbal teasing—and the reader rushes forward, eager to reach the descriptive climax. Okay, we gasp. If it's not this, and it's not this, and it's not this, then what is it? When we finally reach the phrase that actually describes the early autumn sounds, we're not disappointed, though the description consists of only five words: "a barely audible, dreamy chatter." By saving the actual description until the end of the passage, Turgenev holds our suspense.

THE POWER OF ACTIVE, VIVID PROSE

The most basic technique for making descriptions come alive is the use of active, vivid prose. Long before a character begins to move, before any action has begun, descriptive language quivers with life. Its nouns are specific and concrete, its verbs pulsing with movement, its syntax active rather than passive.

In active voice, the subject of the sentence is the doer of the action: "A freckled boy flung the newspaper onto the porch." In passive voice, the object of the action (in this case, the newspaper) becomes the subject of the verb, though the object doesn't actively do anything: "The newspaper was flung by a freckled boy." On rare occasions, the passive voice might be suitable—for instance, when you wish to emphasize a subject's passivity or victimization:

"Walter Milquetoast was buffeted by the slightest breeze of chance." In most cases, however, the active voice is the better choice.

If your descriptions lack vitality, examine your sentences. Are the subjects of your sentences the active doers of action? Or have you twisted your syntax so that a potentially vital act has become passive? Sometimes all you need to do to make a passive sentence active is to move the subject to the front of the sentence.

> PASSIVE: The ship was rocked by rough sea winds.
> ACTIVE: Rough winds rocked the ship.

> PASSIVE: The vote was passed by the neighborhood board of directors.
> ACTIVE: The neighborhood board of directors passed the vote.

Moving the subject to the front of the sentence adds another benefit: Unnecessary words disappear. Often the first to fall are filler phrases that begin with *there* and *it*. Starting your sentence with the most logical and active subject will sweep your sentences clear of unnecessary debris.

> CLUTTERED: It is probable that summer will arrive later this year.
> DIRECT: Summer will probably arrive later this year.

> CLUTTERED: There were four beautiful models waiting outside Tim's office.
> DIRECT: Four beautiful models waited outside Tim's office.

A note of caution: While you're sweeping, be sure you don't sweep away a phrase that might lend drama or rhythm to your description.

REMOVING FILTERING DEVICES

In *The Art of Fiction*, John Gardner mentions another stylistic tic that depletes the energy of a writer's language: needlessly filtering the image "through some observing consciousness." Phrases such as "he noticed" and "she felt" can clutter our sentences and also distance the reader from the sensory image we're trying to convey. In most cases, stating the image directly is more effective than filtering it through the narrator's, or a character's, consciousness, as in this example.

> The boy eyed the contents of his grandmother's room, noticing the tiny figurines arranged in tiers on the mahogany shelf. He saw the bouquet of miniature irises, the ceramic Cinderella slipper, the glass horse with the painted blue eyes. He felt a sadness sweep through him like an autumn breeze.

Once we've established the scene and clarified the point of view, we don't need to constantly supply filtering devices. In the preceding example, the reader knows, after the first few words, who is watching the scene. Unless there's a reason to focus on the boy's consciousness—that is, unless the point of the description is to demonstrate how intensely the boy is watching—the writing loses nothing, and gains much, by removing the filtering mechanisms "noticing," "he saw," and "he felt."

> The boy eyed the contents of his grandmother's room, the tiny figurines arranged in tiers on the mahogany shelf—the bouquet of miniature irises, the ceramic Cinderella slipper, the glass horse with the painted blue eyes. Sadness swept through him like an autumn breeze.

THE IMPORTANCE OF ACTIVE VERBS

Using the active voice and removing filtering devices are important steps toward fresher prose, but they won't guarantee sentences that call forth images. Once you've checked to be sure your sentences are active and direct, examine your verbs. Verbs are the foot soldiers of action-based description. They march in the front lines, toting the heavy artillery. It's hard to imagine a description involving movement that is not supported, in some way, by evocative verbs. Sometimes strong verbs are all it takes to paint a moving picture, as in this short poem by one of my former students, a fifth grader who used an apt pseudonym for his school principal.

> Mr. Grunch storms down the hall,
> Slings open the green door,

Stomps to the front of the room,
Spits out sparks.

An older and more experienced writer, like the novelist Joan Chase in *During the Reign of the Queen of Persia*, embeds verbs more subtly into her prose, but the effect is similar. Both writers succeed in setting their characters in motion, thus allowing the reader to "see" the scene unfolding. In this scene, Chase's narrator describes the actions of a group of boys who have gathered to wait for their beautiful neighbor, Celia, to arrive on the scene.

> One early spring evening when Celia was fourteen and the rest of us girls thirteen or nearly so, Uncle Dan came home, carrying the sack of groceries Aunt Libby had ordered over the phone, and saw a troop of boys sprawled around on the porch or hanging from the railings and balustrades. He stopped and asked them if there was some problem, had their mothers forgotten something at the market. They slunk off sideways and kicked the porch steps. But when Celia walked through the front door they came alive and in a fevered sprint backed away, running and hollering, to the far road, their speeding eyes in retreat still fastened on Celia, who smiled vaguely with a certain regal privilege.

Although setting a character in motion is the most direct way of showing action, a character doesn't have to move in order for verbs to perform their descriptive work. In "For a Godmother," poet Allison Joseph describes the godmother's face, "its bones pushing up under pale skin/like something unrelieved." Here, the bones take on a life of their own through the movement implied by "pushing." In the same way, Pam Durban's opening description in her story "This Heat" comes alive through the use of strong verbs. Even after the character has died, the action continues.

> ... his heart finally set him free, and he staggered and fell and blew one bloody bubble that lingered, rising and shimmering, then burst, leaving a shower of blood like rust spots on his pale skin.

"Rising." "Shimmering." "Burst." Verbs set this picture in motion. Durban not only tells us that Beau Clinton died; she shows it happening. A writer need not be bound by flat statements like "It was a rough sea," when verbs like *tumble* and *roil* and *seethe* wait to spill from her pen. Even inanimate objects come to life when a writer employs strong verbs, as Patricia Hampl does in her essay "Come Eat," describing the food her grandmother has prepared for the extended family.

> We had to eat fast because something was always out there in the kitchen panting and charging the gate, champing at the bit, some mound of rice or a Jell-O fruit salad or vegetable casserole or pie was out there, waiting to be let loose into the dining room.

CAUTIOUS USE OF LINKING AND HELPING VERBS

Although most verbs convey action, not all verbs are created equal. Linking verbs (*appear, seem, was, were,* and other forms of *being*) and even some verbs associated with the five senses (*look, taste, smell, hear,* and *feel*) should not be confused with descriptive verbs that call forth a picture in the reader's mind. For instance, in the sentence "The woman looked strange and distracted to everyone else," *looked* is not an active verb; it merely links the subject (the woman) to labeling adjectives.

It's easy to determine if a particular verb is serving only as a link. A linking verb, one that expresses a state of being, always requires an adjective to complete its meaning, while an active verb does not.

> LINKING: The soup, though creamy and mild, *tasted* funny.
> ACTIVE: Bart *tasted* the soup, curled his lip, and spat.

> LINKING: Beatrice *appeared* sweet-tempered and mild to her co-workers.
> ACTIVE: Beatrice *appeared* in the doorway, wielding a potato peeler.

Although it's often necessary to use them, linking verbs or verbs that refer to states of being cannot take the place of active verbs when it comes to effective description. The same can be said for helping verbs. Helping verbs like *would, can, might, must, should,* and *may* express no action. In addition, helping verbs can clutter your sentences unnecessarily. When they are not necessary for meaning, try removing them, and watch the energy flow into your sentences.

> ORIGINAL: Every Sunday morning Eliza would stand in front of the mirror and sob.
> REVISED: Every Sunday morning Eliza stood in front of the mirror and sobbed.
> OR: Every Sunday morning Eliza stood before the mirror and sobbed.

EXAMINE YOUR ADVERBS AND SUFFIXES

At the beginning of the chapter I warned against using adjectives that merely label or explain. Another kind of modifier to avoid in descriptive writing is the adverb that merely modifies or amplifies. Words like *very, extremely,* and *quite* serve only to show the extent to which a quality is present; they contribute little, if anything, to the word painting. Adverbs can modify a verb, an adjective, or even another adverb, but when it comes to descriptive writing, all adverbs should be examined. (I started to write "examined closely," but how else can one examine?) Adverbs like *closely* sneak up on us, and before we know it, we're writing phrases like "ravishingly stunning" or "hurrying quickly."

Sometimes we insert an adverb because our verb is too weak to stand alone. Trying to conjure up a word picture, we write "walked seductively" or "talked softly." We can avoid using empty adverbs by using stronger verbs to begin with. Rather than "walked seductively," we could write "slinked," perhaps, or "vamped." "Talked softly" could become "whispered" or "murmured."

This isn't to say that adverbs can't contribute to memorable word pictures, as novelist Suzanne Berne demonstrates in her description of a couple who "gazed liquidly" or a pair of Barbie dolls, one of whom "had lost a hand but otherwise appeared haggardly intact." "Liquidly," "haggardly." Berne's choices are not only original and memorable, they also strengthen characterizations, enrich the scene, and reinforce the narrator's eccentric way of looking at the world.

Sometimes we destroy a perfectly good word by adding a suffix like *-ful*, *-ment*, *-tion*, or *-ance*. In the process, verbs become adjectives and adjectives become nouns. Suffix by suffix, our writing expires. Bureaucrats, politicians, educational administrators, and newscasters are known for their ability to turn a concise, direct statement into pure gobbledygook by adding unnecessary suffixes, as are some student writers aiming to impress a teacher.

> **CLUTTERED:** Being *fearful* of every new situation was an *indication* of the *sordidness* of Billy's past.
> **REVISED:** Billy's fear of every new situation indicated his sordid past.
> **OR, MORE DIRECTLY:** Because of his sordid past, Billy feared every new situation.

> **CLUTTERED:** The *experience* of meeting Babs had brought about a *transformation* in the *reality* of Caleb's life.
> **REVISED:** Meeting Babs had transformed Caleb's life, making it seem more real.

Removing cumbersome suffixes can energize your words and force unwieldy sentences into order.

GRANTING METAPHORICAL LIFE TO EMOTIONS AND IDEAS

Through action-based description, almost anything can come alive—human characters, of course, and animals, but also inanimate objects, forces of nature, emotions, and ideas. One way to grant metaphorical life to an abstraction is to use vivid verbs, as in the earlier example in this chapter: "Sadness *swept* through him …" In his memoir *Soul on Ice*, Eldridge Cleaver transforms an abstract idea (the 1960s social and political revolt that began with Rosa Parks's refusal to give up her seat on a segregated bus) into a concrete, pulsing entity.

> And as the spirit of revolt crept across the continent from that wayward bus in Montgomery, Alabama, seeping like new life into the cracks and

nooks of the northern ghettos and sweeping in furious gales across the campuses of southern Negro colleges, erupting, finally, in the sit-ins and freedom rides—as this swirling maelstrom of social change convulsed the nation, shocking an unsuspecting American public, folk music, speaking of fundamental verities, climbed slowly out of the grave; and the hip lobe of the national ear, twitching involuntarily at first, began to listen.

As important as it is in forming memorable description, action becomes meaningless when it is not tempered by its opposite, stillness. Action that continues nonstop, without pause or variation, ceases to hold our attention; it is the *change* in the picture that captures our eye. In puppetry, for instance, stillness can be more dramatic than a forceful or repetitive action. Let's say that a witch puppet is dancing around her cauldron, her pointed hat darting up and down, her shrewish cackle screeching in time to the music. The audience is clapping, bobbing their heads in rhythm, enthralled by the motion onstage—for the moment, at least.

But this moment will not hold.

An inexperienced puppeteer, believing it will, continues shaking his puppets in frenetic, often senseless movement. Soon the audience loses interest, thinking, *Enough already! Let's get back to the story and see what happens next.*

What happens next is often *nothing*—at least, when a skilled professional is manipulating the scene. The witch stops dancing, the hat stops bobbing, the cauldron stops bubbling, the music stops thumping. She freezes, her broom lifted in midair, and holds her pose. One second, two. The eyes of the audience refocus on the stage: silence, suspense. Something is about to happen.

Even the most energetic, vigorous, quick-on-the-trigger prose cannot sustain itself indefinitely. In Cleaver's description, the steady thump of strong verbs and the rollicking, rolling syntax catches our attention and we grab on, riding its power and rhythm. We're heading somewhere, we're not sure where, but we feel the power snowballing, gathering weight as it tumbles headlong toward the end of the paragraph, where "folk music, speaking of fundamental verities, climbed slowly out of the grave; and the hip lobe of the national ear, twitching involuntarily at first, began to listen."

By the time this phrase appears, we've already downshifted, felt the variation in rhythm, the slowing syntax. The verbs recede and soften: "climbed slowly," "began to listen." At the semicolon, we take a breath. The wind changes direction; the action slows, stops. The storm is over for the moment, calming the stage in preparation for the next storm, the next turn in the story.

When Aristotle wrote that description lends "metaphorical life to lifeless objects," he was demonstrating the close, often inseparable, connection between action-based description and figurative language. One often leads to the other. Cleaver's choice of active, often violent diction—"seeping," "sweeping," "swirling," "convulse"—leads inexorably to the image of a whirlpool, signifying the dangerous, churning nature of the 1960s. And his description ends with another brilliant metaphor, "the hip lobe of the national ear." Yet even then, Cleaver does not let up on the verbs. The ear of the nation *twitches*—what a perfect choice for the sudden, spasmodic motion of a nation caught in the turbulence of a decade.

THE IMPORTANCE OF CONCRETE DETAIL

A friend who is fond of slogans, self-help tapes, and refrigerator magnets once gave me a bumper sticker that reads, "Don't sweat the small stuff." I thanked her politely, took the bumper sticker home, excised the "Don't" with a felt-tipped marker, and placed the sticker over my writing desk. A writer's job, after all, is to sweat the small stuff. Without the small stuff, no large stuff can follow. "No ideas but in things," wrote William Carlos Williams, one of the leading practitioners of the Imagist movement in poetry.

Ideas exist, of course, floating noiselessly above our heads, infused with ether. But how does one paint an idea? Or one's idea of an idea? It *is* possible, however, to paint a cow's skull or a white flower—that is, a representation of a cow's skull or a white flower—and allow the idea to rise from the embodied object. When she was asked how she came to paint the famous *Cow's Skull:*

Red, White, and Blue, O'Keeffe responded that she painted "my cow's head because I liked it."

I love the way O'Keeffe calls her painting "my cow's head," taking personal possession of the thing itself and revealing her attachment to it. Why is it that so often in our writing, we fail to describe the *things* of the story, the poem, or the essay? Maybe we don't believe anyone would be interested in the ordinary objects of our world. Or perhaps we feel the task is beneath us. After all, we're trying to make Art with a capital *A*, right? We're trying to move the reader to a new place, to reveal Truth with a capital *T*. Once, in a college writing class, I questioned a student about why he had typed his poem in all caps. I was stalling for time, trying to find something positive to say about the poem, which was filled with phrases like "the anxiety of my being" and "the chaos of undefined modernity." He looked up, his mouth spreading into a smug smile: "I didn't want anyone to miss the obscurity."

I swear, that's what he said. And I had to hand it to him; he'd certainly accomplished his purpose. No reader could possibly miss the obscurity.

I nodded mutely and moved on to the next writer. She'd devoted eight of the twelve lines of her poem to describing a button. It was a small, black plastic button, smooth as a wet stone, slippery to the touch, nothing special, the kind of button you can buy in any fabric store. Painstakingly, the writer had described its shine, its four tiny holes, the way the needle made a "scritching" sound as she tried to stitch the button onto a blue seersucker jacket. The man wearing the jacket was the narrator's dead father, propped up in a casket a few hours before the viewing. The daughter, who had noticed that a button was missing, had hurried to the store for a replacement.

That's all she wrote; those were the twelve lines. But beneath the workman-like description of a button, the poem was living and breathing on its own. The button was a button, yes. But it was also the embodiment of a daughter's grief, her attempt to fill the missing space. Sewing the button was the last task she would ever perform for her father.

I've mentioned that the poet took pains to describe the button. The work of accurate description can be painstaking and difficult, and it often goes unpraised, like most menial labor. In some ways, a writer *is* a menial laborer, laying stone by stone what John Gardner calls the "proofs" of the story, those closely observed details that convince the reader the events really happened or might have happened. Good writers expend much of their energy not in illuminating the deep mysteries of theme and symbol but in performing the physical tasks of the story, such as moving a character from the bed to the refrigerator. Or describing a small black button.

Why spend eight lines of a twelve-line poem describing a button? After all, such description requires valuable time and energy, not only for the writer but for the reader as well. Why not just mention the button, then move on to a memory of the narrator and her father, or to a riff on the joys of the father-daughter bond? Why is it so important to sweat the small stuff?

Keeping alive the fictional dream is the most obvious reason. But it is not the only one. Equally important is the power of concrete detail to engage not only the mind of a reader but his emotions as well. A poet can drone on and on about how her father's death has affected her. She can use abstractions like *grief* and *pain* and *emptiness* until the proverbial cows come home, without moving the reader.

If it is difficult to write about grief, pain, or emptiness without first embodying these concepts, it is equally difficult to write abstractly about a father's death. The subject is too large; the writer cannot compete with it. But let that same poet thread a needle, take a small black button in her hand, and stitch it to a dead man's jacket, and the reader enters the poem with her. Word by carefully crafted word, the world of grief shrinks until it can fit through the eye of a needle. Finally, it is the small things that break our hearts.

The necessity of concrete imagery applies to prose as well as to poetry. "The fiction writer," said Flannery O'Connor, "has to realize that he can't create compassion with compassion, or emotion with emotion, or thought with thought. He has to provide all these things with a body; he has to create a world with weight and extension." Before an idea, emotion, or abstraction can take on imaginative weight and substance, it must be embodied in sensory, concrete detail.

THE WAY TO A READER'S HEART

When a reader fully believes a story, both intellectually and emotionally, he moves in and unpacks his bags. No longer a tourist living out of a suitcase, ordering room service and watching suspiciously from his hotel window as the natives bustle on the street below, he has become, for the moment at least, a native himself. He changes into comfortable clothes, strolls the avenues, eats in open-air cafés, even tries the local catch of the day. He turns another page in the book. Anything is possible. Who knows? He might even fall in love.

When we give careful attention to the things of the story, what Gardner calls "moment by moment authenticating" of detail, our reader is fully engaged. He not only takes in information, he responds emotionally to that information. Like our narrator, the reader, too, wants to kiss the girl with the coral lipstick. He, too, wants to brush the strands of hair from her eyes. Could it be he's falling in love?

If our reader continues turning pages, his blood pressure may rise, his hands tighten into fists. She's been cheating on him all along—he should have known. If he could just get his hands on the guy, he'd …

What has happened is that we have done our job well. Through the use of concrete and sensory detail, through page-by-page rendering of the story's world, we have penetrated layers of the reader's consciousness, blasting right through his neocortex and into the mammalian and reptilian brain.

Human beings have a three-layered brain. The top layer is the most recent layer in terms of evolution. Without this layer, we would not be fully human. The neocortex takes in information and categorizes it. It enables us to reason, to contemplate, to reach intellectual insights, and to process abstractions; words like *grief* and *fear* actually mean something to the neocortex. However, although the neocortex can understand the concept of grief or pain, it cannot *feel* it. I imagine the neocortex as a gentleman in formal attire, sitting upright in a wingback chair, puffing leisurely on a pipe (he is, of course, not inhaling). His head may nod slightly in agreement or detached interest, but be assured he is not keeping time with the music. He is no head banger; he presents no danger on the dance floor. The neocortex is incapable of producing a physical response, a gut reaction.

That ability is housed deeper, in the mesocortex, the early mammalian brain, which is capable of feeling anger, passion, sexual love, and other emotions. When a reader feels desire for a character in your story—say, the girl with the coral lipstick—his mammalian brain is engaged.

And when the reader feels threatened, when his very survival as a fictional lover is called into question, his reptilian brain is activated. He wants to punch the other guy. Although we might like to imagine we're above such brutality, the truth is that no matter how civilized we become, we all possess a reptilian brain capable of almost anything when our survival is threatened. You need look no further than front-page headlines to be reminded of this fact.

Few of us wish to produce such primitive emotions in our readers. However, we *do* want our readers to respond not only intellectually but also emotionally to the words we write, the scenes we set, the characters we create. Without an emotional response, the reader will not sympathize with the plight of our characters or care about what happens to them. And if a reader doesn't care what happens to the character, why turn the next page? If we don't invite the reader into the room of our poem, story, or essay by means of sensory detail, why would he wish to remain? Why spend time in a place you not only can't imagine but also feel nothing for? And *feeling*, remember, resides below the neocortex. It lives beneath abstraction and explanation and analysis, in the living, breathing world of the real, a world created by the writer who patiently and carefully handles, again and again, the objects of her story.

EXERCISES

1. Make a list of terms associated with your vocation, a line of work that interests you, or a job your main character holds. In *On Fire*, Larry Brown lists some of the equipment of his fireman's world.

   > ... ladders, axes, forcible entry tools, rappelling gear, ropes, safety belts, breathing apparatus, nozzles, generators, a Hurst Tool (Jaws of Life), flashlights, pike poles, entry saws, boltcutters, fire extinguishers ...

   After you've made your list, choose several terms from the list and expand them into descriptive phrases. Combine these phrases to make a complete, sensory description. You might try the "I love" listing technique that Brown employs.

   > I love my old torn-up boots, the toes skinned and burned, my wrinkled gloves, soot-streaked and charred, my dirty coat and frayed turnout pants.
   >   I love to go down on the floor and see the smoke over me, worm my way forward to the fire, the hose hard as a brick, the scuffed rubber on the end of the fog nozzle. I love the two-and-a-half-inch hoses and the big chrome nozzles that no man can hold, the red axes and the pry bars and the pike poles that we tear down ceilings with ...

2. Write a description for an article of clothing that will appear in a catalog unaccompanied by an illustration. Your job is not only to describe the item accurately but also to entice a customer to buy it. Begin with the basics: Name the article precisely and list available colors (be inventive!) and fabrics. Then describe, in detail, each distinguishing feature. Finally, set the fantasy scene for the customer. Where might he wear the item? How will this article of clothing change his image, his life?

3. Starting with the same article of clothing (see exercise two), write another description. This time, imagine that you own the item. It is, in fact, your favorite piece of clothing. Your sister (or brother or best friend) has written to you, asking to borrow the item to wear for an upcoming event. She's never seen the item, but she's heard through the grapevine that it's quite a find.

You don't want to loan it to her, but you don't want to tell her that. Write the description you'd include in your response. Remember, you're trying to convince her it's *not* such a find after all.

4. Write descriptions for five different entrees to be served at an upscale restaurant. These are descriptions the waiters will recite, word for word, to diners. Be sure to include not only the name of the dish and its ingredients but also how it will be prepared and served.

5. Choose a piece of furniture in your home that holds at least four objects. I'd probably choose my writing desk, which is crowded with coffee cups, pens, books, rubber bands, a sleeping cat, unsent letters, photographs, and mementos. You might choose your dresser or the dining room table. Before you begin the description, select a method for ordering the details. You might decide, for instance, on spatial ordering, working from right to left or from front to back. You could order the objects in terms of size, shape, texture, or any other sensory quality. Or you might describe the objects in order of their emotional or historical significance to you.

6. Describe a person in action, preferably at a task that has clearly delineated steps. Watch your daughter wash the car, or take notes (mental or actual) as your husband plants a tree. You might also write a description directly from memory. Maybe it's been forty years since you've seen your uncle milk a cow, but the moment remains in your mind as clearly as if it happened yesterday. As you write the description, break the larger action into small, detailed movements. Let the verbs lead the way.

7. Using this chapter's suggestions for using the back-door technique, describe an object or a place in terms of what it is *not*.

8. Following Flannery O'Connor's advice about writers providing a concrete body for emotions, scan your writing for any abstract term for an emotion (words like *love, grief, anxiety,* and *guilt*). Rewrite the section, substituting concrete images that suggest the emotion. If you find it hard to remove the abstraction completely, anchor it with a concrete detail. For instance,

instead of writing, "I feel a heavy guilt every time I go home," you could write, "Guilt comes in the door with me, dragging its heavy suitcase."

9. Choose an inanimate subject—an object, a place, an idea, or an emotion—and describe it using active verbs. Refer to the selections from *Soul on Ice* and *The Gift of Stones* as examples.

10. Using a thesaurus, choose an adjective with several synonyms, each of which might describe a fictional or real-life character. For example, *delicate* (*fragile, exquisite, frail, touchy*); *hairy* (*fleecy, shaggy, hirsute, unshorn*); *flamboyant* (*flashy, lurid, exuberant, showy*). Then write a description of that character, substituting various synonyms until you find the word that represents not only an accurate naming but a significant and musical naming as well.

11. Scan your writing for any sign of passive-voice constructions. Rewrite the phrase or sentence in active voice; then, determine which construction is most effective for your purposes.

12. If you've used adverbs in one of your descriptions, examine them to see if they contribute to the word picture. If not, eliminate them or choose stronger verbs that can stand alone without need of modifiers.

13. Choose a word, phrase, or specific category of words (such as the names of plants in Kathleen Dean Moore's "The McKenzie River") as the basis of a brief essay or poem. Or research the etymology of a significant word or phrase that appears in one of your drafts and, if your research leads you to a new understanding of your subject, include the research in your revised draft.

14. Using Rilke's invented names for variations on the color blue, invent several names to describe a color you are drawn to, perhaps one you've noticed in a particular flower, in an article of clothing, in a person's eyes or hair, or in a landscape you've glimpsed on your travels or in your dreams. Study paint color chips to get you started, noting how slightly different hues call forth different moods or emotion, as in these examples from Benjamin Moore's color wheel: Pumpkin Spice, Citrus Blast, Honeycomb, Nacho Cheese. You might even invent a name that evokes an experience or mood rather than an exact color: Sunrise Hangover, Bridal Regret, Bird-in-the-Hand, Poet's Nightmare.

15. Describe an object that has emotional value to you, including within your description details of its history. For instance, how did you acquire it? What memories are attached to the object? How was the object used in the past? How is it used now? In "The Inheritance of Tools," an essay discussed in this chapter, Scott Russell Sanders embeds such details within concrete, sensory descriptions of his father's hammer, which Sanders explains he now uses for woodworking projects.

> The hammer had belonged to him, and to his father before him. The three of us have used it to build houses and barns and chicken coops, to upholster chairs and crack walnuts, to make doll furniture and bookshelves and jewelry boxes. ... It is a finishing hammer, about the weight of a bread loaf, too light, really, for framing walls, too heavy for cabinet work, with a curved claw for pulling nails, a rounded head for pounding, a fluted neck for looks, and a hickory handle for strength. ...
>
> The grain in hickory is crooked and knotty, and therefore tough, hard to split, like the grain in the two men who owned this hammer before me.

Although this excerpt from Sanders's work goes beyond physical description of the finishing hammer, it nevertheless supports the word pictures he has set in place while also providing historical and emotional context to the object he has named.

CHAPTER FOUR

The Nose and Mouth and Hand and Ear of the Beholder

So far I've spoken mainly about vision, but vision is only one-fifth of the sensory plot. Consider how an infant first encounters the world. Long before the eyes focus—on light, the mother's face, the yellow rattle—the nose and mouth and hands and ears have already begun their work. The taste of first colostrum on the tongue. The milk-scent of Mother, the lilt and pitch of her voice, the Braille of her soft, veined breast.

Since ours is a visually oriented culture, it's natural to think of description solely in terms of seeing. "Paint pictures with your words," we tell our students. "Describe that character so I can really see him." Rarely do we ask to *hear* the character, the rhythms of his dialogue or the squeak of his boots on the linoleum. And we almost never request information about how characters (or places or objects) *feel* to the touch, or how they *smell*. And *taste*? It's barely mentioned in polite company.

Yet to ignore the other four senses in your writing is comparable to sitting in a gourmet restaurant wearing earplugs, work gloves, and a surgical mask over your nose and mouth. Sure, you can still read the menu. You can even enjoy the artist's palette, the purple radicchio curled on top of the mixed greens. You can hold your wineglass to the light and admire its fluted stem. But you can't hear the clink when you raise the glass for a toast. Or the sibilant intimacies from the couple in the next booth. And what about the hot, crusty roll the waiter just placed with a tong on your bread plate? It looks hot, it looks crusty, but how will you know unless you pick it up with your bare hands, feel its weight and shellacked surface, break it open, and feel the steam escaping from the soft center? You swirl the butter knife in the white crock, spread a smear of herb-speckled butter on the bread, lift it to your mouth. Were you not wearing a mask, you might detect the scent of rosemary even before the bread touches your lips.

SMELL

A picture may be worth a thousand words, but a scent is worth a million. Perhaps if we thought of description in terms of a child's scratch-and-sniff book, our writing would be more inviting to the reader, and more evocative. If this were one of those scratch-and-sniff books, you could slide a fingernail across the page and smell the restaurant bread I've just slathered with rosemary butter.

Of the five senses, smell is the one with the longest memory. It's been decades since my high school prom, and I've long forgotten whether my date had blue or brown eyes. I've forgotten the timbre of his voice, too, and the endearments he insinuated into my ear as we were dancing. But each time I catch a whiff of English Leather shaving lotion, he returns to me. It happened just last week. A middle-aged man walked past me on his way to the dairy section, and I had to physically restrain myself from ditching my grocery cart and following him. In that instant, I was transported to the balloon-strewn gymnasium of a Southern California high school. Such is the power of smell, our most primitive sense, the sense most directly linked to memory and emotion.

One of my friends is afflicted with a rare disorder known as anosmia; his sense of smell is absent. It's hard for me to imagine living without the sense of smell. Where would you store your memories? How could you enjoy the present pleasures of the bed, the table, the scented bath?

Smell is why cartoon dogs rise toward the ceiling and float, on visible scent waves, toward their meals.

Smell is why real estate agents advise sellers to bake something—bread or chocolate chip cookies—before a prospective buyer comes to call.

Smell is why some of us marry certain men, and why, after decades, we still want to be near them.

Smell is why cybersex will never wholly catch on.

For even in this scrubbed, disinfected, sanitized, deodorized society, our noses still work fairly well. Some people's noses work better than others, like the noses of perfumers, wine tasters, chefs, firemen, and forensic pathologists who conduct autopsies (only a small percent of the population can detect the odor of arsenic, for example).

Although the rest of us may not use our noses so directly in our work, the sense of smell is nevertheless an important, if subliminal, part of our lives. Many writers rely heavily on this sense during the writing process. "You can smell the poem before you can see it," says Denise Levertov, suggesting that smell not only evokes strong memories but also triggers imagery. Maybe that's why the German poet Schiller stored rotting apples in his writing desk. Their odor, he claimed, helped him write.

Whenever I want to write about adolescence, I need only catch a whiff of vinyl and I'm back in 1962. Vinyl is the smell of September, of fresh beginnings. It's three-ring binders and zippered pouches and collapsible rain bonnets. It's the first day of school. I'm sitting in the front row, sharpened pencil poised. Miss Suchek opens a new box of chalk and removes a piece, long and white and as yet unbroken. She writes the year's first equation on the board. Anything is possible.

Another writing day I'm working on the same story, set in a seventh-grade algebra class. My cat comes in from the rain and leaps onto my lap. Wet fur. Wet wool. It's still 1962, but now it's November. Things have begun to sour. The smell of wet wool brings back cloakrooms, winter coats, cold rain, radiators hissing in the classroom. Already today Miss Suchek has broken two pieces of chalk on the same equation. I feel clammy from the radiator steam seeping into my sweater. Will seventh grade ever be over?

Since smell is the most direct of our senses, you'd think it would be easy to describe a particular scent. On the contrary. In *A Natural History of the Senses*, Diane Ackerman calls smell "the mute sense, the one without words," then goes on to explain the weak connections between the smell center and the language center of our brains: "We can describe a sight using visual adjectives—but when we try to describe smell, it's usually in terms of other things … usually we resort to describing how [scents] make us feel."

If you were to look back at descriptions you've written that include the sense of smell, you'd probably find lots of adjectives suggesting an odor's effect on you or on one of your characters. For example, you might have written that the smell of rotten eggs was nauseating or repulsive, or that the scent of a woman's perfume was intoxicating. You might also have shown a character's physical reaction to a particular smell, writing, "He recoiled from the stench," or "He inhaled deeply the woman's scent." In *As I Lay Dying*, Faulkner uses this method to suggest the stench of Addie's body days after her death. He never directly describes the odor; instead, he mentions such details as the changing direction of the wind and the townspeople covering their noses and mouths as the death wagon passes.

Although these methods—using an adjective to describe a character's feeling toward a particular smell or showing his physical reaction to that smell—can be effective, they are indirect methods of description. They do not call forth directly the quality of the subject. *Nauseating* is not the odor that rotten eggs give off. And although *intoxication* might describe your reaction to smelling a woman's perfume, *intoxication* is not the scent itself (despite the fact that a perfumer names it so).

If this perfumer were asked to describe the qualities of his new scent, "Intoxication," he might press his nose to the test tube. "Musky," he'd say. Or *minty* or *floral* or *acrid*, in the same way a wine taster might describe a particular wine's bouquet as *nutlike* or *fruity* or *oaky*. Yet despite the range of descriptive adjectives at his disposal, the perfumer would still be reduced to naming the aroma in terms of something else. *Floral* suggests that the perfume smells like a flower; *musky*, that it resembles the odor of a musk deer or perhaps a ripe muskmelon.

Writers, also, often evoke smells by describing them in terms of other smells. This works especially well on a reader who has no firsthand experience with a particular scent. For instance, a New Yorker who's never known a summer in the Deep South may not even know what kudzu *is*, let alone how it smells. But after reading Mary Hood's story, "How Far She Went," the reader will be able to imagine it.

> The heat of the day had broken, but the air was thick, sultry, weighted with honeysuckle in second blood and the Nu-Grape scent of kudzu.

By describing the kudzu vine in terms of a grape soda, which most people have smelled, Hood provides the reader with an entry into the sensory territory of the story.

Another descriptive technique for evoking a smell is to confine it to a particular place, especially a place weighted with history. In the following description from Joan Chase's novel *During the Reign of the Queen of Persia*, the smells of the kitchen are intensified by the accumulation of years.

> Both men were smoking; the air held it low because the kitchen was steamy from cooking and the storm windows sealed us in, the smoke blending with the milk smell of the room, that room soured every inch by milk slopped and strained, churned and set by, year after year, maybe seventy of them passed altogether.

Like most readers, you might never have brought pails of milk in from the barn, waited for the cream to rise, or churned butter. But you've known the stale smell of closed-up rooms and the odor of milk left in the carton beyond its expiration date. Because you've witnessed how time has its way with things, you're able to enter the kitchen of Chase's novel.

To evoke the atmosphere of this particular kitchen, Chase also mixes the smell of milk with the smell of cigarettes and the steam of cooking food, thus creating a collage of smells, a layering of senses that takes us deeper into the world of her novel. Mixing two or more smells is another technique for bringing forth the qualities of a place, an object, or a person. One of my college boyfriends smelled like motor oil, cigarettes, and Dial soap. A strange and complex combination, perhaps, but then, most memorable things *are* complex. How would you describe a high school gymnasium during a basketball game? Can you bring forth at least two distinct, even contradictory, smells? How about describing an August afternoon on the beach? Try to get beyond the salt smell of the shallows. Perhaps a scent of coconuts floats by—the girl in the yellow bikini, her body oiled with tanning lotion. Beside you, an opened can of beer warms in the sun. Mix the three smells together, then invite the reader in.

Another way to intensify a description using smell (or any other sense) is to temporarily mute the other senses. I'm not referring to actual mortification of the senses, like poet Gerard Manley Hopkins's temporary refusal to use his eyes, an event I mentioned in chapter two. However, the concept of stripping away the senses is one that writers can apply to descriptive passages. When we refuse to rely solely on one sense—most writers favor the visual—the other senses will naturally come to the foreground. Remember Blind Man's Bluff, the party game of childhood? Suddenly the blindfolded child seemed to grow longer arms, more sensitive fingers. He had to—or risk bumping into a tree.

To call forth sensory description, we can metaphorically darken our characters' worlds. In this excerpt from Naomi Shihab Nye's story "The Cookies," the narrator recalls going door-to-door with her grandmother to sell Girl Scout cookies to elderly neighbors in an old apartment building.

> Hand-in-hand we climbed the dark stairs, knocked on the doors. I shivered, held Grandma tighter, remember still the smell which was curiously fragrant, a sweet soup of talcum powder, folded curtains, roses pressed in a book. Was that what years smelled like?

Because the stairways were dark, the narrator could not rely on her eyes for sensory information. What other circumstances might place a character, literally, in the dark?

Maybe she's in bed trying to sleep. Suddenly smells are more distinct. What *is* that odor? Is something burning?

Or she's bound and blindfolded by kidnappers. For days she tries to identify her surroundings and attackers solely through smell and hearing.

Or maybe she's just blinded by love. (Does closing our eyes when we kiss intensify the aroma of our lover, the flavor of the kiss? Perhaps. At any rate, it cuts down on distractions.)

By refusing to base our descriptions merely on visual imagery, and by placing our characters in situations where vision alone will not serve, we force other sensory possibilities to the surface. A blind man probably isn't born with stronger powers of hearing, smell, taste, or touch than the rest of us; he's just forced to use them more. In his preface to *Eavesdropping: A Memoir of Blindness and Listening*, Stephen Kuusisto calls this phenomenon, as it relates to the sense of hearing, "compensatory listening," explaining that he learned "by necessity how to hear both for content and splendor." And though his memoir primarily explores the auditory sense, he describes smells as well, as in the section "The Horse," when the young, blind Kuusisto enters a horse barn and encounters "a pyramid of fragrances."

"What a thing! To be a young boy smelling hay and leather and turds!"

When discussing techniques for descriptive writing, it's easy to forget the most basic of Aristotle's maxims: "the proper and special name of a thing." Yet this brief example from Kuusisto's memoir reminds us that sometimes the best route to a reader's nose is a precise, accurate, and straightforward naming of the thing itself.

TASTE

Dwelling in close proximity to smell is taste. So close, in fact, that it is difficult to separate the two. As Diane Ackerman writes in *A Natural History of the Senses*, "Smell and taste share a common airshaft, like residents in a high rise who know which is curry, lasagna, or Cajun night for their neighbors." Everything that has been said about describing smells applies to describing tastes. Like smell, taste elicits strong physical and emotional responses. It's not the sight of blood but its scent and taste that draws the shark to its victim. In the same way, the reader can be affected viscerally by a description that employs smell and taste as well as sight. And, like smell, taste conjures up memory. Marcel Proust, a genius of sensory description, wrote that "when from a long-distant past nothing subsists, after the people are dead, after the things are broken and scattered, taste and smell alone … remain poised a long time …"

Although both senses present rich opportunities for evoking emotion and memory, both present challenges when we employ them in descriptive passages. Smell isn't the only "mute" sense; for some writers, the vocabulary of taste extends no further than a mention of a food's name. Sometimes it's enough, as Aristotle suggested, merely to name the object precisely. Fried chicken. Buttermilk biscuits. Merlot. But the effectiveness of that technique depends a great deal upon a reader's associations with the object being named. To launch me directly into bliss, a waiter need only mention Häagen Dazs Chocolate Chocolate Chip, but another diner, say, someone allergic to chocolate or someone who's nursing a toothache, may react quite differently.

Moving beyond a straightforward naming, a writer can describe a taste in terms of the tongue's gustatory map: sweet, salty, sour, and bitter. But tongue-bound adjectives carry a writer only so far. *Sour*, for instance, can describe not only a lemon drop but also buttermilk that's gone bad. The sour of sour cream presents yet another variation, as does a whiskey sour.

These limitations on taste description don't seem to affect the writings of Marcel Proust, whose evocative descriptions elevate tastes and smells almost to the status of characters. For the narrator of *Remembrance of Things Past*, these twin senses are the gateways to the past; in particular, the taste of a madeleine tea cake is the key to evoking memories of his childhood in the village of Combray. With the first taste, the village "rose up like a stage set" in his mind; visual images follow the gustatory.

Years ago my neighbor, a novelist, was so taken with Proust's description of the madeleines that he decided he must learn to bake them. As a result, every few months a package of these delicacies arrived at my doorstep, usually accompanied by a descriptive passage that my neighbor just couldn't resist sharing with a fellow writer. Together, sipping citrus-scented tea, we *ooh*ed and *ahh*ed over Proust's words, agreeing that no writer was more effective in bringing forth the flavors of the world.

Let's return to Proust's treatment of the madeleines, those little cakes soaked in tea. One descriptive technique he uses is to borrow qualities from the other senses. From the sense of sight, he borrows color and shape: the cakes are described as "squat" and "plump," shaped like "the fluted valve of a scallop shell" that is "richly sensual under its severe, religious folds."

From the sense of smell, Proust borrows "a decoction of lime-blossom."

And borrowing from the sense of touch to describe the madeleines soaked in tea, he writes that when "the warm liquid mixed with the crumbs touched my palate … a shudder ran through me." Here, Proust suggests not only the physical properties of the tea—in this case, warmth—but also his bodily reaction to that warmth. If the madeleines had been crunchy, Proust might have included their crispy snap; had they been spicy, he might have described the degree of heat or discomfort that the spiciness induced, perhaps a tingling sting at the edges of his lips.

Another of Proust's techniques is to set the scene in which the cakes are consumed, a childhood scene the adult narrator recounts. The madeleines were served to him on Sunday mornings at Combray, when he went into his aunt's bedroom to wish her good morning. The aunt, after dipping a piece of cake in her tea, would hand it to him. Over time, the taste of the madeleine became inextricably mixed with the memory of those Sunday mornings, the shared intimacy between an aunt and a nephew.

Atmosphere—including time, place, mood, and surrounding details—is an important element in the enjoyment of any food. A chicken salad sandwich, for instance, might be a forgettable lunch when eaten on a paper plate while you're alone on a Saturday afternoon staring at a television screen. Take that same sandwich, put it on a white china plate on a glass-topped table overlooking the Pacific Ocean at dusk while you sit beside your new lover, elbows touching, and it becomes a gourmet feast you'll remember for years.

After a while, the Pacific breeze begins to disturb the latent flavors in the air, so that it isn't only chicken salad you taste, or the slice of Bermuda onion, or even the seeded wheat bread on which the mixture is spread. Is it possible to taste the ocean? My five-year-old nephew can, or so he tells me as he leans his head out the car window—and we're still five miles from the beach. He slurps up a summer evening, too, pronouncing it delicious. He knows the taste of Play-Doh, the dog's fur he presses close, the plastic ball that smacks him in the face. Blood, too, from a cut on his lip. I remember that taste. Once, during a junior high softball game, I tripped over third base and landed face-first: blood rust, mixed with the scent of wild onion and the briny sting of tears.

Our tongues know more flavors than merely those of food and drink. We chew on a blade of grass, bite the end of a cigar, suck on a cinnamon-flavored toothpick. We swish mouthwash, down vitamins that taste of iron, swallow cherry cough syrup. Our mouths know the taste of a dental hygienist's rubber gloves, the cardboard X-ray slide we bite down on, the flat, dry taste of a tongue depressor. Late evening, after giving our baby a bath, we press our mouth affectionately to his stomach, tasting the sweet mixture of talcum and Johnson's Baby Oil and innocence.

Innocence? Well, what else to call the sweetness that rises from the baby's skin? Sometimes, as in the 1960s advertisement for Mounds bars, a taste seems "indescribably delicious." Or merely indescribable. That's when abstractions can come to our aid, helping to complete our descriptions. Struggling to convey the bittersweet taste of a doomed lover's kiss, we might write, "Her mouth tasted like roses and sorrow."

TOUCH

Touch, by definition, is an intimate sense; it requires a body's immediate presence. Eyes can see across long distances, ears hear faraway noises, and noses detect aromas far removed from them. But to touch something or someone, we must be close. A well-written description that employs the sense of touch bridges physical and emotional distances. It can wrap a soft quilt around the reader, deliver a bracing slap across the face, or render her helpless in sensory bliss. Sensory bliss is exactly what I experienced as I listened to Gail Galloway Adams read from her novel-in-progress, *The Eye of Madame X*.

> Next day Madame brushed my hair like Momma does at home. There is real surrender in letting my head be tugged by a rattail comb in someone else's hands. First she parts, scoring my skull like a map, separating strands into smooth threads. Little teeth nip hair by hair out of tangles and the preliminary comb is ritual before the hair brush. That begins with bristles skimming like sea urchins down the contours of my head. Madame lifts the brush quickly off my neck to make the hair fly, like a held music phrase; each strand slips back like a whispered note. With my eyes closed, I pretend I'm underwater, head bumping, and sand scratches my scalp, currents tug me like seaweed ropes; I shiver. Bristles quiver near my ear, tiny nylon nails.
> "You cold?"
> "No, I'm fine. Makes me shiver."

The scene Adams sets is charged with physical intimacy, due in part to the private nature of the act she describes. Unless you're a cosmetologist, you probably don't brush the hair of a stranger, nor do you allow a stranger to brush yours. Not all touch is created equal. We often shake strangers' hands, share crowded subway seats where physical contact is unavoidable, squeeze past fellow airplane passengers on our way to a window seat.

But to allow someone access to your head, your scalp? This requires trust and surrender. At the salon, the stylist greets you, ties a cape around your neck.

You glance in the mirror: You are bibbed like a child. Gently, the stylist lowers your head into the sink, turns on the water, tests it with her hand—a maternal gesture. You close your eyes. If she's a good stylist, she encourages you to let go, not to worry; she'll support your head. Then her hands are working, her fingers scratching, massaging, loosening the scalp. "Marry me," you whisper, and she laughs, wrapping your head in a warm towel.

In her description, Adams so strongly evokes the feeling of being taken care of, of giving oneself over, literally, to another's hands, that I respond as any willing reader responds. I take it personally, extending her scene to include a reverie of my own. I recall that when I first heard Adams's description, and later, when I read her words, I reacted viscerally. Like the narrator, I, too, shivered; I even closed my eyes. Many writers could describe a hair-brushing scene, but how many could cause physical sensations in their readers? And how does Adams accomplish this task, beyond merely choosing a scene of physical intimacy?

First, following Aristotle's suggestion, she accurately names the objects of the story's world: rattail comb, little teeth, bristles, strand, tiny nylon nails. Then she describes, patiently and precisely, the act itself. The hair isn't merely brushed and combed; it is tugged, parted, scored, separated, nipped, untangled, lifted. The writer breaks one broad, generic act into its specific and significant steps, taking time with each one because, in this case, each step matters. Every part of the process is necessary to call forth the emotional quality of this particular scene, in which the narrator first begins to trust Madame, to take her into her confidence.

We know that the narrator is physically affected by Madame's brushing: "I shiver." Madame notices this: "You cold?" Thus the reader is given two proofs of what the narrator is feeling. Since touch is a passive as well as an active sense, describing a speaker's or character's physical reaction is an effective technique for evoking the sense of touch.

When physical terms no longer suffice to describe her sensations, the narrator breaks into metaphor and simile. Madame's brushing has taken her beneath her physical self, into an underwater world where bristles are like sea urchins and "currents tug me like seaweed ropes." The brushed hair, alive with static, is "like a held music phrase; each strand slips back like a whispered note."

It's fitting that Adams describes the scene in terms of music, for much of her description's effectiveness is due to her attention to language, to carefully selected diction, and to musical phrasings. The repetition of the short *i* creates a tingling effect. Lightly and quickly, the words tickle our ears the way a comb tickles our scalp: "nip," "bristles," "skimming," "lifts," "slips," "whispered," "quiver." Adams's phrasing reinforces this effect. During the preliminary parting and scoring, the sentences break into short segments. Then, as the brushing continues and the narrator gives in to the sensual experience, the sentences grow longer, more leisurely, suggesting the rhythms of sex—which happens to be the subject of a subsequent section of Adams's novel.

SOUND

"The ear writes my poems, not the mind," said Stanley Kunitz in a PBS interview. "The ear is the infallible test." Prose writers, too, often speak of the important role sound plays in the writing and revision process. Some claim to hear an inner voice—the narrator's or a particular character's—that dictates the rhythms, diction, and tone of their language. Others focus on the musical interplay among words, on lyrical cadences, a kind of sound for sound's sake that results in stories or essays resembling tone poems. Reading certain lyric essays, I can almost feel the engine of language pulling the train of meaning. Here, I quote from Judith Kitchen's "Blue," using boldface type to emphasize the dominant sounds that caught my attention as I read.

> My father's **eyes, ice** in the center. **Steel**, or something more durable than **steel**. **Still**, they could burst into laughter. Flame. **Heal**-all blue, though in the end they clouded, couldn't **heal**. Blue you could **hear** …

In Kitchen's hands, music and meaning are inseparable. Listen to how "eyes" calls out to "ice," just as "steel" calls out to "still," which calls out to "heal," which leads us to "hear." I'm not suggesting that Kitchen was conscious of the sound echoes working themselves through the text, but it's difficult to miss the musical track playing beneath her words.

Still other writers focus on the sounds of the physical world as a way of pulling the reader into their literary work. Early on in Mary Hood's story, "How Far She Went," the grandmother hears at a distance "the pulpwood cutters sawing through another acre across the lake. Nearer, there was the racket of motorcycles laboring cross-country, insect-like, distracting." Later in the story, after discovering that their lives are threatened by the men on these motorcycles, the woman and her granddaughter hide from the men, crouching in the silence and hearing "the glissando of locusts, the dry crunch of boots on the flinty beach, their low man-talk drifting …" After several terrifying moments, one bike starts up. "The other ratcheted, ratcheted, then coughed, caught, roared." Finally, when the motorcyclists are gone, "crickets resumed and a near frog bic-bic-bicked."

Within these brief passages, Hood demonstrates several methods for evoking the sounds of her fictional world. First, she names specifically the sound the character hears: "the pulpwood cutters sawing." Sometimes merely stating directly what a character or narrator hears is enough—"the screen door slamming" or "a bluebird calling high and sweet"—without attempting to reproduce the particular sound through audio likenesses.

Another common way to suggest a sound is to modify it through the use of adjectives. Rather than "the sound of slippers," for instance, you could write "the soft sound of bedroom slippers." Hood uses this technique with "the dry crunch of boots." Often, however, adjectives merely label the quality rather than bring it to life for the reader. Hood's descriptive phrase escapes cliché partly because she employs an adjective rarely associated with the sense of sound. We expect adjectives like *loud, harsh, high-pitched,* or *deep* to appear in sound descriptions. But *dry*? Hood's choice is surprising and new.

Hood completes the image by giving further descriptive information, thus providing a setting or context for the sound: "the dry crunch of boots *on the flinty beach ...*" By the time this image appears in the story, the reader is ready to receive it, to add it to the other sensory proofs Hood has offered. The dryness of the air has long been established. The reader has learned, by an accumulation of details, that it's August, that there has been no rain in some time, and that there will be none on this day. Even the leaves know it; they have turned over, "quaking, silver."

When Hood names the motorcycles' sound a "racket," she is moving a step closer to imitative sound imagery. Although "racket" does not replicate the exact sound a motorcycle makes, it is nevertheless a more evocative auditory choice than something like *loud sound*; its harsh consonants grate more irritatingly on the ear. In the same way, "crunch," though not strictly onomatopoeic, comes closer to evoking the sound of boots than *noise* would.

Onomatopoeia is one of the most effective ways to help a reader imagine a particular sound. Words like *boink*, *sizzle*, *slosh*, and *yakety-yak* attempt to represent things by the sounds they make. Although no word can reproduce an actual sound, you can sometimes imitate a sound by substituting an onomatopoeic word for a more general word. For example, "the sound of bedroom slippers" could become "the hush of slippers," or "the whisper of slippers," if softness is the quality you wish to evoke.

I encourage my students to keep lists of favorite sound words, those that employ onomatopoeia as well as those that merely suggest a sound's quality. Although adult students occasionally produce interesting lists, the children's lists never fail to startle. After listening to Carl Sandburg's "Jazz Fantasia," one fourth grader, who titled his list "Words with Personality," came up with seventy or eighty during one class period. The list included not only the standard *whiz* and *pop* and other single-syllable explosions fourth-grade boys are so fond of (*burp, belch, fart*, etc.) but also words like *rustle* and *shuffle*, along with the occasional invented word: the *wind-swish* of a weeping willow during a breezy rain, the *honk-shoe* of his father's snoring. My favorite word was *plinkle*, which the boy invented for a story about his sister plucking violin strings. When I asked him why he hadn't used *pluck*, he shook his head adamantly. "*Pluck* is too deep," he said. "Hers is more like the way an angel would do it. You know, *plinkle*."

Although isolated sound words provide an entry into description, they take a writer only so far. After all, how often does a word appear in isolation? Furthermore, a sound word that is overly boisterous may call attention to itself, robbing a phrase or sentence of its overall effectiveness and distracting the reader from the fictional dream. Any word that becomes too big for its own britches should be questioned at length before you let it loose on your story, essay, or poem.

That advice goes double for any word whose sound, however musically intriguing, is not reinforced by its sense. It may be true, as one witty personage noted, that *syphilis* is the most beautiful word in the English language; however, try using it in a story and see how far its musical beauty gets you. The opposite theory also holds true. Some words that purport to suggest beauty simply can't carry the musical message. Take *bucolic*, for instance. Does an uglier word exist? Not for me. It sounds like something a baby would do to a burp rag, or worse. In the case of *bucolic*, for my money at least, sound and sense simply do not make a happy marriage.

On the other hand, some sounds and meanings were meant for one another; Henry James suggested "summer afternoon" as the most beautiful phrase in the English language. The words' meanings not only call forth warmth and leisure and, for some reason I don't quite understand, youth; they also *sound* lazy and languid. "Summer afternoon" takes its time; it's not going anywhere soon. And the living is easy, phonetically speaking—the open vowels, the liquid roll of the repeated *r*s.

Although selecting an evocative sound word is important, more important is how the word operates within a given phrase, sentence, or paragraph. In Mary Hood's story, "ratcheted" helps us hear the motorcycle starting up, but it's the combination of the sputtering phonemes and syntax of "ratcheted, ratcheted, then coughed, caught, roared" that sends the motorcycle, finally, on its way. *Glissando* is a beautiful word in isolation, but Hood's phrase "the glissando of locusts" is even better, not only for the cumulative effect of its sound but also for the surprise of its metaphor.

Just as metaphor can connect a reader to the smells, sights, tastes, and textures in a story, it can also call forth the *sounds* of a fictional world. The motorcycles, the reader learns, were "laboring" through the countryside. They were "insect-like," a description that calls up not only their movement but also their monotonous drone. In contrast, the "glissando of locusts" suggests the graceful slide of music.

Having been presented again and again with the auditory proofs of Hood's story, the reader comes to equate the motorcycles' racket with irritation, cacophony, mechanical intrusion, and finally, terror. When the terror subsides, what remains are the sounds of nature, providing euphony, peace, and release: "Their roaring died away. Crickets resumed …" and, as the grandmother and her granddaughter make their way toward home and safety, insects "sang in the thickets, silencing at their oncoming."

SYNESTHESIA

"It smells like sparkling gases" and "tastes like a mouthful of bees," wrote the little girl. Tammy was a fourth grader in a poetry class I was teaching, and we'd spent the hour writing color poems. She'd chosen silver, which she said was her favorite color. Most of the other children had chosen the expected blue or green or red, and many of their descriptions were good, some even astonishing —"Red is a mad crayon/foaming at the color" and "Green is fresh/like a new pair of lungs." But only Tammy's poem employed synesthesia, the phenomenon in which stimulation to one sensory pathway evokes sensation in another.

I was not in her class long enough to see if her description of silver was typical of the way Tammy perceived the world. Quite possibly it was. She may be one of those rare persons—one out of approximately 500,000—in whom sensory perceptions are mixed. Although some synesthetes claim to "smell" certain colors or musical notes, the auditory-visual mix is the most common. Many famous artists and composers have this ability, as do some writers, Baudelaire and Samuel Johnson among them. Nabokov, a famous synesthete, called his ability "colored hearing," and he often assigned synesthetic powers to his fictional characters. "If I had some paints handy," says a character in his novel *The Gift*, "I would mix burnt sienna and sepia for you as to match the color of a 'ch' sound."

I've never read anything to suggest that Georgia O'Keeffe experienced synesthesia. Why, then, can I almost hear the tones and rhythms pulsing from her painting *Music, Pink and Blue 1*? Perhaps O'Keeffe, although she was not physiologically wired for synesthesia, was emotionally wired to receive multisensory messages. Or maybe, in the process of working long and hard in her medium, she discovered connections she had not known were present. Even those of us who are not synesthetes can write descriptions that mix the senses, following the lead of writers whose literary works employ synesthesia. Think of Emily Dickinson's description of the fly's "Blue - uncertain stumbling Buzz" from "I Heard a Fly Buzz When I Died"; "the scream/Of the reddening bud of the oak tree" from Robert Penn Warren's "Muted Music"; the "yellow cocktail music" Nick Carroway describes in *The Great Gatsby*; or the captivating opening lines to Dave Diotalevi's *Miracle Myx*: "Lemons. The moonlight tasted like lemons. Kind of sour and felt yellow with points."

In her novel *Stones for Ibarra*, Harriet Doerr mixes the visual and tactile with the auditory. Sara and her husband have just arrived in Ibarra. It's dark, too dark for them to see the interior of the house where they will sleep. Although the night is alive with leaves rustling, a coyote crying, the "quick, light feet of possums and raccoons," Sara, having fallen asleep quickly, hears none of these noises. Only when the physical noises cease does she stir from sleep.

> Sara sits up in her cot. "I think I hear frost," she says to her sleeping husband.
> Four hours later they awake shivering to a sudden dawn that floods up behind the eastern mesa and stains half the sky coral.
> Now the house is revealed, and the garden.

It's possible to see frost, touch frost, perhaps even taste frost. But Doerr's character also hears it. Within her highly charged emotional space, her sensory perceptions stir, wake, and leap boundaries, until she is able to hear the unhearable. In the same way, the adolescent narrator Darl, in Faulkner's *As I Lay Dying*, is able to actually *feel* silence.

> Then I would wait until they all went to sleep so I could lie with my shirt-tail up, hearing them asleep, feeling myself without touching myself, feeling the cool silence blowing upon my parts ...

In describing the way silence feels, Faulkner moves a step beyond Doerr, into the realm of abstraction. Frost, although it makes no audible sound, is still an actual object. Silence, on the other hand, has no weight or texture; it is a condition, a quality, an *abstraction* that, in Faulkner's hands, nevertheless manages to evoke a sensory response.

THE PLACE FOR ABSTRACTIONS AND DIRECT STATEMENT

> ... I love abstractions, I love
> to give them a nouny place to live,
> a firm seat in the balcony
> of ideas, while music plays ... —Stephen Dunn, from "Loves"

Literary rules, although not *made* to be broken, often are—even the most basic and sacrosanct dictum of employing sensory, concrete details. In some instances, an abstraction or a direct, telling statement supports our descriptions and serves the larger story, poem, or essay.

Wait a minute, you might be thinking. *I thought you said ...* You're right. In this book's introduction, I *did* say that description is a body composed of three parts: word, story, and *image*. And I'll stick by that assertion. I'll even go so far as to say that the chief quality of description is its ability to make us, as Aristotle put it, "see things." Most of the time—perhaps as much as 90 percent of the time—a concrete, sensory description is the best way to accomplish that task.

But then again, there is that other 10 percent. Consider Chekhov's "The Lady with the Pet Dog," a story filled with passages such as:

> … in his character there was something attractive and elusive that disposed women in his favor and allured them …

Chekhov's description of Gurov meets few of Aristotle's criteria. It fails in "making people see things," it does not show Gurov in a state of activity, and it employs no metaphor. Yet the description effectively supports the story of a man who experiences love through intellect rather than emotion. As readers, we sidetrack Gurov's body and the physical, concrete world his body inhabits, entering the fictional dream through the door of abstract description. We dwell beside Gurov in the room of his intellect, the place where Gurov is most comfortable.

More commonly, writers who use abstract description mix concrete and abstract descriptions within the same passage. Tim O'Brien uses this technique throughout his Vietnam story, "The Things They Carried," in his catalog of the items the American soldiers carried. (The ellipses are mine.)

> They carried Sterno, safety pins, trip flares, signal flares, spools of wire, razor blades … . Taking turns, they carried the big PRC-77 scrambler radio, which weighed 30 pounds with its battery. They shared the weight of memory. They took up what others could no longer bear. Often, they carried each other … . They carried infections. … They carried the sky.

Luke Whisnant, in his novel *Watching TV with the Red Chinese*, employs a similar technique in the narrator's description of his new neighbors, three Chinese men who've recently moved to the States. In the following example, Whisnant not only mixes the concrete and abstract within the same passage but also within the same sentence, so that idea words like "existence" and "approach" share space with "boxer shorts" and "soap scum."

> They wing it, they wing everything: their poverty-line existence, their faded Mao jackets and crisp new white boxer shorts dripping dry on the bathroom radiator, their wobble-legged card-table desk and concrete-block bookcase approach to the Land of Plenty, their soap-scum sinked, bare-lightbulbed, no-Cuisinart kitchen, bottom-line basics—everything rigged, secondhand, cast off, and recycled.

Any writer who has ever attended a workshop, a writers' forum, or a panel of fellow practitioners has probably been warned against *telling* the reader, well, almost anything. We are supposed to describe, to show, to enact, to intimate, to engage by the accumulation of specific and sensory detail, to bring the reader into the scene. And in earlier chapters of this book you've been cautioned against making sweeping abstractions, of *telling* the reader instead of *showing*. (Remember the student who typed his poem in all caps so that the reader wouldn't "miss the obscurity"?) But, in truth, good writing is a dance between the concrete and the abstract, between scene and summary, and between showing and telling.

By *telling*, I'm not referring only to *exposition* as the term is commonly used in discussions of fiction writing—as a technique for providing background information that sets the stage for the story's drama. I'm also referring to the author directly and precisely stating what she means, even if what she means is "Here is what I know. Here is what I believe." And sometimes even "Here is what I feel you should do about it."

How does this genre of writing, often referred to as polemical, fit within our discussion of description? Ask Vicki Hearne, whose essay "What's Wrong with Animal Rights?" might dismantle all your notions about animal rights institutions. Ask Peter Singer, whose essay "The Singer Solution to World Poverty" I have reread many times, hoping he will let me off the hook. He won't. His case is clear, his call to arms even clearer. Yes, Singer's essay makes me uncomfortable. I'd rather be reading about lilies. But many essayists, journalists, and other nonfiction writers are not only working their form but also working their forum, creating a space for public discourse. They are agents of change.

The most effective of these writers manage not only to make their case through logic, argument, example, and opinion but also through use of concrete, sensory details. When Richard Rhodes reports on his visit to an Iowa meatpacking plant in "Watching the Animals," he cites statistics, gives background information, and even comes right out and states his opinion—for instance, that "we are the most expensive of races, able in our affluence to hire others of our kind to do this terribly necessary work of killing another race of creatures so that we may feed our oxygen-rich brains" or "It cannot be heartening to kill animals all day." Reading the essay, I nod in agreement: "… we don't farm any more. The coherence is gone … and so we delegate our killing." But it is his carefully worded, precise, and sensory description that takes me deeply into the world of this "terribly necessary work" and, finally, clinches Rhodes's case. Whether or not I want to witness the scene, I must: the blood that "gushes out … thick as a ship's hawser, pouring directly onto the floor." The "[w]ails from the saws, large and small, that are driven by air like a dentist's drill." The workers who must "gut the carcasses, great tubs of guts, each man taking the third carcass as it goes by." The pigs' "talk: low grunts, quick squeals, a kind of burn sometimes, angry shrieks, high screams of fear."

Later on, in the chapter devoted to plot and structure, I'll discuss the dance between showing and telling in more detail, suggesting ways that description can orchestrate the movement between them.

EXERCISES

1. Keep a sensory journal for a month, devoting each weekday to one of the five senses. For example, if you choose Monday as "scent day," then every Monday during the month you'll describe in detail three things you smelled that day. If Tuesday is "sound day," describe in detail three sounds you heard that day. On Saturday or Sunday, look back over your week's descriptions and combine some of them into longer, more elaborate descriptions. On the second Monday, begin the process again. After a month you'll have at least twelve descriptions for each of the senses. Read over your descriptions, pulling out memorable sections that you might work into a new poem, story, or essay.

2. Make a list of all the items you associate with a particular sensory quality. For instance, if you choose "white," your list might include linens, a bridal veil, a snowy field, vanilla ice cream, bandages, powdered sugar, and eggs. Choose four or five of the items, expand each into a descriptive phrase, and shape your descriptions into list form. Or choose one or two of your items to expand into a fully rendered, stand-alone description.

   If you have trouble expanding your description, use question triggers— who, how, where, when, what kind, in what way—to elicit details. Let's say your first item on your list of white things is an egg. Visualize the egg. Then ask yourself questions about it.

   Where is it? In a straw basket lined with dish towels? Beneath a broody hen? On the top branch of a tree? On the embroidered panel of a child's Easter dress?

   What kind of egg is it? A duck egg, a dinosaur egg, a boiled egg? Is it round, oval, misshapen, tiny?

   Continue asking questions until a complete image begins to form. In this line from his list poem "Varieties of Quiet," John Witte answers the questions: What? What kind? Who? and Where? to form an evocative description.

There is a quiet on the almost invisible eggs the killdeer lay in the dead grass behind our house.

Other sensory categories might include sweet, sour, bumpy, smooth, curly, slick, silent, scratchy, swirly, crunchy, black, swift, slow, bitter, or noisy.

3. Describe a place (a forest, swimming pool, library, etc.) solely in terms of one sense. Mute the other senses while you explore only the smells, for instance, or only the textures of the place.

4. Describe a place or a person by mixing two or more smells—like my description of my college boyfriend, who smelled of motor oil, cigarettes, and Dial soap. Or focus on a sense other than smell, using the same technique of mixing two or more sounds, tastes, textures, or sights to form a complex, perhaps even contradictory, sense impression.

5. Write a short description of a place or person that combines a concrete detail with an abstraction, as Amy Tan does in this sentence from *The Joy Luck Club.*

   And she had a daughter who grew up speaking only English and swallowing more Coca-Cola than sorrow.

After you've written a sentence or two in this manner, write a whole paragraph of description that freely mixes the two. Refer to the passages by Whisnant and O'Brien for examples.

6. Employ synesthesia. Describe an object, a place, a person, or an idea by using one sense to suggest another. What color is the silence in your bedroom? What is the shape of your grandmother's laughter? What smell emanates from fear? What does your name taste like? How would you describe yourself—or a sunset, or an object—to a blind person? What colors and shapes are your dreams? How do they move?

7. Using Proust's description of madeleines as a model, describe a food you particularly enjoy. After exploring taste, borrow from the other senses to expand your details. You might even include the setting in which the food is consumed as well as environmental factors that contribute to your enjoyment.

8. Make a list of words that, as one of my young students put it, "feel good when they land on your ear." They might be onomatopoeic (*buzz*, *sizzle*) or simply words whose sounds suggest particular qualities or emotions. Here's a list of some of my favorites: *whisper*, *rumble*, *slosh*, *shuffle*, *hollow*, *plush*, *slap*, *rustle*, *hiss*, *snap*, *squeak*, *crack*, *glop*, *tweak*, *splat*, *chuckle*, *whoosh*, *willow*, *hush*. After you've listed thirty or more, create sound clusters by combining several words with similar qualities into one descriptive phrase. Using my list, for example, you might write "the plush whisper of her slippers in the hall." Although you can't completely ignore the *sense* (meaning) of the words, for this activity pay more attention to their *sound*. Allow your ear to guide you. (This exercise is a variation on the word basket exercise detailed in the next chapter. With the word basket technique, you use index cards rather than lists. I prefer index cards because I can physically move the words around to form different combinations.)

9. Using the excerpt from Judith Kitchen's "Blue" as an example, write a sensory description propelled primarily, perhaps solely, by language. You might begin with a specific character, place, or object in mind (Kitchen's focus is her father's eyes), but as you write the description, switch your allegiance to the language itself, allowing the words, rhythms, and sentence patterns of your writing to lead you through the description.

10. Choose a public issue that you feel strongly about—for instance, health care, gay marriage, animal rights, abortion, adoption, child labor laws, capital punishment, or zoning laws. Then, write a brief opinion piece on this issue, perhaps something that could be published in the op-ed section of your local newspaper. Use concrete, sensory description to anchor your argument.

CHAPTER FIVE

Figuratively Speaking: A "Perception of Resemblances"

Reality is a cliché
from which we escape by metaphor.
—**WALLACE STEVENS,** FROM *OPUS POSTHUMOUS*

One rainy Wednesday morning, my phone rings. The man at the other end of the line identifies himself as a business writer; a mutual acquaintance has given him my name. "He says you can help me with my writing," the man explains. "It's too cut and dried. It needs something. I'm not too keen on that fancy stuff, but …"

"Fancy stuff?" I say.

"Similes and symbols and all that. I'm just trying to get across information. With me, what you see is what you get."

"How can I help you?"

"I thought you could help make my writing more poetic. You know, more descriptive. I've got all the important stuff down. I just need to stick in some metaphors and similes."

Oh, dear, the dreaded metaphor question. What can I say to let him down easy? "Since you're a friend of a friend," I say, "I'll be happy to look at your writing. But as for metaphors and similes, well, that's just not the way it works. Metaphor isn't something you insert after the fact. It's more than a figure of speech; it's a way of perceiving the world."

Talking about metaphor always has this effect on me. Is any literary term more misunderstood? How many times have I seen students "stick in" a simile or metaphor right before they hand in a first draft? For that matter, how many times have I stared at one of my own dying sentences, laboring to conjure a figure of speech I imagine might save it, only to have the manuscript returned by my editor with the sentence marked, "Seems contrived."

Of course it seemed contrived. It *was* contrived. In my desperation for the telling phrase, the apt image, I forgot my own advice: Metaphor, like all components of successful description, begins in the eye and ear of the beholder. It isn't a fancy embroidery stitch, something with which to embellish the surface of a written piece. Even Aristotle, who tended to view metaphor as separable from language, something that could be grafted onto a piece of writing to achieve a specific effect, nevertheless conceded that the source of metaphor cannot be willed. "It is the mark of great natural ability," he wrote, "for the ability to use metaphor well implies a perception of resemblances."

Does this mean that as far as metaphor is concerned, a writer either has it or he doesn't? Is the ability to perceive metaphors an inborn trait? Some writers do seem to have been born wrapped in a caul of figurative language. Similes seep through their pores; they breathe in metaphor. Although many of these writers are poets, being a poet does not automatically guarantee a "perception of resemblances." Conversely, being a prose writer does not preclude viewing the world through the lens of metaphor. A gift for figurative language seems more closely related to a writer's natural temperament than to the form or content of the writing. Some poets use little or no metaphor, while prose writers like Zora Neale Hurston take long luxurious swims in its waters.

Janie stood where he left her for unmeasured time and thought. She stood there until something fell off the shelf inside her. Then she went inside there to see what it was. It was her image of Jody tumbled down and shattered. But looking at it she saw that it never was the flesh and blood figure of her dreams. Just something she had grabbed up to drape her dreams over. … She had no more blossomy openings dusting pollen over her man, neither any glistening young fruit where the petals used to be. She found that she had a host of thoughts she had never expressed to him, and numerous emotions she had never let Jody know about. Things packed up and put away in parts of her heart where he could never find them. —from *Their Eyes Were Watching God*

Like the ongoing debate of nature vs. nurture, the debate of whether metaphor can be learned could go on indefinitely. For our purposes, let's consider that both nature and nurture play a role in a writer's use of figurative language. Yes, it appears that some people are more naturally tuned to receive messages from the universe of metaphor. But we can all learn to recognize resemblances in the world around us. And once we recognize these resemblances, we can learn to shape and reshape the expression of the resemblances, the metaphors we have been given.

WHAT IS METAPHOR?

Thus far, I've been using *metaphor* and *figurative language* synonymously. Because metaphor is the mother of universal connections, I view all forms of figurative language—in fact, all original turns of phrases—as metaphor's offspring. *Figurative language* is too cold and confining to describe the "perception of resemblances" that radiates from the natural world and the world of the imagination; the phrase places too much emphasis on the words being used rather than on the perception beneath the words. However, for purposes of clarity I'll defer to centuries of literary criticism and define my terms in more traditional ways.

Literal language means, literally, what it says. It follows the denotation of words—their meanings as defined by the dictionary. *Figurative language*, on the other hand, doesn't mean exactly what it says. It strays from denotation and moves toward connotation—those overtones a word acquires over time. Figurative language usually implies (or overtly states) a comparison between two things. These comparisons are called *figures of speech*.

Metaphor has traditionally been considered the most prominent figure of speech. It derives from the Greek *metaphora*, which breaks into two parts: *meta* ("over") and *pherein* ("to carry"). Moving vans in Greece are often marked with the word *metaphora* to suggest the transfer of items from one place to another. Metaphor occurs when one thing, or part of one thing, is carried over into another. An imaginative transfer takes place.

Usually this carrying over is accomplished through images. These need not be visual images, although figures of speech usually form sense impressions; abstractions almost never act as transfers. The earliest uses of *metaphor* stretch to include any transfer of a word from its ordinary application to another application, whether or not that transfer involves a comparison. In contemporary usage, however, metaphor suggests a comparison between two seemingly unlike things.

A metaphor always requires two parts, two sides, to complete its equation. The critic I.A. Richards names these two sides the "tenor" and the "vehicle." The tenor, the main subject or the "general drift," is usually a thing but can also be an idea, an emotion, or some other abstraction. The vehicle is the concrete image that embodies the main subject, supplying it with weight, shape, and substance. For instance, in the sentence "He carried his guilt like a heavy suitcase," *guilt* is the tenor and *suitcase* is the vehicle.

In the passage from *Their Eyes Were Watching God* quoted earlier, Hurston's tenors (main ideas) include time, thought, emotions, and dreams. Her vehicles (concrete objects and images that carry the main ideas) include a shelf, a drape or blanket, pollen, fruit, petals, and "things packed away." But Hurston does more than simply show relationships between tenors and vehicles. Reading the passage, I didn't think, *Oh yes, Janie's heart is like a closet lined with shelves of memories.* I didn't visualize a blanket draped over a dream or pollen floating down on a man. Instead I was taken into a world I'd never entered before: Janie's inner world of disillusionment and lost dreams.

Effective metaphor does more than shed light on the two things being compared. It actually brings to the mind's eye something that has never before been seen. Metaphor is not just the marriage ceremony linking two things; it is the child born from their union. An original and imaginative metaphor brings something fresh into the world. In the interaction between two things being compared, a new image or idea is formed.

METAPHOR AND SIMILE: FRATERNAL TWINS

Some scholars don't distinguish between simile and metaphor, or between metaphor and other figures of speech, considering the differences among figures of speech to be mostly surface differences. However, if we dig beneath even these surface differences, we discover variations that, however slight, affect our writing in important ways. Take simile and metaphor. At first glance, they seem to differ little from one another. Both are comparisons between two things.

> SIMILE: Your hair is like a dark river.
> METAPHOR: Your hair is a dark river.

In this example, the surface difference between the two statements is the inclusion of *like*, which calls to mind the definition I memorized in sixth grade: *A simile is a comparison using* like *or* as. Actually this is an inadequate definition. *Like* and *as* aren't the only connectives that appear in similes. *Than* is another; so are verbs like *resembles.* The sixth-grade definition is inadequate also because it suggests that any phrase comparing two things using *like* or *as* is a simile. Not true. "Your hair is like your sister's hair" is not a simile. Both simile and metaphor require comparisons between things that are unlike in kind.

By its very construction, a simile calls attention to itself as a figure of speech. It not only shows the relation between the two things being compared, it *explains* the relationship through *like* or *as,* or some other connective. Simile is comparison made explicit. In metaphor, however, one thing is not explicitly being compared to another; it *is* the other. Metaphor suggests that the imaginative transfer (from one thing to another) has already occurred. For this reason, metaphor often carries more imaginative weight than simile.

The use of connectives isn't the only quality that distinguishes metaphor from simile; the two differ also in the degree of likeness they suggest. Simile is usually limited to one likeness, whereas metaphor often invites a whole range of like qualities. In metaphor, the reader is free to imagine additional qualities the two things might share.

Another form of metaphor, implied metaphor, carries the reader's associations a step further. In traditional simile and metaphor, both parts of the comparison are stated.

> SIMILE: Your *hair* is like a dark *river.*
> METAPHOR: Your *hair* is a dark *river.*

Both statements contain *hair* and *river,* the two sides of the metaphorical equation.

In implied metaphor, however, only one side of the equation is stated.

> IMPLIED METAPHOR: Your hair twists and meanders across the landscape of your shoulders.

Here, the tenor of the metaphor (*hair*) is present, but the vehicle (*river*) is merely implied through the use of *twists, meanders,* and *landscape.* An implied metaphor uses neither a connective (such as *like* or *as*) nor any form of the verb *to be.* Skilled writers often employ several different levels of figurative language within the same work—similes and metaphors in which both sides of the equation are obvious, and also more subtle, implied metaphors.

For instance, in the early segments of Lia Purpura's essay "Autopsy Report," we note the startling, effective similes that open the scene to our eyes and ears: the bladder "cupped in hand like a water balloon" and the "whisking and shushing of knives over skin, a sound like tearing silk." Her metaphors are equally effective—the "shield of ribs," and the organs on the hanging scale "a cornucopia of dripping fruits." But Purpura's figurative language doesn't stop with one-on-one correspondences, noun aligned with noun: bladder = water balloon; sound of knives = sound of tearing silk; ribs = shield; organs = cornucopia. At the end of the essay, once the narrator leaves the autopsy room and re-enters her accustomed world of grocery store and city street, Purpura's metaphors keep right on coming, though they are now so subtly stated as to be almost invisible at first glance. It is as if the narrator, having been changed by her experience, no longer draws a visible line between the dead and the living. Stepping into fresh, cold, rainy March air, she notices "the milky blueness" scent lingering from her earlier encounter in the autopsy room. "Yes," begins the final sentence of the essay, "everything looked as it always had—bright and pearly, lush and arterial after the rain."

"Pearly." "Arterial." Implied metaphor. Firm evidence that an imaginative transfer has taken place in the narrator's perception, a transfer that Purpura's carefully worded metaphors make available to the reader as well.

DISCOVERING ORIGINAL METAPHORS

The excerpt from Zora Neale Hurston's novel, quoted earlier in this chapter, succeeds not only because of its striking and sustained metaphors but also because those metaphors appear to be deeply felt, springing organically from an authentic source. The writer has not "stuck in" metaphors after the fact; rather they appear as natural outgrowths of the way the narrator sees, and feels, her way through the world. Hurston's metaphors reflect a "perception of resemblances" richer and deeper than any mere figure of speech.

When images emerge naturally, when the "perception of resemblances" makes itself known, it's not *fancy* at work, but imagination. (The distinction between fancy and imagination was first made by Samuel Taylor Coleridge in *Biographia Literaria*.) In fancy, the writer is concerned with making or assembling images; fancy is a mechanical facility that calls attention to its own construction. When my editor wrote, "Seems contrived," in the margin of my manuscript beside the drummed-up metaphor I'd written, she was distinguishing between imagination and fancy. Fancy relies solely on labor. When we employ fancy, we feel ourselves reaching out, fetching. That's why our results often seem far-fetched; we've fetched them from afar.

Imagination, on the other hand, isn't a mere assembling of likenesses but a seemingly effortless blending of images into a unified whole. But how does this blending occur? How can we encourage metaphors to emerge organically in our writing? Coleridge offers a hint: The difference between fancy and imagination depends, in great degree, upon the emotional involvement of the writer. Images, he says, "become proofs of original genius only as far as they are modified by a predominant passion."

"Original genius." Hmm. The subject of originality comes up often in literary discussions. My writing students, especially those of college age and beyond, talk a lot about originality, by which they seem to mean something weird or odd or completely, dazzlingly incoherent. Some complain that their metaphors are hopeless, that they just can't think of anything that's new enough, strange enough.

"Everything's already been said," one student moans. "And by better minds than mine."

"I don't have an original bone in my body," says another.

"Did you hear what you just said?" I say. "That's exactly where your originality lies. In each bone of your body." I go on to explain the root of *originality*: *origin*. Origin, as in source, spring, primary being. We are most original when we are most ourselves. Only then are we close to our first source, our fueling passions.

Discovering the source of original passion should be the most natural thing in the world, right? "It's as clear as the nose on your face," my grandmother used to say. In fact, the nose on our face isn't clear to us at all. It's clear only to others, or to ourselves when we're looking in a mirror. Sometimes we are simply too close to our origins to recognize them. When our writing is going well, it's often because we have connected with our original source, our ruling passions. As a result, our metaphors are organic and unforced, springing from imagination rather than fancy.

Beginning writers, especially children, usually draw naturally on original sources. They don't know any better, and ignorance serves them well. They write only, as Samuel Butler once advised, "what refuses to go away," what matters most to them. Those of us who have been writing for a while sometimes lose our way. The act of writing—that solitary, sometimes joyous and sometimes agonizing act—gets mixed up with publishing and competition and success and failure and reviews and deadlines. We forget why we began writing in the first place. Like the nouveau millionaire who leaves the little town that formed him, we forget where we came from. We lose our origins—and with it, our originality.

FINDING YOUR PERSONAL "CONSTELLATION OF IMAGES"

The poet Stanley Kunitz, who wrote and published for over eighty years, once called the sources of a writer's originality her "constellation of images," a constellation that is sometimes traceable within her work by the repetition of certain images that reflect her passions or obsessions. If a writer never discovers her constellation, Kunitz said, she may produce adequate, even good, work, but the work will never rise above superficiality. In Kunitz's poems, his "constellation of images" revolves around a central star, his father. The loss surrounding his father's death (his father committed suicide six weeks before Kunitz was born) supplies the metaphor that informs almost everything he writes. Kunitz calls his father's suicide the "nexus" linking every image, every metaphor, of his work.

An early event in your life can shape the "constellation of images" that emerges in your work. For me, it was the death of an infant sister the year I was born, an event that shaped not only my role in the family drama but also the images of death and survivorship that eventually emerged in my poetry, fiction, and nonfiction. For many years after I began writing, I was not conscious of my personal metaphor, my "one small grief" as I would later call it. I discovered my "constellation of images" partly through the writing process itself and partly through the comments of editors and readers; it was as plain as the nose on my face, at least to them.

Little by little, as I studied the metaphors running through my work, the clues came together: sidekicks, sisters, decoys, hand-me-downs, skin grafts, rubber dolls, twins, doubles, even my penchant for compound words. Dead and lost children haunted my fiction, as did childless women and men. Even my comic stories contained images of the double—remember my reference, in an earlier chapter, to the freemartin, the female calf of a twin bull? To this day, I continue to work and rework the central myth of the double. If my metaphors are original, it's simply because they arise organically from my origin, my life source.

Childhood events aren't the only forces that shape a writer's vision. Your present-day preoccupations, interests, and obsessions provide original metaphors, as do subjects discovered through research or accident. Look back over your writing. Reread your stories, poems, and essays, noting successful images or metaphors, those passages that seem to have sprung from imagination, not fancy. Notice what you've taken time and care to describe—description is one of the entries into metaphor. If you keep a journal or a writer's notebook, reread old entries. Circle recurring images, descriptions, or isolated words; if the entries are stored in a computer, you can do a search to see how often a particular word or phrase occurs. From a sample of text, online resources can even create virtual "word clouds," visual representations that depict the prominence of certain words based on how many times they appear.

Such studies of your writing can help you discover your inner "constellation of images," the ruling passions that fuel your most original work. But they can also help you locate the constellation that appears in other writers' works, or in early drafts of your own. Uncovering the constellation—of images, sounds, particular words or rhythms—can help you understand the deeper pattern of meaning or theme trying to push through the surface. Imagine the following words scattered in random fashion across your desk: *torn, broken, graves, gone, buried, ruts, no, left, blown, litter, rubble, patina*. What pattern of meaning begins to emerge as you study these words in relation to each other? If each of these words were a star in a galaxy, what constellation might they form?

I composed this list of words from Ted Kooser's "In Nebraska," a brief meditation (excerpted from *Local Wonders: Seasons in the Bohemian Alps*) in which the careful placement of particular words, some of which are repeated, forms a constellation of meaning. You could also think of Kooser's essay as a tapestry, woven with intricate loops or braids or netting, or as a web of small but elaborate design, a web that captures and holds his main subject of loss.

Repeated patterns of any kind in our work—words, phrases, objects, colors, places, events, people, sounds—are there for a reason. We should pay attention to them. However, too cold hearted or objective an assessment won't help at this delicate stage. Like the centipede in "The Centipede's Dilemma," (a poem usually attributed to Katherine Craster) who is proceeding quite nicely, thank you, until he stops to consider which leg goes after which, we don't want to become too preoccupied with the how and why of each step of the writing process. But a calm, inquisitive approach to our own processes can instruct us. Paying attention to recurring motifs in our work can help us discover the sources of our originality. It can also increase our ability to extend isolated metaphors, resulting in richer, fuller descriptions.

EXTENDING METAPHORS

Once you've discovered your original images, you can use and reuse those images in new ways. Monet's overwhelming passion for water served him well throughout his career. Even when he wasn't painting water he was painting water. His smokestacks and meadows seem liquid, his trees mastlike, his trunks and branches like rivers. In the self-portrait of 1917, his cheekbones seem to be made of wave-like particles. Even his brushstrokes are watery. Monet extended his ruling metaphor to include not only ordinary water but also mist, fog, ice, and even steam from passing locomotives.

One way to write richer descriptions is to extend one of your original metaphors. Let's say you've discovered images of plants recurring in your work. But the images are merely mentioned, then abandoned; they aren't leading to full-fledged descriptions. Try writing down all the words or phrases you associate with plants. Free-associate, listing everything that comes to mind. Your list might include *leaf, bud, stem, seed, water, roots, compost, moss, darkness, green, swamp, trowel, greenhouse, oxygen, rubber boots, roses, thorns*. As you continue, allow one detail to lead to another; *thorns* might lead you to write *blood*, for instance, which might lead to *circulation*.

If the words in your list begin to diverge from your original idea, don't worry. You can always return to your root word—or the free association might lead to more interesting connections than you'd planned. In chapter four, we discussed how the engine of language seems to pull the train of meaning in Judith Kitchen's lyric essay "Blue." The engine of language can also pull the train of metaphor. If you're especially tuned to the sounds of words, their musical qualities can lead you further into the metaphorical world. This happens to me often, and it always surprises me. When I began "Sidekick," which later evolved into a long catalog poem, I thought it would be a short lyric. After all, I had only two images—that of a comic's straight man, and Michelangelo's image of the martyred St. Bartholomew reuniting with his flayed skin. But as I began to write, one word called up another. "Straight man" led to "ploy," which led to the rhymed "decoy." The image of "decoy" demanded "bobbing," which called, musically and visually, for "backup singers with their benign doo-wops." The metaphors kept growing in this way, propelled not by an overall idea or motif but rather by the actual process of placing one word after the other. With this method, the shapes, rhythms, and sounds of words suggest other shapes, rhythms, and sounds, which can extend a single metaphor, forming a universe of connections.

We can also extend a metaphor by studying the technical world from which the metaphor emerged. Your isolated and spotty plant images, for instance, might expand into full descriptions if you consult a gardening book, a botany text, or schematic drawings that depict a plant's inner workings. In his novel *Ingenious Pain*, Andrew Miller describes a boy's fascination with William Harvey's sketches of the human body.

> But it is the pictures which snare him: the world beneath the skin; the skein of guts, the globes and bulbs of the great organs; the sheets of muscle strapped around the trellis of the bones; the intricate house of the heart, veins and arteries radiating, curling, branching into tiny tributaries.

Although the boy is presented as a character and not the author himself, the description has the feel of firsthand observation. Perhaps, like the curious boy, Miller stared at Harvey's sketches until he began to see the other worlds contained within the world of the body—the skein and globes and trellises and houses. Our metaphors can grow out of research, eye-search, and even I-search, that ransacking of memory that so often yields surprise treasures. In the case of your plant images, for instance, can you recall an early experience that shaped the obsession? The memory may contain within it details you'd temporarily forgotten.

An isolated metaphor, when given attention, can yield a whole family of metaphors, resulting in rich and sensual descriptions. Sometimes we're not sure where an image is leading, but we feel instinctively that it is important. At this point, we may feel the way Ingmar Bergman says he feels when he conceives a film.

> It is a mental state ... abounding in fertile associations and images. Most of all, it is a brightly colored thread sticking out of the dark sack of the unconscious. If I begin to wind up this thread, and do it carefully, a complete film will emerge.

Winding up the thread of a metaphor requires patience and trust. We must believe that connections will be made along the way. Provided that our metaphor has emerged from imagination rather than fancy, these connections will probably grow naturally as the writing proceeds.

Bergman likens the artist's process of discovery to winding up a thread; Eudora Welty describes the process in a different way. When a writer is "into a story," she once told a *Paris Review* interviewer, "everything seems to apply. … Wherever you go, you meet part of the story. I guess you're tuned in for it, and the right things are sort of magnetized."

I imagine these "right things" as iron filings drawn to the magnetic field of a writer's work. For Welty, the iron filings were usually overheard conversations stored in her memory until they reemerged as dialogue spoken by her characters. For other writers, these iron filings might be plot twists, specific details about characters, the final lines that complete a sonnet-in-progress, or the extended metaphor that unifies seemingly disparate elements. The "right things" differ from writer to writer. However, as Welty suggests, one principle remains constant: For the right things to be magnetized, the writer must first be "into a story." My own experience confirms this theory. My magnetic field is activated only when I am fully engaged in the writing process.

Depending on the scope and nature of the text, a writer's iron filings might align rather quickly or the process might take months, even years. I was nearly a decade into researching and writing a multigenerational memoir before I discovered the metaphor that illuminated my central theme and helped me shape the material into a unified whole. The work-in-progress focused on the intersecting lives of my Indiana ancestors and how their relationships played out against larger historical, societal, and cultural contexts.

This obsession with family and with the myriad ways that lives intersect was nothing new for me; I'd been writing about family, in various forms and genres, for thirty years. But never before had I questioned the value of familial connections—not only of blood relations but also the ties that bind extended families in the form of neighbors, friends, church congregations, fraternal and other like-minded societies, and communities of every kind. Do these connections create more harm than good? Does individuality trump community? Should it? Where do I leave off and others begin?

These are some of the questions that kept rising out of the material, which included hundreds of letters, documents, and artifacts spanning more than a century, as well as interviews, oral histories, and site visits. The material itself was interesting enough to draw the attention of editors and readers who sampled early versions of the book, but as any writer knows, all the material in the world does not a book make. Despite extensive research, personal passion for the subject, and thousands of hours of drafting and redrafting, I still had no vision of what to leave in, what to leave out, or how to structure the book to reveal its deepest concerns. I didn't even have a working title. My center was not magnetized.

Then one morning, while conducting an interview with a distant cousin about a family murder-suicide that occurred in the 1930s, the iron filings aligned. In Welty's words, I was "tuned in for it." I knew, even as the cousin spoke, that the image she described was exactly what I needed; more important, it was what the book needed. In my cousin's version of the murder-suicide, pieced together from her own investigations and corroborated by testimony of several people who had been close to the events, a family "hair picture" was an important factor in the fatal altercation between an uncle and his son. I was familiar with Victorian hair art and had researched ancestral hair weavings, but I had not heard, until that moment, of the existence of an artifact woven from the hair of thirteen members of my Mounts family tribe, including the murdered son and his deceased mother, Mary Mounts. As the interview progressed, the cousin reported that as the son was packing to leave the farm he worked alongside his father, he tried to take the "hair picture," saying that it belonged more to him than to the father, since the father had only married into the Mounts family, while he himself was related by blood. At that point, so the story goes, the father killed his son and then himself. End of story.

Or, beginning of story, depending on how you look at it. For me, a writer who had struggled for a decade to find the center of the story she was trying to tell, the hair art image was a gift from the writing gods, complete with a title for the book: *The Tribal Knot*. The image had drawn itself to my magnetic center. Where do I leave off and others begin? Study the hair art: Each family member has her own strand of individuality, yet when all these strands are woven together, the design they form is more intricate than any individual design could be. The metaphor of the family "hair picture" was the physical incarnation of the deepest issue I'd been grappling with; once I discovered it, I knew how to proceed to finish the book.

Not every literary work requires an extended metaphor. But when a metaphor arises organically out of the material, we do well to pay attention to that metaphor and to allow it to guide us in finding the center of the essay, poem, or story we are struggling to write.

ENCOURAGING METAPHORICAL CONNECTIONS IN OUR WORK

What about those times when our metaphors do not grow naturally, when an isolated image remains a single thread we're unable to wind into a fully developed description, or when a metaphor fails to magnetize our center?

Sometimes the best thing to do is to stop worrying about it. Metaphor is only one of many methods for achieving effective description. In fact, using too many metaphors can harm our writing, calling attention to the metaphors at the expense of the literary dream. In *Writing Fiction*, Janet Burroway suggests that "metaphor is to some degree always self-conscious" and that a bad metaphor "produces a sort of hiccup in the reader's involvement." Prose writers, especially, might wish to heed Aristotle's advice: Overuse of metaphor can make prose too much like poetry. Even if your aim is to craft more poetic prose, metaphor may not be the best way to achieve the goal. Your reader may suffer for your overindulgence.

However, if you wish to increase your perception of metaphoric resemblances, you can take some practical steps. Two have already been suggested—that you write directly from your passions, those things that "refuse to go away," and that you begin to trace the "constellation of images" that emerges in your life and work.

Another step is to respect your natural writing style and stay true to it, trusting that metaphors will emerge in their own good time. My friend, the writer Frye Gaillard, confesses that metaphor does not come easily to him. Instead he focuses on word choice and on the cadences of his sentences, two of his natural gifts. By focusing on what he does well and avoiding any self-conscious "sticking in" of metaphor simply for the sake of metaphor, his writing proceeds smoothly. Occasionally he's even rewarded by the appearance of an apt, original figure of speech that grows organically from his attention to the diction and rhythms of his language.

As in John Lennon's adage about life, metaphor sometimes happens while you're busy doing something else. You can exercise the muscles of metaphor even when you're not writing, through any activity that tricks your mind into making connections between seemingly unlike things.

- Play games that require divergent thinking. My favorite is "Object," where participants sit in a circle and pass around common household utensils like colanders, eggbeaters, and chopsticks, miming imaginative uses for each object. Chopsticks, for instance, can become antennae or drumsticks or tiny oars.
- Spend time with children. Build forts from Popsicle sticks, whittle swords from broomsticks, or create self-portrait collages out of vegetables, fruits, seeds, and pods.
- Each day, move something in your house to a different spot. Turn it upside down or inside out, or use it for a new purpose. A quilt can become a tablecloth; an ashtray, a soap dish.
- Visit an art gallery or a craft fair and enjoy the creations of artists who see the surreal, whimsical, and extraordinary worlds hidden within the ordinary.

- Every morning, instead of reading the newspaper or checking e-mail and phone texts, read a poem, especially one rich in metaphor. When Gina Berriault was interviewed after winning the National Book Critics Circle Award for *Women in Their Beds: New and Selected Stories*, she said that she often reads poetry as a way of preparing herself to write. She even cited a line from the Chilean poet Pablo Neruda—"There is no space wider than that of grief"—as inspiration for one of the stories in the collection. Poetry reminds us of the metaphorical connections in our world.

The characters in our stories can also inspire metaphor, opening up possibilities our "author selves" fail to see. By imagining ourselves inside the skin of someone else—which is what fiction writers do all the time—we free ourselves to see things in a new way. Viewing the world through the lens of our character allows dormant parts of our personality to emerge. For example, in my daily public life, my speech is, for the most part, carefully considered; I don't trust myself with spontaneous outbursts, one-liners, and colorful epithets.

My writing self is another story. It creates characters like Regina Ratcher, a feisty fourteen-year-old from a poverty-pocked town in North Carolina. Regina capitalizes on her love of hyperbole, puns, clichés, and other forms of figurative language by writing advertising copy for local businesses. What a delight to speak through her mouth. All the silly phrases I deny myself are freed from bondage, like Regina's motto for Gotch's taxidermy (*Forever Yours: The Look of Life Without the Trouble*) or her newspaper ad for Lloyd Batson's Full Service Exxon (*Jesus is Lord. We pump, you relax.*).

Perhaps one of your characters is fond of simile or paradox, or his speech is more colorful than yours. Let him have his say. He may surprise you with a striking metaphor. Looking through his eyes, you may begin to see the ordinary world anew, noticing connections you have never seen before. The connections are there, just waiting to be discovered. "Life," as Regina is fond of saying, "is just one big extension cord."

THE EXTENDED FAMILY: OTHER FIGURES OF SPEECH

Metaphor and simile, though the most fundamental figures of speech, aren't the only possibilities open to us. Choices abound.

Hyperbole is an exaggerated metaphor or simile. In hyperbole, you overstate the comparison. Your boss is a weasel or a rat or pond scum. Your lover is more stunning than heaven's brightest star. James Lewis MacLeod's story, "The Jesus Flag," opens with hyperbolic brilliance.

> If God, in cursing Lot's wife, had turned her into a pillar of sugar, instead of salt, Mrs. Wilhelper would have fit the bill. With her tight bun hairdo and her squat body resembling a bush, she was five feet three inches of sweetness as determined as a dump truck. She had two sayings—"Too Sweet for Words" and "Perfectly Marvelous" —which she unloaded on every aspect of the universe as relentlessly as a manure spreader covering a green field.

Although hyperbole is used primarily for comic touches, it can also be employed for serious, even tragic effects, as in these lines describing a gifted child pianist.

> He was born with the ears of a dog.
> He could hear his mother's skin decay,
> the soft give
> as her cheeks sagged just barely more. —Lola Haskins, from "The Prodigy"

In **personification**, an inanimate object, a force of nature, or an abstract term is spoken of as if it were a person. Although the critic John Ruskin disapproved of phrases that ascribe emotion to nonhuman phenomenon (he named this figure of speech "pathetic fallacy"), modern writers often employ personification, with stunning results.

> When laborers imported from Haiti came to clear the land, clouds and fish were convinced that the world was over …. Only the champion daisy trees were serene. … It took the river to persuade them that indeed the

world was altered. That never again would the rain be equal, and by the time they realized it and had run their roots deeper, clutching the earth like lost boys found, it was too late. The men had already folded the earth where there had been no fold and hollowed her where there had been no hollow, which explains what happened to the river. It crested, then lost its course, and finally its head. Evicted from the place where it lived, and forced into unknown turf, it could not form its pools or waterfalls, and ran every which way. —Toni Morrison, from *Tar Baby*

Since most writers are persons (chimps write, too, and some baboons), personification comes naturally to us. We know how people feel and act, so we can easily extend those feelings and actions to the world of vegetables, minerals, or forces of nature. Personification also works in the opposite way. By describing the emotional worlds of inanimate objects or aspects of nature, you can suggest the emotional worlds of your characters without overtly stating them.

Animism, closely related to personification, also attributes life to an inanimate thing, an idea, or a natural object; the difference is that animism does not imply *human* life. One of the most famous literary examples of animism appears in the first line of Robert Frost's "Out, Out," a narrative poem in which a boy's hand is severed by a saw.

The buzz-saw snarled and rattled in the yard …

Notice that the "buzz-saw" does not purr; it does not woof. The animal sounds that come from the saw are angry, dangerous, portending imminent harm: a dog straining at a leash, a snake about to strike.

Cathy Smith Bowers employs animism in her poem "The Love." In Bowers's first line, which alludes to a Thomas Wolfe quote, she begins with an abstraction, but the abstraction soon grows a body. Though not a human body, it is nevertheless a living entity capable of emotion.

The love that ended yesterday in Texas
crawled out of the sea
fresh-eared and barnacled,

his lashed eyes astonished
at the shook-out world …

Animism avoids the "pathetic fallacy" inherent in most uses of personification, while still infusing descriptions with energy. In both personification and animism, this energy stems predominantly from the use of strong verbs.

Paradox creates a relationship that seems, at first, to be contradictory, but upon reflection, expresses a possible truth. Thus the use of paradox can suggest emotional complexities and provide the mystery all good writing requires. "She loved John too much to stay with him" gets our attention; it makes us want to know more, and we continue reading in part to unravel the paradox. Paradox can also suggest conflicts that will emerge later in the story. If you're having trouble finding the center of conflict within your plot or character, try writing an opening sentence that contains a paradox.

In **metonymy**, we refer to something not by its own name but by something closely related to it. The President is "the White House." "From birth to death" becomes "from cradle to grave." And who's watching the baby? Not a mother, but "the hand that rocks the cradle." In **synecdoche**, a subset of metonymy, we use part of something to stand for the whole, or vice versa. "Lend a hand," we cry, although we require more help than a single hand could provide. As you can see from these examples, it's difficult to find a fresh example of metonymy and nearly impossible to come up with one of your own. But that doesn't mean you can't try.

An **analogy** is a comparison between two relationships, and it contains four parts: A is to B as C is to D. Although many writers are fond of analogy, for my money, analogic constructions seem overly clever and complicated, too reminiscent of standardized tests and No. 2 pencils and empty bubbles waiting to be filled. When it comes to proportional metaphor, I'll step aside and let better minds than mine have their say. My favorite analogy is from Franz Kafka: "A book must be the axe for the frozen sea inside us."

An **allegory** is a story or description in which each element—each person, place, thing, and idea—is metaphorical. In addition to providing one-on-one correspondences, the elements add up to something greater than the sum of their parts, that is, some overriding idea or message. Bunyan's *Pilgrim's Progress* and Kafka's "In the Penal Colony" are classic examples of allegorical narratives. The problem with allegory is that its literal elements aren't necessarily important in their own right. The objects, characters, and places in an allegory stand more for abstract ideas than they do for themselves. Whereas a story using symbols has two independent lives, the literal and the symbolic, an allegory often can't stand alone as a literal story.

A **conceit** is a long, complex comparison between two things that are otherwise extremely unlike. Like allegory and analogy, conceit requires a great deal of ingenuity and logical plotting on the part of the writer. When conceit isn't skillfully accomplished, it calls attention to itself, thus distracting the reader from the fictional dream. However, in the hands of a master such as the metaphysical poet John Donne, this technique yields literary surprises, as in "A Valediction: Forbidding Mourning," in which separated lovers are compared to the twinned legs of a compass.

Symbols are such important and complex figures in poetry, fiction, and nonfiction that they warrant more than a brief explanation. Remember our discussion of tenor and vehicle, the two sides of a metaphor? The tenor is the general idea that requires concreteness before it can be fully understood; the vehicle is the embodiment of the tenor. In both metaphor and simile, the tenor is stated. In symbolism, it is not. In symbolism, only the *vehicle* shows itself. A symbol is a visible sign—an object or action—that points to a world of meaning beyond itself.

Although symbolism works by the power of suggestion, a symbol is not the same as meaning or a moral. A symbol cannot be an abstraction. Rather a symbol is the thing that points to the abstraction. In Poe's "The Raven," death isn't the symbol; the bird is. In Crane's *The Red Badge of Courage*, courage isn't the symbol; blood is. Symbols are usually objects, but actions can also work as symbols—thus the term *symbolic gesture*. Since actions speak louder than words, a single symbolic gesture can reveal more about a character than

WORD PAINTING

pages of dialogue. Anna Karenina throws herself under the wheels of a train, Cinderella's stepsister slices off her toes so her foot can fit into the slipper, and Steinbeck's Kino finds the pearl of great price.

An object or action may come to symbolize a world greater than itself, but first it must justify its existence—as an object or an action—in the world of the story, the poem, or the nonfiction work. For a symbol to work effectively, the real world must precede the symbolic. The necklace in Guy de Maupassant's story "The Necklace" may come to symbolize surface appearances and human vanity, but first it must be a necklace. The laundry in Richard Wilbur's "Love Calls Us to the Things of This World" may come to represent angels or souls "bodiless and simple/As false dawn," but first it must be washed, rinsed, and hung out to dry.

A symbol means *more* than itself, but first it means *itself*. Like a developing image in a photographer's tray, a symbol reveals itself slowly. It's been there all along, waiting to emerge from the story, the poem, the essay—and from the writer herself. Symbols are powerful figures, capable of bearing the weight of a hundred metaphors. When a symbol grows organically from its source—character, setting, conflict, plot, language, and from our own passions—it enriches our writing. But when it feels forced, self-conscious, or merely *placed* over a piece of writing, it brings the whole house down with it.

AVOIDING THE PITFALLS OF METAPHOR

Let's say you've begun to explore your personal "constellation of images," that "perception of resemblances" that lies beneath any successful use of figurative language. Your metaphorical well is filling from within, and these connections are emerging in your writing. Since you're writing from your passions and origins, your metaphors are original. But are they fresh? Beyond that, are they effective? Do they contribute to the larger story, poem, or essay?

The most obvious test of an effective metaphor is its freshness—not only of vision but of expression as well. Clichés are dead metaphors. When they were first born, they were lively, original figures of speech. The first time someone wrote "proud as a peacock," the expression was fresh; the second time, it was imitative. Now it's a cliché. It's hard to escape cliché—it's as comfortable as an old shoe. (The old-shoe cliché sneaked up on me. That's how clichés work. If you aren't vigilant, they'll sneak into your writing.) Unless you're using a cliché intentionally—for purposes of humor, irony, or as an integral part of character development—it doesn't belong in your work.

Sometimes we don't realize we're using a cliché. Maybe it hasn't been around long enough to acquire full cliché status, like old has-beens such as "white as snow" or "silver-tongued devil." It might be an expression borrowed from politicians, pop culture, or the media, like "my plate is full," "getting in touch with your inner child," "couch potato," "thinking outside the box," or "surfing the Internet." A metaphor doesn't have to be decades old to be stale; any overused expression qualifies, however recently it might have been coined. There I go again with another cliché: "to coin a phrase." Actually, coining a phrase might not be such a bad idea. If we had to pay every time we used a stale expression—a kind of syntax sin tax—we might be more careful about allowing clichés into our descriptions.

In our attempt to use fresh expressions and to avoid clichés, we may go too far in the opposite direction. *Far* is the operative word here. You've already been warned against fetching metaphors from afar—that is, straying too far from your origins and passions. Far-fetched also refers to anything that seems strained, improbable, or unnatural. A far-fetched metaphor not only calls attention to itself; it calls attention to the differences between the two things being compared rather than to the likenesses. Although a metaphor, by definition, compares two unlike things, if they are *too* unlike, the reader will focus on the strangeness of the metaphor rather than on the images being created. Yes, perhaps a character's teeth *could* be compared to stalactites or stalagmites. But do you really want your reader to fixate on subterranean images, when all you are trying to show is that the teeth are sharp?

The main goal in using metaphor is not merely to point out resemblances but also to create, through these resemblances, a fresh and vivid image. Like other descriptive techniques, metaphor usually accomplishes this task through concrete, sensory details. Although I've never actually seen an eagle dive off a cliff into the ocean, when I read the second stanza of Tennyson's "The Eagle," I feel as though I have.

> The wrinkled sea beneath him crawls;
> He watches from his mountain walls,
> And like a thunderbolt he falls.

Tennyson's figures of speech—the wrinkled sea crawling and the falling thunderbolt—appeal to my senses, bringing the imagined picture into sharp focus. They clarify, rather than blur, the picture. His metaphors and simile, instead of calling attention to themselves as figures of speech, illuminate the scene, bringing it vividly to the eye of my imagination.

Tennyson's metaphors and simile are not only concrete and sensory; they are also precise. Not literally precise, of course. Figurative language, by definition, deviates from the literal. Literally speaking, waves are not wrinkles, and the sea has no knees on which to crawl. But within the world Tennyson creates, the figures of speech are accurate; they follow natural laws. In contrast, a phrase like "her tears gushed like a geyser" is inaccurate. Tears might trickle, drip, even flow, but they cannot gush like a geyser, and saying that they do distracts the reader from the sense impression you're trying to create—unless you're intentionally employing hyperbole to accomplish some literary purpose.

Figurative language is not a screen to hide behind. Using metaphor does not absolve us from writing clearly and accurately. Unfortunately government officials, businessmen, academics, and advertisers so often use figures of speech as substitutes for clear communication—or worse, to deceive, evade, or manipulate—that it's tempting to think of metaphor as an easy way out. Clear, direct thinking is hard; communicating those thoughts precisely is even harder. It's far easier to take cover behind clichés, vague or mixed metaphors, or overworked figures of speech.

"Dazzle me with clarity," the poet Cathy Smith Bowers tells her students. It's easy to dazzle without clarity, to fill our poems and stories with figures of speech that leave the reader stunned, yet confused, as in this example.

> A vacuum waits to be filled, if not with precious stones, with scarabs, fat and scarred. Birds of crimson plume, sky blue, or white fluff with rufous trim, compete for precious gems beneath a sunflower moon. The stylish meet at first light for revels. Yardbirds rush in to fill a void like circus clowns.

This description may dazzle, but it doesn't dazzle with clarity. It took three readings for me to figure out what is happening: Birds are gathering at an almost-empty bird feeder. The writer, carried away by metaphor, does not anchor his metaphors with clear, direct language. Nor does he consider how the metaphors interact with one another. Not only is the description crowded with details—vacuums, scarabs, sunflowers, moons, gems, and clowns—the details don't work together for an overall effect. The writer has scattered his forces.

We scatter our forces when we use too many metaphors or when our metaphors cancel each other out. This happens in succinct passages as well as in long descriptions.

> The neighborhood bullies hover like vultures, plunging in names like daggers and carting away the bones.

In this example, *vultures* and *bones* work well together, but *daggers* cancels out a potentially effective image. The reader is left not knowing where to put his attention. Just when he's conjured up a mob of vultures, he's asked to provide them with knives.

Figures of speech require space and time in which to accumulate meaning, and the reader needs room to imagine the connections. If you write "The woman brandished a hairbrush, skipping toward him like a schoolgirl on holiday," you'll derail the reader. Which meaning is intended? Is the woman warlike or girlish? Is her gesture a physical threat or a playful tease? *Warlike?* you think. *Oh, no, I didn't mean warlike. I just meant that she's swinging the hairbrush as she moves toward him.*

The problem here is more fundamental than a mixed metaphor; it's a problem with word choice. In an earlier chapter we discussed the importance of naming an object precisely and accurately. The same principle applies to effective figures of speech. Any word used in a simile or metaphor must pass the precision test; figurative language is no excuse for sloppy diction. *Brandish* suggests that a weapon is being used. If you're going to use *brandish*, you need to know both its denotation and its connotation, to ensure that your diction is precise.

Knowing the precise meaning of words will help you avoid mixed metaphors like "He was steeped in the aurora of her hair." *Aurora* is not just a pretty word. If you look it up in a dictionary, you'll see that it means "a flashing luminosity visible in the night sky." And *steep* has nothing to do with the night sky—or any sky, for that matter. It means "to soak in liquid, to be immersed."

Writing a mixed metaphor isn't the worst sin a writer can commit. We're all allowed a few along the way. Even the most successful writers, whose editors are paid to catch such things, sometimes fail to be accurate. Here's Ian Fleming at his metaphorical worst: "Bond's knees, the Achilles' heel of all skiers, were beginning to ache." The problem with such writing isn't simply that the metaphors are mixed. The real problem is that *since* the metaphors are mixed, the reader is unable to conjure the word picture in her mind's eye. Should she visualize a knee or a heel? An imprecise metaphor, or one in which two or more vehicles fight for dominance, cannot create a unified impression in the reader's mind.

PRECISE, ORIGINAL, AND EFFECTIVE METAPHOR

In the earlier discussion of "the proper and special name of a thing," we noted the importance not only of a precise naming but of a significant and musical naming as well. The same principles apply to figurative language. An effective metaphor or simile is *significant* when it calls forth an image that reinforces the overall description. When John Edgar Wideman, in his memoir *Brothers and Keepers*, describes the grass surrounding the penitentiary where his brother is incarcerated, his simile is not only precise but also significant. It reinforces the regulated sameness of such institutions, a soulless uniformity evident in the prison's physical property as well as in its human property.

> Grass grows in the margin between the spiked fence paralleling the river and the asphalt lot. Grass clipped harshly, uniformly as the bristle heads of convicts in old movies about prison. Plots of manicured green define a path leading to steps we must climb to enter the visitors' building.

Because of Wideman's precise simile, we can visualize both the grass and the convicts' severe haircuts; each side of the simile supports the other. The significant details that surround the simile—"spiked," "clipped," and "manicured"— further support the simile rather than canceling it out. The larger constellation of words and images—"margin," "between," "define," "plot," even the seemingly innocuous "we"—is also significant, suggesting the boundaries not only between convict and visitor but between brother and brother as well.

Wideman's description also passes the third test of "the proper and special naming of a thing"—it is musically appropriate. "Spiked," "bristle," and "clipped" appeal to our ear as well as to our eye. The repetition of *i* provides musical unity, while the harsh, brittle consonants reinforce the brusque treatment both the grass and the prisoners receive.

Wideman's use of figurative language succeeds on every level. His simile is *original* because it appears to spring naturally from his origins, the source of his passions. It is *effective* in its precision, in the suggestiveness of its sound, and in the significance of its details. Every element extends and deepens the simile, the larger descriptive passage, and finally, the entire memoir. We are left with a "perception of resemblances," each one illuminating the other, and all of them illuminating the whole.

EXERCISES

1. Make a "word basket" for your writing desk. Fill it with words recorded individually on index cards or slips of paper, one word per card; the more cards, the more possibilities. (You can also purchase ready-made word kits; some are magnetized so you can create poems and stories on your refrigerator. I prefer to create my own list of words from my personal "constellation of images.") Concrete nouns, strong verbs, and sensory adjectives work best for me, but I also include some abstract words. Here's a partial list of the words in my basket: *blossom, moon, plow, white, melt, deep, stream, edge, hollow, circle, wave, willow, root, parting, hand, crown, hayloft, kites, pianos, mirror, follow, gloss, nibble, home, song, sorrow, mercy, skin, window, wonder.*

    The object of the exercise is to trick your mind into making metaphorical leaps. Once you've filled your word basket, select at random four or five cards, spread them out on your desk, and combine two or more to form a simile, metaphor, or other figure of speech. For instance, from the list above you might combine *nibble* and *kites* to form "kites nibble at the sky." *Blossom, sorrow,* and *song* might form "Sorrow blossoms into song." Once the metaphorical connection is made, you can reword your metaphor: "Yellow kites take bites of the sky" or "Sorrow's song is a blossom."

    You may find that this exercise produces far-fetched or mixed metaphors, which you've been warned against using (like the one above, in which *song* competes with *blossom*). However, the word basket is merely an exercise for your metaphor muscles; once you get used to freely associating disparate images, you may find that metaphors arise more naturally in the context of your work.

2. Locate a simile in one of your stories, poems, or essays. Rewrite the simile first as a metaphor and then as an implied metaphor. You'll probably find that the conversion requires more than simply removing *like* or *as*, particularly when you're writing an implied metaphor, which relies solely on

supporting details. (Verbs may be your best route into implied metaphor.) After you've written all three versions, choose the one that most effectively serves your literary purpose.

3. Select from one of your stories a character to develop more fully. Using hyperbole, describe her physical appearance, demeanor, personality, or movement. Limit yourself to one main vehicle for your hyperbole; then expand it. For instance, rather than saying that Gloria is slim as a willow reed, pale as the far side of the moon, and aggressive as a pit bull in heat, choose one of the hyperboles and expand it into a full description.

4. Write a description of a natural object, idea, or emotion using personification or animism. Again, verbs are natural entries into both figures of speech. If you're animating greed, for instance, ask yourself how greed moves or acts. Does it grab, clutch, or seize? Does it devour? The verbs might be enough to suggest personification or animism, or you can allow the verbs to lead you further in the writing process. If greed grabs, perhaps it has tentacles. If it devours, it might have a mouth. What kind of mouth?

5. Using paradox, write a description of one of your characters. You can apply the paradox to a physical description of your character or to your character's motives or emotions. In either case, choose two qualities that seem to be contradictory; then place them side by side. For instance, you might write that Eloise's face was "scarred and beautiful" or "beautifully scarred." Thinking in paradox requires engaging the all-accepting eye we discussed in chapter two. When you use paradox, you allow both sides of the mystery equal weight. One way to do this is to join the two sides with *and* (which is a democratic, equal-opportunity conjunction) rather than with conjunctions like *but*, *or*, or *yet* (which emphasize the opposition between the two sides). Another way is to use a modifier (an adjective or adverb) that seems opposed to the word it modifies (as in Eloise's "beautifully scarred" face).

The same principles hold if you describe a paradox in your character's emotions or motives. What does your character want? Rather than state it as a single, unequivocal desire, break the desire into two opposing parts and give each of them equal weight.

6. If you haven't begun to identify your personal "constellation of images," search through your stories or poems for recurring images or motifs, or ask someone familiar with your work to point them out. If you suspect that a certain word or phrase is part of your constellation, use your writing program's "find" feature to search your writing for evidence of a pattern. Once you've identified recurring patterns, you can use this knowledge for "seeding" new stories or poems.

7. Search your work for a metaphor that seems clichéd, strained, far-fetched, or simply inaccurate. Either rewrite the metaphor in a fresh way or remove it altogether. If a passage contains several metaphors close together, none of which relates to the others, consider removing all except the most effective one. Or expand the passage so that the metaphors are spread over more area, giving the reader time to let one metaphor fully settle before moving on to the next.

8. In chapter three we discussed Georgia O'Keeffe's "treasures," the objects she carried with her or arranged, in various ways, to inspire her as she painted. Make a list of your own treasures, or list objects significant to one of your fictional characters. Better yet, arrange an actual still life of the objects, or several still lifes. Study works by visual artists that group disparate objects, such as Susan Jane Walp's *Bread in a Tin Bowl with Fork, Shell, and Xeroxes, 1998*. Then draft a piece of prose or poetry that describes that particular artist's still life or that incorporates your own (or your character's) list of treasures.

9. Study published poetry that uses objects in significant ways, such as Gertrude Stein's *Tender Buttons*, which one critic described as a "verbal collage." You can also study segmented essays organized with the names of objects, or collections of objects, such as Brenda Miller's "Artifacts," in which the following subtitles appear: Angel, Shell, An Unearthed Crystal, Dead People's Things, Empty Vessels. Although each segment in Miller's essay is separate,

all five work together to suggest a unified theme. Using examples like these as models, write several separate segments of poetry or prose, focusing on one particular object at a time. Then arrange and rearrange the segments until they form a larger meaning, something greater than the sum of separate parts. Don't worry about transitions. Let the order and arrangement of the segments create a collage of meaning, a "constellation of images."

CHAPTER SIX

Bringing Characters to Life Through Description

When Broadway composer Stephen Sondheim was asked about his creative process, he replied, "If you told me to write a love song tonight, I'd have a lot of trouble. But if you tell me to write a love song about a girl with a red dress who goes into a bar and is on her fifth martini and is falling off her chair, that's a lot easier, and it makes me free to say anything I want." As we've already noted, it's hard to write effectively about a large, abstract subject—grief or anger or love—without first "sweating the small stuff." Remember the student writer who demonstrated, through a description of a small black button, the grief over her father's death? In Sondheim's case, the concept of love is embodied in a girl, but not just any girl. This is a particular girl in a particular place wearing a particular dress and drinking a particular drink. By the time the song is over, the girl may come to signify love, but first she has to put on the dress, take her place on the bar stool, and order a drink.

The characters in our stories, songs, poems, and essays *embody* our writing. They are our words made flesh. Sometimes they even speak for us, carrying much of the burden of plot, theme, mood, idea, and emotion. But they do not exist until we describe them on the page. Until we anchor them with words, they drift, bodiless and ethereal. They weigh nothing; they have no voice. Once we've written the first words—"Belinda Beatrice," perhaps, or "the dark-eyed salesman in the back of the room," or simply "the girl"—our characters begin to take form. Soon they'll be more than mere names. They'll put on jeans or rubber hip boots, light thin cigarettes or thick cigars; they'll stutter or shout, buy a townhouse on the Upper East Side or a studio in the Village; they'll marry for life or survive a series of happy affairs; they'll beat their children or embrace them. What they become, on the page, is up to us.

The girl in Sondheim's scenario acquires weight and substance through the physical details Sondheim supplies. First he provides a setting. In our mind's eye we see the girl sitting at the bar, wearing a dress that Sondheim also provides. But it's not just any dress. This dress is *red*—a detail both sensory and significant, suggesting a certain kind of girl (passionate or showy perhaps) or suggesting, at the very least, the passionate and showy aspects of the girl's nature. The drink is another significant detail. Other girls might drink chardonnay or light beer or frothy pink drinks with paper umbrellas on the side. The girl in the red dress drinks martinis. Note the plural. Not one martini, but five.

Sondheim doesn't stop with identifying the girl and providing her with weight and substance through significant details. He also sets her in motion, thus following another of Aristotle's dictums for vivid descriptions—that whenever possible, we show our subjects in a state of activity. As a result, the reader not only sees a picture in his mind's eye; he sees a *moving* picture. The girl in the red dress is falling off her chair.

If the description were to continue, we might hear the girl speak. Her choice of words, her syntax, the timbre of her voice, and the rhythms of her speech would add other elements to her characterization. We might also overhear what others at the bar are whispering about her. We might even gain access to the girl's inner world—hearing her unspoken words, feeling her fears, dreaming her dreams. Once we're situated inside, we might look out through her eyes and describe the world as it appears to her (and now to us) from our unsteady perch on the bar stool.

Our characters, whether fictional or nonfictional, come alive through all of these descriptive methods, and more. We establish a character by direct physical description, by our choice of sensory and significant details about the character's surroundings, and through description of the character's movements and speech. Less directly, we describe our character through the eyes of other characters, by evoking his private world of thoughts and feelings, and by describing what he sees through his own eyes.

CHRISTENING YOUR CHARACTERS

We begin by naming our characters or by identifying them in some way—"the grocer," "my aunt," "the little girl in the front row"—so the reader can keep track of them. If you're writing fiction, choices abound. Like a prospective parent, you have the power to name your child anything you want. Not that you would, of course. A loving parent doesn't slap just any old name on her child. She carefully considers her choice. How will each possibility sound when coupled with the surname? Should she choose a name with ethnic flavor, one that suggests the family heritage? Maybe she should name him after his father or after a famous person—a heavyweight boxer, a saint, an actor. What impression will the name make later on—on teachers, peers, future employers?

When we name our fictional characters, we should use the same care we'd use in naming our children. A name is often the reader's first introduction to a character, and first impressions are important. "Queen Esther Alexander Pratt" announces itself, while "Sybil Rumple" stands in the shadows. An "Alfred J. Petticoat" might take mincing steps toward us; a "Sam Slade" probably won't. (If he does, however, or if Alfred turns out to hold a black belt in karate, you may still be on firm fictional ground, particularly if your goal is to surprise the reader.)

If you have trouble thinking of appropriate names for your characters, start by scanning the phone book, the obituary pages, or online lists of names, some of which include derivations and variations. As you browse, you might run across names that, though inappropriate for your character, are just too good to pass up. File them away for future stories.

Once you've used a character's name in a story, keep a record of the name and any other important details about the character you might be apt to forget. Good recordkeeping will help ensure that you don't reuse the name, or use a name too close in sound or flavor, in other stories; this technique also comes in handy if you're writing a long novel, a group of interrelated stories, or a novel series in which the same characters reappear. Mystery writer Margaret Maron records all the important information about her characters—physical descriptions, biographical data, and other details revealed through dialogue and summary—to ensure consistency from book to book.

Occasionally real-life encounters provide us with better names than we'd find in the phone book or obituary pages. Some names seem too good to be true, which probably means we can't use them. I once taught a student named Tarantula, a small girl who liked to bite her classmates. True story. But there's no way I could use that name, coupled with those details, in a story. It would feel forced, as if I'd thought of The Big Idea first, then hunted around for a name to serve my idea.

Certain names suggest larger ideas and themes, even symbols: Destiny, Beulah, Pandora, Jesus. But unless you're writing an allegory or a parable, be cautious about using a name that works only on the symbolic level. Eudora Welty often used names with symbolic overtones, but she was quick to defend her choices. When a critic asked if the character name "Phoenix" in her story "A Worn Path" was consciously chosen to work as a symbol, Welty responded, "It's boring to think that things would be offered for symbolic reasons only, and it would be ridiculous, too." She chose the name, she said, because it was "an appropriate Mississippi name," and because it fit not only the locale but also the time period in which the story takes place. The names we give characters do more than merely suggest personality traits. They also establish characters in time and place, and suggest ethnic and religious backgrounds, social and financial status, even parental aspirations (much is expected of a "Muhammed Ali Johnson," for instance).

A character's nickname also provides clues for our readers. "Stretch" and "Spider" bring forth visual images; "Butter Bean" and "Buffy" suggest geographical and social classes. Since a nickname is usually bestowed by close friends or family, it offers insight into a character's personal relationships while also suggesting her history and the events that have shaped her. Relating how a character got her nickname can open up a straightforward narrative, providing background information that might otherwise be difficult to insert. In one of my stories, I wanted to show the close relationship between the orphaned teenaged narrator and her older brother, but I didn't want to use flashbacks. His nickname, "Brick," not only provided a way to insert background information; it also focused the details of my physical description. Since physical description of a character is such an important element of most fiction, and since it's often difficult to select the telling detail from so many possibilities, I was happy when the name "Brick" came along to help.

If you're writing nonfiction, you have little choice as to what to name your characters (unless you use pseudonyms, in which case you would probably still choose an appropriate name to stand in for the real name). However, actual names of nonfiction characters often provide rich opportunities for characterization. Isabel Wilkerson's nonfiction narrative, *The Warmth of Other Suns: The Epic Story of America's Great Migration*, is structured in part on the names of three main characters whose individual stories suggest the stories of millions of black Americans who migrated from the South to northern and western cities from 1915 to 1970. To keep readers situated in time and place, and to help monitor the movement among the three stories, Wilkerson uses the characters' names for some of the chapter titles and subtitles. And although she employs multiple techniques to build fully rendered characterizations over the course of the long narrative, first she names the characters, and their names provide important clues for the reader. Ida Mae Brandon Gladney is the first character we meet, an elderly woman living on the South Side of Chicago, a neighborhood, Wilkerson writes, "so danger-ously absurd that it is living entertainment in her old age," a place where "the hustlers and pushers playing out their lives beneath her window" have a nick-name for Ida—"you watch yourself now, Grandma."

Already, barely two pages into a book of nearly 600 pages, we already know much about Ida Mae, and although Wilkerson inserts direct physical descrip-tions and provides bits of backstory in this opening segment, much of Ida's characterization grows directly out of her name. The reader will quickly fig-ure out that the young man named George Gladney, who appears on the scene when Ida Mae is only fifteen, will become her husband, thus adding Gladney to her family name of Brandon.

Then, within a few more pages, we learn even more. As it turns out, Ida Mae was not her given name. When she was born in 1913, her mother, Miss Theenie, named her Mae Ida after Miss Theenie's mother-in-law, Ida.

> There was a spark inside of her, and when she got big enough, she told peo-ple to call her Ida Mae instead of Mae Ida. She would later say it sounded less old-timey to her, but it was an early indication that she could think for herself when she chose to.

Names continue to provide essential clues to Ida Mae's character—for in-stance, she names her first son James, after a boy she took care of, hoping that naming him after a white boy would bring him good luck. She names her daughter, born in 1938, after the First Lady, Eleanor Roosevelt. Ida Mae's choices act as more than time and place markers for the reader. They also re-veal her belief system, her political leanings, and her hopes and dreams for her children's future. As the book progresses, the character of Ida Mae will grow, thanks to Wilkerson's close attention to every aspect of character de-scription mentioned elsewhere in this chapter. First, however, in the spirit of Aristotle's advice, she provides the most basic of all elements, the "proper and special name of a thing."

PHYSICAL DESCRIPTION OF CHARACTERS

Once we've named a character, we provide him with a body—how else will he move through the world of the story? Unfortunately description that relies solely on physical attributes too often turns into what Janet Burroway calls the "all-points bulletin," which reads something like this: "My father is a tall, middle-aged man of average build. He has green eyes and brown hair and usually wears khakis and oxford shirts."

This description is so mundane, it barely qualifies as an "all-points bulletin." Can you imagine the police searching for this suspect? No identifying marks, no scars or tattoos, nothing to distinguish him. He appears as a cardboard cutout rather than as a living, breathing character. Yes, the details are accurate. Some even border on sensory—"green eyes and brown hair." But they don't call forth vivid images. We can barely make out this character's form; how can we be expected to remember him?

When we describe a character, factual information alone is not sufficient, no matter how accurate it might be. The details must appeal to our senses. Phrases that merely label (like *tall*, *middle-aged*, and *average*) bring no clear image to our minds. Since most people form their first impression of someone through visual clues, it makes sense to describe our characters using visual images. *Green eyes* is a beginning, but it doesn't go far enough. Are they pale green or dark green? Even a simple adjective can strengthen a detail. If the adjective also suggests a metaphor—*forest green, pea green,* or *emerald green*—the reader not only begins to make associations (positive or negative) but also visualizes in her mind's eye the vehicle of the metaphor—forest trees, peas, or glittering gems.

The problem with intensifying an image only by adjectives, as you can see from these examples, is that adjectives encourage cliché. It's hard to think of adjective descriptors that haven't been overused: bulging or ropy muscles, clean-cut good looks, frizzy hair. If you use an adjective to describe a physical attribute, make sure that the phrase is not only accurate and sensory but also fresh. In her short story "Flowering Judas," Katherine Anne Porter describes Braggioni's singing voice as a "furry, mournful voice" that takes the high notes "in a prolonged painful squeal." Often the easiest way to avoid an adjective-based cliché is to free the phrase entirely from its adjective modifier. For example, rather than describing her eyes merely as "hazel," Emily Dickinson remarked that they were "the color of the sherry the guests leave in the glasses."

Making details more specific is another way to strengthen physical descriptions. In my earlier "all-points bulletin" example, the description of the father's hair might be improved with a detail such as "a military buzz-cut, prickly to the touch" or "the aging hippie's last chance—a long ponytail striated with gray." Either of these descriptions would paint a stronger picture than the bland phrase *brown hair*. In the same way, his oxford shirt could become "a white oxford button-down that he'd steam-pleated just minutes before" or "the same style of baby blue oxford he'd worn since prep school, rolled carelessly at the elbows." These descriptions not only bring forth images, they also suggest the background and the personality of the father.

Specific details can strengthen our descriptions, but if we include too many specific details, we defeat the purpose of providing a visual image of our character. Here's the kind of description I wrote after my first creative writing teacher advised me to make my details more specific.

> Rosa Guy stood in the doorway, dressed in a blue denim jumpsuit with silver braid. Her face was bright and shiny, as if she'd just scrubbed it with complexion cream or Dove soap. Yellow earrings, in the shape of sunflowers, dangled from her tiny pink ears. Her neck was thick and veiny. She was broad-chested, like a female wrestler from Channel Nine's Monday Night Wrestling. Her hips were wide, but her feet were as long and narrow as the oars my grandfather uses when he rows his canoe.

Yikes! Where is the reader supposed to focus attention? True, the details are sensory and specific, but are they significant? What overall impression was I trying to make? In the previous chapter we discussed how a figure of speech fails when images are too far-fetched or mixed, or when one image cancels out the other. The same principle applies to physical descriptions. Too many details, however sensory and specific, overload the reader.

In describing characters, we need to select details carefully, choosing only those that create the strongest, most revealing impression. One well-chosen physical trait, item of clothing, or idiosyncratic mannerism can reveal character more effectively than a dozen random images. This applies to characters in nonfiction as well as fiction. When I write about my grandmother, I usually focus on her strong, jutting chin—not only because it was her most dominant feature but also because it suggests her stubbornness and determination. When I write about Uncle Leland, I describe the wandering eye that gave him a perpetually distracted look, as if only his body was present. His spirit, it seemed, had already left on some journey he'd glimpsed peripherally, a place the rest of us were unable to see. As you describe real-life characters, zero in on distinguishing characteristics that reveal personality: gnarled, arthritic hands always busy at some task; a habit of covering her mouth each time a giggle rises up; a lopsided swagger as he makes his way to the horse barn; the scent of coconut suntan oil, cigarettes, and leather each time she sashays past your chair.

Besides including too many details, beginning writers also tend to clump details of physical description together, usually at the beginning of the story or when the character is first mentioned. There's no need to front-load your story with physical descriptions or to reveal all your details at once. Details can accumulate as the story progresses. This technique protects your readers from overly long or static passages, while providing the series of proofs that help sustain the fictional dream. According to Flaubert, an object in a story must be mentioned three times in order for the reader to be convinced of its existence. The same can be said for details of physical description. If you describe a character's freckled skin only once, the reader may not remember it. But if you mention it again, even briefly, you increase the chances that the detail will be not only remembered but also believed. Look back at the passages of physical description in your stories or essays. Are all of your descriptive details about a character lumped together at the beginning of the piece or when the character is first introduced? If so, try breaking up the passage into smaller sections, then scattering these sections throughout the work.

You don't have to confine your descriptive proofs to scenes in which the character appears. Photographs can provide a smooth entry into physical descriptions. In Tim O'Brien's story "The Things They Carried," he introduces Martha through one of the photographs Lieutenant Cross carries in his wallet.

> It was an action shot—women's volleyball—and Martha was bent horizontal to the floor, reaching, the palms of her hands in sharp focus, the tongue taut, the expression frank and competitive. There was no visible sweat. She wore white gym shorts. Her legs, he thought, were almost certainly the legs of a virgin, dry and without hair, the left knee cocked and carrying her entire weight, which was just over one hundred pounds.

Photographs offer rich opportunities for nonfiction writers as well, particularly family historians or memoirists searching for details to flesh out real-life characters. If you have access to photographs of people who appear in your work, study them closely in search of character-defining clues such as perfectly creased trousers or an Army jacket that has seen better days. Half-closed eyes, a pouty mouth, or arms crossed tightly across his chest? Where is she positioned in relation to others? If you have access to home movies, videos, or audio recordings, mine them for even more details. And if these particular details contribute to your character portrait and help support the larger work you are creating, include them.

Photographs supply visual clues to a character's past, but we can also portray characters by imagining how they might look in the future, a form of literary time travel. In Andrew Miller's novel *Ingenious Pain*, the narrator describes a young boy named Sam, "an agile, scrawny, wonderfully ugly boy of eleven years." The description continues.

At fifteen he will be untellable from a red-faced son of the plough in spotted neckerchief and leather breeches, roaring in some market town. By thirty he will be one of these at the table; still lusty, but already half broken by work and worry, drinking to forget.

The Limitations of Visual Description

Although visual physical description is the most common way to create memorable, believable characters, it's not always the most effective way. As we discussed in an earlier chapter, description that involves smell, hearing, touch, or taste often draws the reader in more closely than description that relies only on sight. Rich, sensory descriptions can also provide important background information that reinforces our characterizations.

A character's scent, for instance, can reveal his age, background, lifestyle, and environment. (Helen Keller claimed to be able to tell a person's occupation by the way he smelled.) When my nephew comes in from outside and climbs onto my lap, I can tell not only where he's been but also what the weather is like. When he smells fresh, like pine or cedar, I know it's cool and windy, and he's been swinging on the tree swing out back; when he smells like a wet puppy, I know the afternoon has turned hot and steamy, and he's been running hard. Great Aunt Bessie, a recurring character in my essays, appears not through the world of smells but through sounds I associate with her oldness—the swish of taffeta down the hall, the clonk of heavy heels, and the mechanical clack of her loose dentures.

Study your descriptions. If you find you've included only visual description, try adding other sensory details. What smells might suggest your character's occupation or preoccupation? Formaldehyde, paint thinner, motor oil, furniture polish, Lava soap, bourbon, wintergreen breath mints, wood smoke? How does his wife's skin feel? Silky and smooth, or dry and scaly? When he holds her, does he sink into womanly flesh or impale himself on bone? Is her laugh shrill as a whistle or low and raspy, a lifetime smoker's laugh? Our characters are more than mere holograms or still photographs in an album.

Their bodies are microcosms of texture and aroma and sound, reflecting the private and public worlds in which they move.

SPECIAL CHALLENGES OF DESCRIBING REAL-LIFE CHARACTERS

In any literary work that involves characters, the writer must decide which characters will appear, what role each will play, and how to make each character come alive on the page. Decisions depend on the writer's intentions and the requirements of the work. In fiction or poetry, characters can be created solely from imagination; in nonfiction genres, characters are usually selected from a cast of real-life people.

At first thought, bristling-with-life characterizations seem like natural outgrowths of the nonfiction genre. After all, the people we're writing about actually existed, or still do, so it follows that they will automatically spring to life on the page, right? Not at all. Just because characters exist in real life does not mean that they will exist as believable characters on the page. Nonfiction writers must work as hard as fiction writers to create characters that feel real to the reader. Sometimes they have to work even harder. For fiction writers are neither bound by fact nor limited by lack of information about their characters; they can construct them from imagination's whole cloth. And, as tailors will tell you, it is often easier to construct a new garment than it is to reshape what is already in place. Memoirists, journalists, and other nonfiction writers work with materials already in place—factual details about characters gathered through observation, research, interviews, or memory. Of course, many fiction writers base their stories on real-life people, but they can include disclaimers regarding characters' identities. And poets, many of whom include autobiographical details in their poems, can claim poetic license.

Not so for nonfiction writers, who in most cases must deal with the consequences of identifying and describing real-life characters. In "To Fashion a Text," Annie Dillard discusses the many choices she made when writing *An American Childhood*, including her choice to omit "anything that might trouble my family. ... Everybody I'm writing about is alive and well, in full possession of their faculties, and possibly willing to sue. Things were simpler when I wrote about muskrats."

As Dillard's quotation suggests, writing about people close to you, especially friends or family members, is fraught with complications. Let's say you're writing an essay about your brother, whose most distinguishing characteristics are his bald spot, his paunch, and his stutter, none of which he likes to be reminded of. If he were a fictional character, you'd have no problem including such details. A fictional character won't show up at two o'clock in the morning, demanding to know what right you have to embarrass him in this way. A fictional character won't weep, slam a door in your face, or disown you. A brother might. All writers who include real-life people in their work will have to balance their obligations to create accurate, sensory, and significant character descriptions with their obligations to the flesh-and-blood person.

Another character description challenge, which all writers face to some degree, is how to portray the character *behind* the words, the authorial presence that presides over the work. Sometimes this presence is a character in the story, the "I" teller of the tale; sometimes it is the authorial "eye" that guides the reader through the work. In chapter seven's discussion of point of view, we focus on various literary stances and consider particular issues writers face when describing the self behind the words. For now, it is enough to consider that although self-description is a consideration in some fiction and poetry, it is an essential element in most memoirs and personal essays. Part of what draws a reader into a memoir or essay is the sense that a flesh-and-blood character stands behind the words. As Phillip Lopate observes in "Writing Personal Essays: On the Necessity of Turning Oneself Into a Character," "The point is to begin to take inventory of yourself so that you can present that self to the reader as a specific, legible character."

Turning oneself into a character? Yes. The personal essayist or memoirist, in effect, must create a self on the page, a character as believable and lifelike as other characters who appear in the work.

MULTIPLE AND GROUP PORTRAITS

Although this chapter deals primarily with techniques for individual characterizations, some literary works include a large cast of characters and may require you to write multiple portraits or group portraits. Writing multiple portraits differs little from writing individual portraits. Each character, whether major or minor, is described with sufficient detail to make him or her recognizable to the reader and distinguishable from other characters. The main challenge with multiple portraits is in monitoring the proportion and placement of individual portraits so the reader can keep track of the large cast of characters.

In a group portrait, however, characters are described not as individuals but rather as part of a collective body: think *flock, herd, fraternity, team, tribe*. Members of this collective body might be described elsewhere in a work as individuals (especially in a novel or other long form) but in the group portrait their individuality is subsumed, at least momentarily, within the collective body.

The group or collective portrait should not be confused with the composite portrait. In fiction, a composite character is created by combining the qualities of two or more real-life or fictional characters and presenting them as a single character; in journalism and in most nonfiction genres, this technique raises ethical concerns and is highly controversial.

The group portrait should also not be confused with the first-person plural narrator (the *we* as opposed to the first-person singular *I*), a point-of-view choice discussed in chapter seven.

Sometimes a group portrait shapes an entire literary work such as a short poem or brief prose piece. More often, the group portrait appears as a brief segment of a larger work. For instance, in a few paragraphs of Richard Selzer's essay "Amazons," he describes a team of female hospital workers he observes in an operating room as they perform a mastectomy. First he compares them to a herd of deer with long necks that turn gracefully. The sound their voices make, he writes, is "a kind of choir, a blending. … Working together, they are parts of a unified whole, just as colonies and cities comprise a great empire, or as the organs of a single body pulse within the same membrane."

In a longer work, such as a novel or sustained nonfiction narrative, group portraits are often fully developed, as in Suzanne Berne's novel *A Crime in the Neighborhood*. "My grandmother used to say that she had given birth to one daughter with four heads," the narrator recalls, adding that as a child she saw her mother and aunts as "a hilarious, vindictive sorority: Fran, Claire, Lois, and Ada, the fabulous Mayhew girls. …" Although at times Berne describes each woman individually, often they appear in the novel as a collective body, as in this segment where the narrator relates details from her mother's stories.

> … the Mayhew Girls, those resilient sisters in scarlet lipstick, hiding pillowcase underwear under black shantung skirts, declining Latin verbs (*amaveram, amaveras*) with the clipped, dedicated arrogance of queens. All sitting together on one bed, painting one another's toenails. Smoking cigarettes under the pink insulation in the eaves of their mother's house, coughing and laughing in the camphorous, nicotine fug. A tangle of long arms, long legs—one daughter, four heads. You know Fran-Claire-Lois-Ada.

DESCRIBING CHARACTERS THROUGH THEIR ENVIRONMENTS

As the old saying goes, everybody has to be *somewhere*. Literary characters are no exception. Once we give our character a name and body, we put a roof over his head or, at the very least, give him a place to roam. The world we create for the character includes not only physical spaces—a home, work-place, neighborhood—but historical settings as well. Since I'll be discussing setting in chapter eight, I'll focus here on those elements of setting that directly reveal a character's character—not only his occupational and personal environment but also his belongings, those objects that fill his world.

Often when I'm having trouble developing three-dimensional characters, it's because I haven't provided them with a suitable background against which to shine. For a long time, one of my characters refused to show herself. Her name was fitting, her actions believable, and her internal conflict absorbing. But I could not visualize her; she did not feel real. She lacked a world in which to move. Once I discovered the right workplace for her (a greenhouse) and the right digs (a basement apartment on the premises) she fleshed out nicely, and the plot thickened. The greenhouse provided a space for her first meeting with the man who would become the father of her child. And since he happened to be a *married* man, the underground apartment mirrored their illicit relationship, deepening the internal conflict that drove the story to its conclusion.

A character's immediate surroundings can provide the backdrop for the sensory and significant details that shape the description of the character himself. Environment can also mirror a character's emotional state. If your character doesn't yet have a job, a hobby, a place to live, or a place to wander, you might need to supply these things. Once your character is situated comfortably, he may relax enough to reveal his secrets. On the other hand, you might purposely make your character uncomfortable—that is, put him in an environment where he definitely doesn't fit, just to see how he'll respond. Let's say you've written several descriptions of an elderly woman working in the kitchen, yet she hasn't begun to ripen into the three-dimensional character you know she could become. Try putting her at a gay bar on a Saturday night, or in a tattoo parlor, or (if you're up for a little time travel) at Appomattox, serving her famous buttermilk biscuits to Grant and Lee.

Fiction writers and poets aren't the only writers who can time travel or enter what I like to call "The Land of What If." As we noted in chapter two's discussion of "the gift of perhaps," nonfiction writers can enter imaginary worlds through speculation and conjecture, as long as readers are given the tools to navigate the territory. In "The American Man at Age Ten," Susan Orlean employs several journalistic techniques in the extended profile of fifth-grader Colin Duffy, including straight reporting of facts gained through observation and research; direct and indirect dialogue; and descriptions of characters, places, and events. But in her opening paragraph, she also employs conjecture, creating imagined scenarios based on what she has learned about how one particular ten-year-old views the world.

> If Colin Duffy and I were to get married, we would have matching superhero notebooks. We would wear shorts, big sneakers, and long, baggy T-shirts depicting famous athletes ... . We would sleep in our clothes. We would both be good at Nintendo Street Fighter II, but Colin would be better than me. We would have some homework, but it would never be too hard and we would always have just finished it. ... We wouldn't have sex, but we would have crushes on each other and, magically, babies would appear in our home.

This is where "the gift of perhaps" can take us, as readers and as writers. "What if?" the writer asks, then commences to imagine her way into the answer, creating, through speculation and conjecture, more fully developed characterizations than she might have created through more conventional techniques.

In describing a character's surroundings, you don't have to limit yourself to a character's present life. Early environments shape fictional characters as well as flesh-and-blood people. In Flaubert's description of Emma Bovary's adolescent years in the convent, he foreshadows the woman she will become, a woman who moves through life in a romantic malaise, dreaming of faraway lands and loves. We learn about Madame Bovary through concrete, sensory descriptions of the place that formed her. In addition, Flaubert describes the book that held her attention during mass and the images that she particularly loved—a sick lamb, a pierced heart.

Living among those white-faced women with their rosaries and copper crosses, never getting away from the stuffy schoolroom atmosphere, she gradually succumbed to the mystic languor exhaled by the perfumes of the altar, the coolness of the holy-water fonts and the radiance of the tapers. Instead of following the Mass, she used to gaze at the azure-bordered religious drawings in her book. She loved the sick lamb, the Sacred Heart pierced with sharp arrows, and poor Jesus falling beneath His cross.

Characters reveal their inner lives—their preoccupations, values, lifestyles, likes and dislikes, fears and aspirations—by the objects that fill their hands, houses, offices, cars, suitcases, grocery carts, and dreams. In the opening scenes of the film *The Big Chill*, we're introduced to the main characters by watching them unpack the bags they've brought for a weekend trip to a mutual friend's funeral. One character has packed enough pills to stock a drugstore; another has packed a calculator; still another, several packages of condoms. Before a word is spoken—even before we know anyone's name—we catch glimpses of the characters' lives through the objects that define them.

What items would your character pack for a weekend away? What would she use for luggage? A leather valise with a gold monogram on the handle? An old accordion case with decals from every theme park she's visited? A duffel bag? Make a list of everything your character would pack: a "Save the Whales" T-shirt; a white cotton nursing bra, size 36D; a breast pump; a Mickey Mouse alarm clock; a photograph of her husband rocking a child to sleep; a can of Mace; three Hershey bars.

We already know many things about your character, and you haven't even described her yet. Or have you? Description doesn't have to be direct to be effective. Techniques abound for describing a character indirectly, for instance, through the objects that fill her world. Create a grocery list for your character—or two or three, depending on who's coming for dinner. Show us the character's credit card bill or the itemized deductions on her income tax forms. Let your character host a garage sale and watch her squirm while neighbors and strangers rifle through her stuff. Which items is she practically giving away? What has she overpriced, secretly hoping no one will buy it? Write your character's Last Will and Testament. Which niece gets the Steinway? Who gets the lake cottage—the stepson or the daughter? If your main characters are divorcing, how will they divide their assets? Which one will fight hardest to keep the dog?

Nonfiction writers also employ indirect description to flesh out real-life characters, using details gathered through research: the tools that fill a character's garage, the items listed on the auction sheet, inscriptions in his books, the names he gives his hunting dogs, stories others tell about him, important documents gone missing, and even dreams. Mikal Gilmore's memoir, *Shot in the Heart*, opens and closes with descriptions of dreams in which the author's brother, convicted murderer Gary Gilmore, appears. These dream sequences work alongside the author's research—interviews, letters, school records, tape recordings, site visits, and firsthand observation—to expand Gary's characterization so that he emerges as a three-dimensional presence on the page.

SETTING CHARACTERS INTO MOTION

As we said earlier, characters do not exist on the page until we describe them; this applies to real-life people as well as to fictional characters. As characters (composed not of flesh and blood but of black marks on paper), they cannot actually walk, talk, make love or war, scramble eggs, or strum guitars. But in order to be believable to the reader, they must *appear* to. So after we've provided characters with substance—bodies, names, histories, occupations, preoccupations, houses, and cars—we set them in motion. One character flicks cigarette ash onto the carpet; another character vacuums it up. Poets and nonfiction writers, too, create characters through action-based description. In writing, as in life, actions speak louder than words. We learn about characters by watching them move.

The earlier "all-points bulletin" description of the father failed not only because the details were mundane and the prose stilted; it also suffered from lack of movement. To enlarge the description, imagine that same father in a particular setting—not just in the house but also sitting in the brown recliner. Then, because setting implies time as well as place, choose a particular time in which to place him. The time may be bound by the clock (six o'clock, sunrise, early afternoon) or bound only by the father's personal history (after the divorce, the day he lost his job, two weeks before his sixtieth birthday).

Then, following Aristotle's dictum of "using expressions that represent things as in a state of activity," set the father in motion. Again, be as specific as possible. "Reading the newspaper" is a start, but it does little more than label a generic activity. In order for readers to enter the fictional dream, the activity must be *shown*. Often this means breaking a large, generic activity into smaller, more particular parts: "scowling at the Dow Jones averages," perhaps, or "skimming the used-car ads" or "wiping his ink-stained fingers on the monogrammed handkerchief." Besides providing visual images for the reader, specific and representative actions also suggest the personality of the character, his habits and desires, and even the emotional life hidden beneath the physical details.

As we've said earlier, verbs are the foot soldiers of action-based description. However, we don't need to confine our use of verbs to the actions a character performs. Well-placed verbs can sharpen almost any physical description of a character. In the following passage from Marilynne Robinson's novel *Housekeeping*, verbs enliven the description even when the grandmother isn't in motion.

> … in the last years she continued to settle and began to shrink. Her mouth bowed forward and her brow sloped back, and her skull shone pink and speckled within a mere haze of hair, which hovered about her head like the remembered shape of an altered thing. She looked as if the nimbus of humanity were fading away and she were turning monkey. Tendrils grew from her eyebrows and coarse white hairs sprouted on her lip and chin. When she put on an old dress the bosom hung empty and the hem swept the floor. Old hats fell down over her eyes. Sometimes she put her hand over her mouth and laughed, her eyes closed and her shoulder shaking.

Notice the strong verbs Robinson uses throughout the description. The mouth "bowed" forward; the brow "sloped" back; the hair "hovered," then "sprouted"; the hem "swept" the floor; hats "fell" down over her eyes. Even when the grandmother's body is at rest, the description pulses with activity. And when the grandmother finally does move—putting a hand over her mouth, closing her eyes, laughing until her shoulders shake—we visualize her in our mind's eye because the actions are concrete and specific. They are what the playwright David Mamet calls "actable actions." Opening a window is an actable action, as is slamming a door. "Coming to terms with himself" or "understanding that he's been wrong all along" are not actable actions. This distinction between nonactable and actable actions echoes our earlier distinction between showing and telling. For the most part, a character's movements must be rendered concretely—that is, shown—before the reader can participate in the fictional dream.

Actable actions are important elements in many fiction and nonfiction scenes that include dialogue. In some cases, actions, along with environmental clues, are even more important to character development than the words the characters speak. Writers of effective dialogue include pauses, voice inflections, repetitions, gestures, and other details to suggest the psychological and emotional subtext of a scene. Journalists and other nonfiction writers do the same. Let's say you've just interviewed your cousin about his military service during the Vietnam War. You have a transcript of the interview, based on audio or video recordings, but you also took notes about what else was going on in that room. As you write, include nonverbal clues as well as your cousin's actual words. When you asked him about his tour of duty, did he look out the window, light another cigarette, and change the subject? Was it a stormy afternoon? What song was playing on the radio? If his ancient dog was asleep on your cousin's lap, did he stroke the dog as he spoke? When the phone rang, did your cousin ignore it or jump up to answer it, looking relieved for the interruption? Including details such as these will deepen your character description.

Action-based description does more than bring a character to life by painting a vivid, moving picture. A character's actions also reflect how a character navigates the moral and psychological terrain of the story. Mystery writer Margaret Maron says that there are some things a character simply cannot do as part of his moral landscape. The writer, she says, cannot successfully force a character to perform an action that goes against his personal morality without first changing the character himself. We can't simply wind up our characters as if they were spring-loaded toys. The actions we give our characters must be chosen carefully to represent not only the character's outer life but his inner life as well.

DESCRIBING A CHARACTER'S INNER LANDSCAPE

When Hollywood announces the opening of a movie made from a wonderful novel, my first reaction is to climb into the pages of the book, pull the cover over my head, and fall back into the fictional dream. The last thing I want to do is see the movie. For months I've lived within the world of the novel, wearing the character's skin and looking out through his green, penetrating eyes. Now, on the forty-foot screen, it's Harrison Ford or Liam Neeson or Tommy Lee Jones, and no matter how skilled his portrayal, he can never be more than an actor playing a role. He stomps or stumbles or rolls onto the scene, wearing a three-dimensional body that leaves nothing to my imagination. The character that breathed from the pages of the novel is dead, and nothing short of opening the book and climbing back into its pages will revive him.

Although the novelist described the character well, what was left unsaid was as important as what was said. My imagination completed the rest. Like all absorbed readers, I created the character partly in my own image. Such is the power of the written word. Novels, short stories, essays, and poems allow the reader to complete what the author began.

Those of us who write for the page can learn much from the fields of playwriting, cinematography, scripting, and oration—about showing instead of telling, setting the stage, and bringing a character to life through actions, dialogue, and stage directions. But at a certain point, our paths diverge. Although the road of the filmmaker or screenwriter may be broader, more public and populated, and more likely to be paved with coins, our road has more twists and turns, more hidden entries and exits, and more possibilities for revealing the mysteries of the human heart. Those of us who write for the page can travel to places a camera can never travel, the internal landscape and mindscape of thoughts and feelings.

Description does not rely solely on external proofs. We don't always have to use concrete, sensory details to describe our characters, and we aren't limited to describing actable actions. We don't even have to follow Aristotle's dictums of making people "see things" or of "using expressions that represent things as in a state of activity." Aristotle, after all, was schooled in drama and rhetoric, which are public, oral traditions that rely solely on outward signs to achieve their effects. Since he'd never read a novel—there were no novels to read in his time—Aristotle most likely had no idea of how to portray the inner life of a character.

I wonder what Aristotle would have thought of the novels of Milan Kundera, who uses little outward description of characters or their actions. Kundera is more concerned with a character's interior landscape, with what he calls a character's "existential problem," than with sensory description of person or action. In *The Unbearable Lightness of Being*, Tomas's body is not described at all, since the idea of *body* does not constitute Tomas's internal dilemma. Teresa's body *is* described in physical, concrete terms (though not with the degree of detail most novelists would employ) only because her body represents one of her existential preoccupations. For Kundera, a novel is more a meditation on ideas and the private world of the mind than a realistic depiction of characters. Reading Kundera, I always feel that I'm living inside the characters rather than watching them move, bodily, through the world.

With writers like Kundera, we learn about characters through the themes and obsessions of their inner lives, their "existential problems" as depicted primarily through dreams, visions, memories, and thoughts. Other writers probe characters' inner lives through what characters see through their eyes. A writer who describes what a character sees also reveals, in part, a character's inner drama. In *The Madness of a Seduced Woman*, Susan Fromberg Schaeffer describes a farm through the eyes of the novel's main character, Agnes, who has just fallen in love and is anticipating her first sexual encounter, which she simultaneously longs for and fears.

> ... and I saw how the smooth, white curve of the snow as it lay on the ground was like the curve of a woman's body, and I saw how the farm was like the body of a woman which lay down under the sun and under the freezing snow and perpetually and relentlessly produced uncountable swarms of living things, all born with mouths open and cries rising from them into the air, long-boned muzzles opening ... as if they would swallow the world whole ...

Later in the book, when Agnes's sexual relationship has led to pregnancy, then to a life-threatening abortion, she describes the farm in quite different terms.

> It was August, high summer, but there was something definite and curiously insubstantial in the air. ... In the fields near me, the cattle were untroubled, their jaws grinding the last of the grass, their large, fat tongues drinking the clear brook water. But there was something in the air, a sad note the weather played upon the instrument of the bone-stretched skin. ... In October, the leaves would be off the trees; the fallen leaves would be beaten flat by heavy rains and the first fall of snow. The bony ledges of the earth would begin to show, the earth's skeleton shedding its unnecessary flesh.

By describing the farm through Agnes's eyes, Schaeffer not only shows us Agnes's inner landscape—her ongoing obsession with sex and pregnancy—but also demonstrates a turning point in Agnes's view of sexuality. In the first passage, which depicts a farm in winter, Agnes sees images of beginnings and births. The earth is curved and full like a woman's fleshy body. In the second scene, described as occurring in "high summer," images of death prevail. Agnes's mind jumps ahead to autumn, to dying leaves and heavy rains, a time when the earth, no longer curved in a womanly shape, is little more than a skeleton, having shed the flesh it no longer needs.

When a character describes a place, in effect we get two descriptions for the price of one: a glimpse of the external location as well as insight into the describer's internal world. The same principle applies when one character describes another character. The reader not only glimpses the second character through the eyes of the first but also gains insight into the inner life of the describer, as well as to the relationship between the two characters. In Tom Wolfe's novel *The Bonfire of the Vanities*, we are introduced to Lawrence Kramer's wife through the eyes of her husband, who has been fantasizing about having an affair with a young woman. The Kramers live in a small apartment, and their bed is almost as wide as the bedroom, which means they have to crawl to the edge of the bed to reach the floor. His wife is doing just that as Kramer awakes.

> He woke up to the pitch and roll of his wife crawling down to the foot of the bed. … Now she was standing on the floor and bending over a chair to pick up her bathrobe. The way her flannel nightgown came down over her hips, she looked a mile wide.

A third, more subtle method of indirect description involves rendering a character's inner landscape through cadence, syntax, and diction. In this method, the writer imagines herself into a character's mind, then attempts to reproduce the internal rhythms of a character's thought patterns. In *Praying for Sheetrock: A Work of Nonfiction*, Melissa Fay Greene takes us inside Fanny's mind as she recalls a difficult childhood "in a world that consisted of her cot, the field, the kitchen, and the church."

> Night, dawn, noon, dusk, night. Bed, field, table, field, church. Sleep, pick, eat, pick, pray …

Bed, field, table, field, church. Bed. Field. Table: a hollow gallop of wooden bowls on a wooden table. Field. Church: a chase through dark woods and clinging vines, barefoot behind her grandmother, who carried a pair of church shoes for the girl in one hand. Bed. Field. Table. Field. Church: dry, upright, mumbling heat. She slumped against her sisters and snored. Bed. Field: endless. Table. Field: dirt filled her fingernails, eyes, ears, nose, hair. Church. Bed. Field: she weeded, hoed, and picked until the sky and air whirled brown and thistly around her, and her small fingers moved, delicately plucking so as not to get pricked, even in her sleep. Bed.

Through the use of repetition, cycling and recycling the same words through recurring staccato rhythms, Greene describes Fanny's world from the inside out. Rather than being told what Fanny looks like from the outside, we feel the weight of Fanny's weariness and the monotony of her days.

All three of these techniques—showing a character's inner life through thoughts, dreams, and fantasies; describing the world that passes before a character's eyes; and rendering a character's interior rhythms—are indirect methods of description. That is, the writer does not directly describe a person, scene, or event, but rather processes the description through the character's consciousness. Once we depart from direct authorial methods (such as physical description of a character, his environment, and his actions) and enter a character's internal world, we must consider how the character's consciousness filters the description and shapes the telling of the tale.

EXERCISES

1. If one of your fictional characters doesn't yet have a full name, give him one, including a last name and a middle name or initial. Try out different names to see which best fits his personality and actions, or give him a completely inappropriate name, one that goes against expectations. Then give him a nickname and invent the story behind it; describe him in terms of his nickname.

2. Choose one physical feature of your character—hair, eyes, hands, etc.—and describe it metaphorically. (Remember Emily Dickinson's eyes, the "color of the sherry the guests leave in the glasses"?) If you wish to take the metaphor further, describe the feature in terms of a setting you associate with your character.

3. Write a long description of a character, or locate one in a story or an essay you've written. Break the description into three sections, and place each section in a different part of the story. You might wish to start with the most obvious details and save the more intimate or evocative details for later, so that the character is revealed a little at a time.

4. Describe a photograph or video of your character that reveals something about her that your story or essay does not yet reveal. If the photograph was taken during a time period not covered in the story, your description might serve as a flashback.

5. Write a description of a character as he might appear in the future. The description could be from the character's own imagination ("Henry saw himself years from today ...") or from another character's viewpoint (see the passage from *Ingenious Pain* quoted in this chapter).

6. Describe a character as a blind person might describe her; use every sense *except* sight.

7. Describe the same character in three different environments—say, the grocery store, a hockey game, and the locker room. Notice how the setting affects the character's appearance, posture, mannerisms, speech, and

thoughts. In which place does your character seem most relaxed, youthful, worried, or lighthearted?

8. Write down a particular trait, emotion, or attitude your character possesses. Then list at least three actable actions that reveal that quality. For instance, if you wish to show Darla's vanity, your list might include glancing at her reflection in storefronts, wearing turtlenecks and scarves to hide the wrinkles in her neck, undergoing liposuction on her thighs. Expand one of these actions into a full description that *reveals* Darla's vanity rather than merely *tells* the reader about it.

9. If you want to learn more about your characters' inner lives, write a description of how each would react given the same situation. Choose a situation that will reveal the characters' values, attitudes, or other qualities of their inner landscape: being accosted by a panhandler, being given too much change by a cashier, being seduced by a beautiful stranger. Which of your characters would fail to report cash earnings to the IRS? Which ones would refuse to have an affair, even if their spouse couldn't possibly find out?

10. Write a description of a person, a place, an object, or an event in the language of one of your characters. Use his vocabulary, his grammar and syntax, and the rhythms of his sentences. (For an example, study the passage quoted from *Praying for Sheetrock*.)

11. Employing the "gift of perhaps," choose an alternate name for yourself, a name you wish, or once wished, you had. Imagine how your life might have been different had you been given this name. Who might you have married? Where would you live, and what job would you have? You can expand the "gift of perhaps" technique beyond naming to describe other paths your life might have taken. How would your life have been different had you moved to Wyoming rather than to Baltimore, if you'd been a triplet rather than a twin, or if you'd studied nursing instead of accounting? (You can use the same technique to describe an alternate life of a character in one of your stories, essays, or poems.)

12. Interview a family member or distant relative about a particular aspect of his or her history. Record the interview, transcribe it, and incorporate significant responses into a brief character profile. If you videotape the interview or take detailed notes that include gestures, silences, hesitations, or other nonverbal clues, include these details in the profile, as well as details about the surroundings in which the interview took place.

13. After reviewing the passages from "Amazons" and *A Crime in the Neighborhood* quoted in this chapter, write a group portrait that describes several individuals as if they comprised one collective body.

14. Using Phillip Lopate's notion of "turning oneself into a character," write a few paragraphs in which you introduce yourself to the reader. Use any technique that appeals to you: direct, physical description of your body; discussion of your obsessions, quirks, idiosyncrasies, opinions, and frustrations; or indirect characterization through lists of the jobs you've held, for instance, or cars you've owned, pets you've acquired, the contents of your refrigerator, the items of clothing you're preparing to donate to Goodwill, the items you just can't part with, and so on.

CHAPTER SEVEN

The Eye of the Teller: How Point of View Affects Description

Throughout this book, we've discussed the importance of writers paying attention, of giving full and thoughtful consideration to three components of descriptive writing: eye, word, and story. We attend to the images in the sensory world and the world of the imagination; we shape precise, vivid, and fresh descriptions of these images; and we consider how our descriptions serve the larger story, poem, or nonfiction work.

Attention also refers to a position taken and held. Each time we put pen to paper, we assume a literary position—call it our posture, angle, stance, persona, or point of view. Point of view, in this case, does not mean *opinion* but rather the position from which we describe the details of our literary work; it also concerns how a work makes its journey from author to reader.

Point of view is arguably the most complex of literary conventions. Countless dissertations have been written on the subject, and almost every writing text devotes a chapter or two to point-of-view issues, including how point of view affects a work's form, content, plot, voice, tone, and reliability. For our purposes, we'll focus mainly on point-of-view issues that directly affect description. We'll show how description frames the narrator's point of view, how shifts in the descriptive frame (or eye) signal viewpoint shifts, and how point-of-view description can organize our work. Finally, we'll discuss the strengths and limitations of different point-of-view methods as they relate to description. But first we'll briefly define various point-of-view choices and review basic issues concerning each choice.

POINT-OF-VIEW BASICS

There are three main point-of-view methods: first person, second person, and third person, each of which contains variations.

In first-person point of view, an "I" or "we" narrates the work, and everything is filtered through the consciousness of this "I" or "we." The first-person singular is the "I" voice behind the work, a common point-of-view choice for fiction writers, nonfiction writers, and poets alike. The first-person plural narrator is not an "I" but rather a "we." However, this narrator is not the mere rhetorical "we" (as in "We will now move on to our discussion of penguins") but rather what I sometimes refer to as the "tribal we," identified not as an individual but rather as part of a communal unit, a shared consciousness. Like the group portrait we discussed in chapter six, the first-person plural choice is rare in literature.

In fiction, first-person narrators are characters in the story; they may be the main characters around which the story revolves, or they may be peripheral characters, but in both cases they are the tellers of the tale. In poetry, the first-person narrator is sometimes called the "speaker." In nonfiction, the first-person narrator is often so closely aligned with the flesh-and-blood author that it's easy to overlook the fact that the narrator of a nonfiction work is also a character who, as we noted in chapter six, must be constructed on the page. The main thing to remember about first-person narration, whether used in fiction, poetry, or nonfiction, is that the work is filtered through the consciousness of the "I" or "we."

In second-person narration, a character in the literary work is referred to as "you." Usually this "you" is the protagonist of the story, the main character around which the events revolve. Second-person narration goes beyond merely addressing your reader as "you," a technique I've used throughout this book; it actually places the "you" within the events of the story. Like first-person plural narration, second person is a rare point-of-view choice.

In third-person narration, the speaker does not appear as an actual character in the story, poem, or essay. Rather a third-person narrator uses third-person pronouns—*he, she, it,* or *they*—to tell a story about someone else. (A first-person narrator also uses third-person pronouns, but only to refer to other characters in his own story.)

There are three main variations on third-person narration. The *objective narrator* relates a story solely through outward signs—dialogue, action, and description. The *omniscient* or *godlike narrator* knows everything that a god might know. He not only sees and describes outward signs; he can also see into the minds of all his characters, move freely through time and space, and insert authorial comments. The *limited-omniscient narrator* can do everything an objective narrator can do but less than an omniscient narrator. He can describe outward signs—actions, dialogue, setting—but usually inhabits only one character's mind.

ESTABLISHING POINT OF VIEW

An effective literary work usually reveals its point of view early on, positioning the reader in the appropriate seat from which to view the show. The eye of the describer focuses the telling, often within the first sentence.

> We get married in two days: Charles and me. — Clyde Edgerton, from *Raney*

> The day after Thanksgiving my mother was arrested outside the doors of JC Penney's, Los Angeles, and when I went to get her I considered leaving her at the security desk. — Ethan Canin, from "Pitch Memory"

> Lloyd Abbott wasn't the richest man in our town, but he had, in his daughters, a vehicle for displaying his wealth that some of the richer men didn't have. — Sue Miller, from "The Lover of Women"

With all three of these opening sentences, we learn right away (from the first-person pronouns "me," "my," "I," and "our") that we'll be viewing the story through the eyes of a first- person narrator who is a character in the story. We don't yet know whether the speaker will be the main character or a peripheral character, but we do know that the speaker will place himself, to some degree, *within* the story rather than outside it.

Sometimes it takes longer than one paragraph to establish point of view, but in most cases the reader knows by the end of a story's first page who will be narrating the tale and whether the speaker will be a character in the story or a third-person narrator.

> "Yes, of course, if it's fine tomorrow," said Mrs. Ramsay. "But you'll have to be up with the lark," she added.
>
> To her son these words conveyed an extraordinary joy, as if it were settled, the expedition were bound to take place, and the wonder to which he had looked forward, for years and years it seemed, was, after a night's darkness and a day's sail, within touch. — Virginia Woolf, from *To the Lighthouse*

The first sentence of Woolf's novel suggests a third-person narrator; Mrs. Ramsey is named as a third party. But the point of view isn't firmly established at this point. The narrator might be a first-person "I," a character in the story who is telling us about Mrs. Ramsey. It's only when the narrator enters the son's mind that we know for sure this is third-person narration rather than first. A first-person narrator cannot inhabit another character's mind, only his own.

Most contemporary stories are told either from first-person point of view or from third-person limited omniscient. Since there usually isn't space within a short work for multiple viewpoints to be shown well, very few short works use a third-person narrator who is totally omniscient, capable of entering all characters' minds. Novelists, however, often use this technique, dipping in and out of several characters' minds over the course of the story. Multiple viewpoints can also be accomplished through several first-person narrators, as in Faulkner's *As I Lay Dying*.

In the case of multiple narrators (in third-person narration as well as first) we may not know for several pages, or even several chapters, how many minds we'll be inhabiting. Faulkner's opening sentence—"Jewel and I come up from the field, following the path in single file"—announces a first-person narrator, Darl. We don't know until the next chapter, when another first-person narrator speaks, that we'll be entering the mind of more than one character. Thankfully, Faulkner's opening chapters are short, so it doesn't take us long to recognize Faulkner's pattern. In addition, his chapter headings ("Darl," "Cora," "Darl," "Jewel," etc.) provide early hints to his viewpoint structure. Simply by skimming the novel's pages, we can surmise that more than one teller will be relating the tale.

Like most novels and short stories, essays and poems also announce their point of view early on. With some poems, the clues come even before the first line, with titles like W.S. Merwin's "Grandmother Watching at Her Window" or Patricia Hubbell's "The Streetcleaner's Lament." And by the end of the first paragraph of an essay, we usually know whether the writer will be using the first-person narration characteristic of personal essays, opinion pieces, and memoirs, or the third-person narration that shapes some biographies, profiles, and journalistic investigations.

Through effective use of pronouns, names, and other clues, you can reveal early on whether your speaker is a first-person narrator or a third-person narrator. It may take a bit longer to establish whether your first-person narrator is a main character or a peripheral character, or whether your third-person narrator is objective, omniscient, or limited omniscient. Even so, establishing your narrator's point of view is a fairly straightforward procedure. Maintaining your point of view is more difficult, as is sensing when to subtly shift viewpoints to achieve literary effects. Shifts in points of view can be likened to the nursery-rhyme girl with the curl in the middle of her forehead. When they are good, they can be very, very good. But when they are bad, they are horrid.

TROUBLING SHIFTS IN POINT OF VIEW

The reader needs time to position herself in a story and to focus her imaginative eye. If that focus changes abruptly, for no apparent reason, her energies are diverted. Radical, awkward, or inappropriate shifts confuse and frustrate the reader, making her unsure of whose story she's reading.

One of the most common ways to frustrate your reader is to abruptly switch point of view from one character to another. Let's say that for the first several pages of your story, you've been situated inside Linda's mind, looking out.

> Linda lit a cigarette and watched her mother cram another forkful of chocolate cake into her mouth. *I'll never let myself get that fat*, Linda thought. *Never. I'll starve myself first.* Linda inhaled deeply, holding the cigarette between two thin fingers.

Linda's mother has been present in the scene also, but only as described through Linda's eyes. Since the reader has been living solely within Linda's consciousness, she's made an intellectual and emotional investment in Linda; you've given no clue that the story belongs to anyone else.

Then suddenly, you ask the reader to slip inside the mother's mind, to feel her emotions.

> Linda's mother looked up from her plate and smiled, hoping that Linda hadn't noticed how big a bite she'd taken.

Until the point of view shifted, the reader had been immersed in your fictional dream. One small word—*hoping*—was all it took to distract him. *Hoping* betrays emotion and thought on the part of the mother. It moves the reader inside another character's mind, violating the limited-omniscient point of view you'd established.

Luckily this kind of viewpoint shift is easy to correct. Simply remove the subjective, internalized word or phrase (*"hoping* that Linda hadn't noticed ...") and replace it with an objective, actable action that Linda could witness ("Her mother lowered her eyes," perhaps, or "Her mother laid the fork down quickly and wiped the crumbs of chocolate from her mouth"). We'll still get a notion of what the mother is feeling, but the evidence will be filtered through Linda's consciousness. We'll remain inside her mind, securely centered in Linda's story.

Another way to distract or confuse your reader is to switch visual points of reference too often or too quickly. This can happen even when you're firmly centered in one consciousness and don't stray from it. Let's say you open with a phrase like "From where he lay, Simon could see the flat Illinois sky, stretched between two silos." So far, so good. The reader mentally lies on his back next to Simon, peering up into the sky.

In the next sentence, Simon watches an ant crawl over his big toe. The reader is still with you. Granted, the reader might have enjoyed dwelling a while longer on sky images, experiencing more detailed proofs, but one abrupt switch won't hurt your description too much. The reader can shift vantage points from the Illinois sky to the ant without suffering whiplash.

Sentence three: "Simon stared at the ant, then stretched and sighed, remembering the last time he'd seen Flora, her long lean legs pedaling away from him as she disappeared down the country road." By now the reader is dizzy. It's like those three manic minutes on your sister's wedding video. (Remember? You'd set the camera down for a minute, just long enough to get another glass of champagne, and your four-year-old grabbed the camera. Now you've got three minutes of spinning linoleum tiles, stiletto heels, then swoop! a quick pan of the ceiling, your uncle's mouth, an unidentified hand reaching for the punch bowl.) By the time Simon rises to his feet in sentence four, your reader is grabbing a chair for balance. You've shifted visual viewpoints so abruptly that the reader has lost all sense of perspective.

More often, shifts in perspective are not visual but rather what novelist John Gardner calls shifts in "psychic distance." Psychic shifts are harder to pinpoint than visual shifts, but they are even more disturbing to the reader because they erode the emotional ground of the story. Here's a sentence from Ivan Turgenev's "The Tryst," followed in italics by two sentences which, had they appeared in the story (they didn't—I invented them) would have eroded the psychic ground Turgenev had established.

> I cannot tell how long I slept, but when I opened my eyes, the whole interior of the forest was filled with sunlight, and in all directions, athwart the joyously rustling foliage, the bright blue sky seemed to be sparkling. *The weather report had been accurate after all*, I thought. *It was indeed a mild day to venture outdoors.*

Turgenev's description is intimate and highly charged with emotion. The narrator is psychically close to the scene and pulls the reader in with him. It's as if the forest is alive, wrapping itself around both narrator and reader. The two sentences that follow, on the other hand, are objectively reported, as if spoken by someone totally removed from the scene. The psychic distance between the two voices is staggering. Any shift in point of view—in visual perspective, psychic distance, or a shift from the vantage point of one character to another—must be carefully executed.

SUBTLE, EFFECTIVE SHIFTS IN POINT OF VIEW

Troubling viewpoint shifts are just that: troubling. But carefully executed, subtle viewpoint shifts can serve your writing in many ways. They can act as gearshifts to vary and monitor a story's pace, or to transition among various characters' stories. They can visually enlarge a scene or shrink it; close in tightly on a character's inner landscape and then, when that space becomes too claustrophobic for the reader's comfort, open a window to allow outside air in. In some texts, especially memoir, different viewpoints can even dwell inside one another, like Russian nesting dolls, each segment of the memoir opening up yet another figure until multiple versions of the same self appear. And although shifting viewpoints occur most often in novels or other long, sustained works, many authors of brief works move seamlessly among various points of view. In some brief essays, for example, the "I" is absent at first, then emerges after a page or two, as in Jane Brox's "Bread" or Dinty W. Moore's "Son of Mr. Green Jeans," an essay structured on the template of the alphabet, which withholds the first-person narrator until the letter "I" is introduced. Although a casual reader may not notice Moore's subtle viewpoint shifts, they nevertheless shape the essay's movement and affect the reader's intellectual and emotional response to the work.

Sometimes what seems to be a shift in viewpoint is actually a kind of settling, a gradual descent into the story, like a hawk circling before moving in for the kill. In this technique, the author slowly brings the story into focus through description. This gradual settling can be likened to the opening frames of some movies—the camera taking in the large view, its eye sweeping over the terrain. Joan Chase's novel *During the Reign of the Queen of Persia* begins in this cinematic manner.

> In northern Ohio there is a county of some hundred thousand arable acres
> which breaks with the lake region flatland and begins to roll and climb,
> and to change into rural settings ...

Chase's description continues in this way, a luxurious rendering of the countryside, complete with concrete and sensory details like "water shoots that rapidly lose themselves in gladed ravines," "the hump of railroad lines," and "the jeweled dust of crushed quartz." Chase describes the setting first—the time and locale in which the story takes place. Only after the setting is established do we begin to settle into the teller's visual and psychological point of view.

Another way to settle gradually into point of view is to describe the opening scene from the eye of a removed or objective first-person narrator who stands on the outskirts, physically or psychologically. This technique is especially effective in certain nonfiction forms where you wish to establish yourself as a witness to the events, a presence with the "I" of authority. Once you establish this authority, you can slip from the scene, allowing the reader to focus on a character or subject other than yourself.

In fiction, too, beginning with a first-person peripheral narrator is a way to establish the storyteller's authority. Flaubert uses this technique in *Madame Bovary*. Although the bulk of the novel is told from the third-person limited-omniscient point of view, it actually opens with first-person narration. "We were at preparation," the novel begins. The narrator is a schoolboy speaking in first-person plural, as if through the communal voice of all the schoolboys present when the new boy, Charles Bovary, arrives on the scene. First-person narration continues for a few pages, but once Charles Bovary is described in detail, the first-person narrator slips from the scene and the third-person narrator takes over. The novel never returns to first-person point of view, for, in fact, it was never firmly situated there. The novelist was simply circling the scene, fluttering briefly but not landing: The permanent nest was third-person narration.

Flaubert's technique—shifting from first person to third—is relatively rare in fiction. More often, subtle shifts in opening points of view occur when a third-person narrator circles the scene objectively, lighting briefly here and there—on setting, minor characters, scenes—before settling into one character's consciousness. Truman Capote's story "A Tree of Night" opens with a description of a depot. We're not yet sure who is telling the tale or whose story it is. The narrator seems removed both physically and psychically, positioned far enough from the scene in space and time to describe the large picture.

> It was winter. A string of naked light bulbs, from which it seemed all warmth had been drained, illuminated the little depot's cold, windy platform. Earlier in the evening it had rained, and now icicles hung along the station-house eaves like some crystal monster's vicious teeth. Except for a girl, young and rather tall, the platform was deserted.

Up to this point, the eye of the narrator is objective. We've not entered any character's mind. The girl on the platform may not be a character at all; at this point, she's merely part of the still life the narrator has painted. As the paragraph continues, the eye of the narrator moves closer to the girl. He describes her clothing and belongings, proceeding from the most obvious and generic details (a gray flannel suit, a raincoat) to the particular and telling (a green Western guitar and "a gray suede purse on which elaborate brass letters spelled Kay"). He also describes her hair and face. With each detail, the narrator moves closer to the girl, bringing us with him. Through the description of the purse, we even learn her name.

In the second paragraph, the train enters the depot and the girl springs into action. No longer merely part of the still life, she's an actor in the drama—thus far, the only actor. We sense that something is going to happen on that train and that the girl will be a part of it: "Kay assembled her paraphernalia and climbed up into the last coach."

In the third paragraph, the narrator once again refocuses his descriptive lens. It is no longer trained, close up, on Kay; it has moved into the coach. The next four or five sentences describe in detail the coach's interior, including its velvet, balding seats, litter-strewn aisles, and leaky water cooler. Coach passengers are mentioned briefly, but they remain in the background, generic and unnamed, seeming to exist only to provide a backdrop for Kay's entrance into the car.

In the fourth paragraph, the narrator moves from an external description of Kay to an internal one. In a few words, he settles into the limited-omniscient point of view that will frame the rest of the story.

> Kay resisted a temptation to hold her nose ...

We are now inside Kay's mind, looking out. "Resisted a temptation" is not an external, actable action; it reveals an internal thought process. This kind of phrase will pepper the story from this point on, keeping us centered in Kay's consciousness. Although much of the story will be told through objective action, dialogue, and description, every now and then the narrator will move back into Kay's mind, revealing her thoughts or emotions.

> … she wished she had a pillow for her back.
>
> … the way he was looking at her made her squeamish …
>
> She wondered if there might be a seat in a car up ahead.

As the story progresses, other characters move into action. The narrator describes them fully, sometimes objectively and sometimes through Kay's eyes. But the narrator never enters their minds. Every detail of description or action is filtered through either the narrator's point of view or through Kay's. When another character's thought processes or feelings are suggested, the suggestion is qualified through objective phrases such as "it seemed" or "as if." (In the follow example, I've used italics to mark the qualifying phrases.)

> [The woman] began to unscrew the cap but, *seeming to think better of this,* handed the bottle to Kay.

> *As if to deny it,* the man made a queer, furry sound deep in his throat …

Capote, having chosen the limited-omniscient point of view and established residence in only one character's mind, does not deviate from that viewpoint. He may take his time circling the scene, but once he settles into Kay's mind, he does not violate his point-of-view method by entering another character's mind or by radically altering visual or psychic perspectives.

HOW POINT-OF-VIEW METHOD AFFECTS DESCRIPTION

First-Person Narrator

The advantages of describing through the eyes of a first-person narrator are clear. First-person narration narrows the field of vision, providing a single focal point for your descriptions. Descriptions from a single viewpoint can also unify your story's theme and tighten the storyline, especially if your story is loosely plotted or episodic. And in most cases, limiting yourself to one consciousness can create instant intimacy between narrator and reader, thus intensifying your story's emotional effects.

When my students begin writing stories, most of them choose the "I" point of view. It's easier, they tell me—and more freeing. To a point, I agree. The "I" voice, especially when it closely resembles our own voice, may feel more natural than the voice in a second- or third-person narration. We relax into our first-person narrator's descriptions because they so closely align with our personal view of the world. We are in control of our descriptions—or so it appears on the surface. In truth, first-person narration presents challenges that no other point-of-view method presents, and before we choose to write a story in first person, we need to consider these challenges.

Since everything in first-person narration must be filtered through the "I," every description in our story must be something the "I" has either witnessed firsthand or learned through some other source. If you choose a first-person narrator, he must be present in every scene in the story, or if he describes a scene in which he wasn't present, he must rely on secondhand information. A first-person narrator cannot describe what another character is thinking or feeling unless this information is reported to him; he cannot enter another character's consciousness, except through fantasy, conjecture, or extrasensory perception. For these reasons, descriptions filtered through the eye of a first-person narrator often feel more limited, fragmented, and subjective than those of a third-person narrator.

Although it may appear on the surface that first-person narration gives us supreme control over our descriptions, in reality when we choose a first-person narrator, we relinquish much of our control. We relinquish our right to inhabit more than one mind, to describe places and events outside the narrator's experience, and to intrude with our own authorial opinions and reflections (unless, of course, we are writing a memoir or personal essay in which the narrator and author are indistinguishable from each other).

If we choose a first-person fictional narrator, we may also have to set aside concrete, sensory, and significant descriptive passages—those passages we've labored so hard to achieve—to make way for our narrator's descriptions. If our point-of-view narrator is less articulate or educated or ironic or sympathetic than we are, we may also have to relinquish our authorial egos, muting our own voice in order to speak through the voice of our narrator. When Daniel Keyes chose to speak through the voice of a mentally retarded man in *Flowers for Algernon*, he gave up the right to speak as the highly intelligent, articulate writer he is. Whereas the *writer* Daniel Keyes might describe a Rorschach test in stunning, brilliant prose, his first-person *narrator* can describe the test (misspellings and all) only as "some white cards with ink spilled all over them."

The costs of using a first-person describer may be even higher if your narrator is someone whose values are quite different from your own. You must relinquish your own prose style as well as your moral landscape so your narrator can describe the world through his own lens. Here is the narrator of Tom McAfee's story "This Is My Living Room" describing his wife and mistress, his daughter, and one of the customers in his store.

> ROSIE
> ain't exactly good-looking. She got to be dried-up but once was on the fat side. She makes a good wife. ... Sometimes I get fed up with her and go to my woman in South Town. I take her a couple of cans of beans and some hose or a pair of bloomers. There ain't nothing much a woman won't do for food or clothes.
>
> Ellen Jean, the oldest, is a right good-looking girl but sassy and you can't hardly do anything with her. ... Like as not she's got a baby starting in her belly right now. She's a sassy bitch-girl and don't take after her ma or me. Sometimes I wonder if she's mine.
>
> OLD EZMO
> was what you'd call a low class of nigger. ... You're a crooked, low-down nigger, I told him, and they ain't nothing much worse than that. You ain't fit for making side meat out of.

If you're considering using a first-person narrator, especially a fictional character who is quite different from you, here are some questions to ask yourself.

- How will the character's limitations (age, sex, intelligence, ability to perceive irony or humor, etc.) affect her descriptions?
- Am I capable of telling the character's story solely through her words? (Her voice, including her descriptions, must sound authentic.)
- Is the character interesting enough to warrant the time a reader spends in her presence? (First-person narrators can't be boring. Theirs is the only voice our reader will hear. Who wants to listen to a boring storyteller?)
- How will I include essential information that the narrator cannot possibly know?
- Am I willing to give up my own voice in exchange for the narrator's voice? What if I can describe a river in liquid, sparkling prose, but my narrator can say only, "Wow, what a—I mean, it's like, well, really cool, huh?" Whose voice will win out?

After considering these questions, you may decide that despite its inherent difficulties and limitations, first person is the most appropriate viewpoint for your story. Whereas an omniscient narrator is expected to know everything God knows (a daunting challenge, since God is seldom wrong) and an objective narrator is expected to report events with computer accuracy, a first-person narrator is allowed to be human. As such, we accept that her descriptions are colored by her ignorance, prejudices, misconceptions, and all those other warty inadequacies that make human beings so fascinating. If you decide on first-person narration, you'll be in good company. Many of the most brilliant and moving literary pieces—novels, short stories, essays, and poems—are written in first person.

First-Person, Main Character Narrator

Think of first-person description as a convertible camera lens attached to the eyes of your character. The lens can do two things, and only two things.

Flipped one way, the lens can focus inside the character's head. We see what he is thinking, feeling, remembering, dreaming. Flipped the other way, the lens records everything the character sees through his own eyes.

That's it. In terms of description, that's all a first-person lens can do. It can't focus on the character's whole body or view his actions, unless he's looking in a mirror or at a photograph or a video of himself. That's one reason first-person narrators are often the most thinly described characters in the story, novel, or poem. And as we noted in chapter six, self-description is also an important consideration in most memoirs, essays, and other nonfiction works. The convertible-lens principle applies to all literary works employing a first-person narrator.

One of the hardest challenges you'll face if you choose a main character as your teller is how to physically describe him. This is also true with peripheral narrators, but since a peripheral narrator is not the center of the action, readers aren't usually as eager to "see" him as they are to see the main character. Some highly imaginative readers require no bodily description of the narrator; they climb right inside his skin without stopping to wonder what he looks like on the outside. Most readers, however, need descriptive clues to help visualize the narrator, especially if that narrator is the main character in the story.

If you're using a first-person narrator and wish to describe him visually, how will you do it? We've already mentioned one way: having your narrator describe himself while looking in a mirror or studying a photograph, sketch, painting, video, or home movie of himself. The mirror technique has been used so much in literature that it has become hackneyed; it also limits your description to the present time period. A photograph, however, can reveal how your character looked in the past, and a moving picture (a video or home movie, for instance) can show your character in action. You might even travel into the future by having your character view a computer-generated image of himself, like those age-progression images the FBI uses to track missing persons.

Sometimes a first-person narrator, rather than revealing himself visually through a scene in the story, simply tells us about himself. (First-person narration lends itself to telling rather than showing—another challenge for the "I" point of view.) In Reynolds Price's novel *Kate Vaiden*, the title character starts talking in the first sentence; by the second sentence, we begin to visualize her through the details she supplies.

> The best thing about my life up to here is, nobody believes it. I stopped trying to make people hear it long ago, and I'm nothing but a real middle-sized white woman that has kept on going with strong eyes and teeth for fifty-seven years. You can touch me; I answer.

Price's details aren't intended to be visually specific but rather to reveal Kate's sense of being "nothing but" an ordinary woman. The two distinguishing characteristics she mentions—her strong eyes and teeth—are not details an outside observer would notice. Instead they're what a woman might *feel* about herself from the inside out. Kate tells us not that her eyes are blue or her teeth crooked, yellow, or gleaming white (visual details a third-person narrator might mention) but that they are *strong*, a fact she knows from living within her own skin. "You can touch me," she says. "I answer." Although first-person narrators cannot *see* themselves, they can *experience* themselves as physical bodies and describe the sensations of moving physically through their world.

If you don't want your first-person narrator to study himself through mirrors, photographs, or other graphic tools, you can give the reader a physical sense of the character by describing how she experiences her body from the inside out, as Kate Vaiden does. A first-person narrator can also report what others say about her physical appearance, or even what she imagines others see when they look at her. To give readers a sense of a first-person narrator's physical appearance, you don't need to supply a blow-by-blow description of every physical feature. As in other kinds of description, a few telling details go a long way.

First-Person Peripheral Narrator

Not all first-person narrators are main characters. Some stand off to one side, relating someone else's story. Willa Cather employs this form of narration in *My Ántonia*, as does F. Scott Fitzgerald in *The Great Gatsby*. First-person peripheral narration provides many of the benefits of first-person narration while avoiding some of its limitations. Because the telling is filtered through a single consciousness, the writer can engage the reader emotionally, relate events efficiently, and focus descriptions through a single lens. At the same time, a peripheral narrator can lend an air of objectivity and psychic distance that a main character cannot; because the peripheral narrator is not the center of the action, she is free to observe events from her box seat. An added benefit is that a peripheral narrator can describe the main character's physical attributes and actions as viewed from the outside, something that a first-person main character can rarely accomplish for himself.

Although all successful descriptions require some knowledge of the things of this world—its places, persons, and things—first-person narrators, especially peripheral narrators, can be forgiven for not knowing everything. Let's say I want to write a story about an Italian chef, but my knowledge of sauces is limited to sautéing onions and garlic in a skillet, then dumping in a can of Ragú. Well sure, I could do the research—go online, visit my neighborhood restaurant and quiz the chef, maybe even take a six-week course in Italian cooking. Even so, my knowledge might still be too limited to justify telling the story from the chef's point of view. However, I could tell the chef's story through another character's point of view, someone standing in the doorway of the kitchen, a character whose knowledge of Italian cooking is as limited as my own.

As a peripheral narrator, my descriptions of pasta primavera might not be as thorough or accurate or gastronomically enticing as those of a trained chef, but they would at least sound authentic. And my ignorance might lend just the amount of interest, humor, or mystery my story requires. A first-person peripheral narrator is like a student learning a difficult subject, putting the puzzle together piece by piece. He catches glimpses of the central character and events, then reveals them to the reader little by little. This puts him in cahoots with the reader, who may know even less and who enjoys unraveling the mystery. As a reader, I hate to be lectured to by a know-it-all. I prefer to be taken by the hand and led through the story's terrain, even if my guide appears to be discovering the terrain step by step.

Reading a story that employs a peripheral narrator allows me this privilege. And writing a story, an essay, or a poem from this point of view allows me to use my partial ignorance as a helpful guide for my reader. In descriptions by a peripheral narrator, a certain amount of ignorance can be bliss—for the writer as well as for the reader. A peripheral narrator is, by definition, an outsider—a stance that comes naturally to most writers. Many of my students tell me that they often feel they are standing outside their own lives, looking in. Some can remember feeling this way since childhood. "That's the way most writers are," I tell them. "That's how we make stories out of our lives." Perhaps this outsider stance makes first-person peripheral narration a natural choice for many of us. The problem comes when the peripheral narrator remains only an observer, without becoming intellectually or emotionally involved in the story's outcome.

Although the first-person peripheral narrator is not the center of the action, he *is* the center of the telling. He witnesses the main events of the story, and through his eyes we watch the drama unfold. Cather's title, *My Ántonia*, illustrates the principle that governs a story told by a first-person peripheral narrator. "Ántonia" tells us this story centers on someone else, in this case a girl named Ántonia; "my" stakes the narrator's claim to the telling. Both of these elements must be present in any successful narration employing a peripheral narrator. As Rust Hills points out in *Writing in General and the Short Story in Particular*, when point of view fails, it is often because the point-of-view character is not the character moved by the action.

This principle applies to nonfiction works as well as to novels and short stories. In Beverly Lowry's *Crossed Over: A Murder, A Memoir*, the main character is convicted murderer Karla Faye Tucker; it is Karla's story that focuses the narrative. However, Lowry, as the peripheral narrator, is an important part of the story as well—not so much as a character, though her own story parallels Karla's in many ways, but rather as the "eye" that shapes Karla's story and also as the "I" who is changed by the story's events.

A peripheral narrator must do more than merely report the story's events. He must also be changed, in some degree, by what he witnesses, and his descriptions should reveal this change. Why else employ a peripheral narrator? Why spend time and effort setting up housekeeping in your narrator's head, seeing through his eyes and hearing with his ears, if you don't also reveal the narrator's stake in the story? The choice of a first-person peripheral narrator is also a choice to explore the impact of the story's events on that narrator.

First-Person Plural Narrator

As we mentioned earlier, first-person plural narration is a rare point-of-view choice, but when used effectively it offers opportunities for description that no other viewpoint offers. The "we" viewpoint is an excellent vehicle for describing experiences in which the individuals comprising the "we" are tightly bonded, connected to each other so strongly that they live, breathe, and move as one unit. Think twins, linked through shared DNA; survivors of an earthquake, crouched together in the rubble; naturalized citizens gathered in a courtroom to confirm their oath of allegiance. Think soldiers in a platoon, camouflaging themselves from the enemy.

> We tied branches to our helmets.
> We painted our faces & rifles
> with mud from a riverbank,
>
> blades of grass hung from the pockets
> of our tiger suits … — Yusef Komunyakaa, from "Camouflaging the Chimera"

The first-person plural viewpoint often governs brief works, such as Komunyakaa's poem, or short stories, like Faulkner's classic "A Rose for Emily." Brief first-person plural passages also appear as breakaway sections in many long works of first-person singular or third-person narration. As the primary viewpoint choice for a book-length work, however, first-person plural is extremely rare. David Huddle's novel *The Faulkes Chronicles* is a notable exception, told from the point of view of a large group of siblings (uncounted and perhaps uncountable) who witness their mother's struggle with the cancer that will kill her. The opening lines establish the plural viewpoint.

> In her last year of life our mother betrayed us by becoming pretty. We are a homely family. For generations we've been that way.

Note the pronouns: "our," "us," "we." The speaker is not a single child of this mother, but the entire tribe of children, "the largest Faulkes family on record," descended from a long line of Faulkeses who often appear in Huddle's pages as one single unit.

> You won't find a simpering Faulkes anywhere on the planet. We don't flirt, we don't small-talk, we don't suck up, we don't flatter, we don't shoot the breeze. We have thrived because we are notably competent and dependable.

Now and then in *The Faulkes Chronicles*, the names of the siblings appear, along with detailed cameo descriptions and passages of dialogue that help distinguish individual characters. But only for brief passages. Turn the page, and the individual is again subsumed within the group and the communal narrator resumes the tale: "Our mother usually takes two of us with her to Price Chopper ..."; "Most of us aren't sleeping well ..."; "The ones of us who are sitting around the table this evening nod our heads ..."

"Two of us"; "most of us"; "the ones of us." For this reader, the first-person plural viewpoint is the perfect choice for Huddle's novel. A first-person singular narrator would have to carry not only the whole story but also the whole weight of grief occasioned by the impending death of the mother. And though each child's experience with the mother is unique ("She gave each of us a way to defend ourselves from discouragement and squalor ...") and each must navigate the loss in his or her own way, in the end, we sense that the loss is a communal loss, more than the sum of its separate parts.

In successful first-person plural description, the reader in effect gets two descriptions for the price of one. A voice, or eye, still guides the reader through the text (as in other viewpoints) but in first-person plural, this voice is actually a choir of voices singing in unison, and its eye is the focused vision of many eyes witnessing the events through a single lens.

Second-Person Narrator

Like first-person plural narration, second person is an idiosyncratic choice, rarely used for book-length works but sometimes appearing in brief poems or prose pieces, or in the form of breakaway passages in longer, sustained works that employ more conventional viewpoints. As we stated earlier, in second-person narration the "you" is an actual character in the literary work, not just a grammatical construct. Writers often insert casual "you" references within texts that are not second-person narratives: "When I entered the room, I noticed the head waiter was wearing one of those frilly aprons you usually see in shows like *Upstairs, Downstairs*." The use of "you" in that sentence does not constitute second-person narration. Nor does merely addressing the reader as "you," as I did in the following passage from chapter four.

> And what about the hot crusty roll the waiter just placed with a tong on your bread plate? It looks hot, it looks crusty, but how will you know unless you pick it up with your bare hands, feel its weight and shellacked surface, break it open and feel the steam escaping from the soft center?

If I had continued in this manner, however, and if the "you" had become a character in a story, I would have been writing in second person, as Jay McInerney does in his novel *Bright Lights, Big City*, which includes these opening sentences (ellipses mine).

> You are not the kind of guy who would be at a place like this at this time of the morning. ... You are at a nightclub talking to a girl with a shaved head. The club is either Heartbreak or the Lizard Lounge.

Although McInerney's main character is unnamed, identified only by the second-person "you," it becomes clear as the novel progresses that this "you" is the teller of the tale. His own tale. A tale set in a specific place (New York City) during a particular time (the mid-1980s). The characters ("a girl with a shaved head," etc.) and events the "you" describes are part of his story.

The "you" in second-person narration is sometimes considered little more than a substitute for the more common first-person "I" or the third-person "he" or "she." However, the literary effect of second-person narration is quite different from the effect of other viewpoint choices. (Try substituting "he" or "I" for "you" in the excerpt above, and you'll sense the difference.) When a writer employs a second-person narrator, especially one who is also the main character in the narrative, many readers immediately identify with this "you" even more closely than they might with a first-person narrator or a third-person character. It's almost as if by removing the "he" or the "I" the writer frees up physical and psychic space so the reader can place herself in the central role. The effect is similar to point-of-view camera shots in film, shots that place the viewer in the position of the character. In a point-of-view shot, we do not see the character; rather, we see what the character sees. In a literary work, this sense of firsthand participation can extend beyond the visual to include sounds, smells, tastes, and textures, thus intensifying the reader's experience in the fictional dream.

Third-Person Objective Narrator

Although no human being can be totally objective, if a writer wishes to create a fictional dream that appears strictly reportorial, she can employ an objective narrator to tell her tale. The objective point of view is also referred to as "dramatic" or "scenic," suggesting that a story told by an objective narrator unfolds like a stage play. Most stage plays—*Our Town* is a notable exception—do not include a narrator or other authorial presence. The story is told solely through onstage dialogue and action.

With a third-person objective narrator, what you see is what you get. An objective narrator cannot intrude on the story by giving his opinion or by lapsing into reverie. He is also banned from entering characters' minds or commenting on characters' thoughts or motives. He can't write phrases like "he thought" or "she wishes." All descriptions must be based on concrete, external evidence.

At first glance this point-of-view method seems overly restrictive. In practice, however, it is a flexible form that allows for much freedom, especially in matters of description. An objective narrator is free to relate any external information, including information about observable events happening to anyone, anywhere. Objective narration is like having an unlimited number of cameras available, each one taking pictures for the reader. An objective narrator can also move freely into the past, supplying information about the histories of places, people, and actions. He can describe—people, places, objects, actions—to his heart's content. There are only two things an objective narrator cannot do: enter any character's consciousness and reveal directly what he (as a writer or narrator) thinks or feels.

The third-person objective point of view is especially suited to works in which an event itself is unusual, suspenseful, or otherwise intriguing, an event such as a hostage standoff, suicide attempt, rock-climbing expedition, or dangerous surgical procedure. The power of the action, coupled with the author's skillful use of description and dialogue, is often enough to propel such a story; the reader won't miss authorial comment or access to characters' inner worlds.

External event alone, however, can't hold our attention forever, and physical action alone doesn't guarantee a forward-moving story. Some of the most successful objectively narrated stories—Hemingway's "The Killers" or "Hills Like White Elephants," for example—rely more on psychological action than on physical activity. The impersonal, reportorial quality of the third-person objective point of view works well to suggest ironies of situations and speech, those understated subtleties of discovery and reversal that make for psychological suspense.

Shirley Jackson's story "The Lottery" is fundamentally an objective description of an event that appears at first to be nothing more than an ordinary town gathering. The narrator reports the event in detached, understated prose, thereby creating psychic distance between reader and story; we feel we're watching the scene from afar. As the story progresses, Jackson begins dropping hints—a stone in a boy's hand, nervous laughter—suggesting that perhaps this event is not so ordinary after all. Each detail is described with clinical precision, and with each description the tension mounts, the very ordinariness of the details belying the horror unfolding sentence by sentence. As each of the townspeople draws a slip of paper from the wooden box, we watch breathlessly. Who will draw the paper with the black mark? We don't yet know what the mark signifies, but by now we fear the worst.

Yet however suspenseful Jackson's tale-telling and however sharp her use of ironic dialogue, "The Lottery" could not succeed without her precisely rendered descriptions of people, place, objects, and action. Although all descriptions should pass the tests of precision and significance, descriptions written from the objective point of view must fairly *sing* with clarity and truth. An author using objective narration can't divert our attention with a character's musings or with authorial flights of existential angst; our attention must remain focused on the scene at hand. Because an objective narrator's tale is built solely on externals, she must give her utmost attention to the objects, people, and places that make up this external reality. The characters are the actors in her drama; the objects and places are the set pieces. All elements of the outward scene must be chosen carefully, rendered with clarity and precision, and directed with a firm, even hand.

Jackson selects only those details that contribute to the mounting horror, and she reports these details in spare, detached language. In the following selection from "The Lottery," we are introduced to the black box, carried into the town square by Mr. Summers.

> When he arrived in the square, carrying the black wooden box, there
> was a murmur of conversation among the villagers, and he waved and

called, "Little late today, folks." The postmaster, Mr. Graves, followed him, carrying a three-legged stool, and the stool was put in the center of the square and Mr. Summers set the black box down on it.

Jackson follows this no-nonsense description with a paragraph detailing the history of the black box. (That's one of the prerogatives of the objective narrator; she can fill us in on all external events, even those in the past.) When we return to the present-day box, we're given another succinct description of the box.

> The black box grew shabbier each year; by now it was no longer completely black but splintered badly along one side to show the original wood color, and in some places faded or stained.

In objective narration, descriptions of actions must be as carefully selected, functional, and significant as descriptions of objects, places, and people. Since we readers aren't allowed access into characters' minds, we must surmise everything about their thoughts and emotions through outward signs. We can't overhear their unspoken language; we can hear only what they say through body language or dialogue. At the climax of Jackson's story the lottery has been narrowed to the Hutchinson family and five slips of paper have been placed in the box, one for each family member to draw. Through precise descriptions of the family's gestures and speech, Jackson succeeds in revealing the powerful emotions roiling beneath the surface.

First to draw is the youngest son, Davy, who holds the folded paper tightly in his fist, then looks "wonderingly" up to Mr. Summers. Next is twelve-year-old Nancy, who "breathed heavily as she went forward, switching her skirt, and took a slip daintily from the box." Bill Jr. lunges clumsily for the box, "his face red and his feet over-large." Mr. Hutchinson is silent and calm as he reaches for his slip. Only Mrs. Hutchinson hesitates, studying the crowd with defiance. Then, we are told, she "set her lips and went up to the box … snatched a paper out and held it behind her."

By this point, we are fairly certain whose slip is marked with an *x*. We've not looked into any character's mind, nor has the author supplied her own suspicions. Relying solely on descriptions of external action, people, and setting, Jackson has provided all the clues we need to enter her fictional dream.

Third-Person Omniscient Narrator

To know everything; to move freely in time and space; to look into the heart of every person, tree, and insect; to opine or praise or condemn with impunity: What power! It's no wonder so many authors have chosen, and still choose, to speak through an omniscient narrator. Omniscience was the point-of-view choice for classic writers like Chekhov, Tolstoy, Dickens, and Dreiser, and though omniscient narration is less popular today, some modern writers continue to explore its boundaries.

Omniscient narration provides for ease of exposition, panoramic views of time and space, and psychological complexities. Since it allows access into any and all characters' minds, it also helps guard against the creation of one-dimensional characters. Once we've glimpsed a character's individual dreams, fears, memories, and joys, it's difficult to think of her in stereotypes; the omniscient method can round her out.

When we read a novel with an omniscient narrator, we can relax and enjoy the scenery, secure that a godlike presence is leading us, someone more knowledgeable and reliable than any one character might be. After all, the omniscient author knows everything all his characters know, and more. If our narrator is also brilliant, witty, wise, or otherwise fascinating, and if he chooses to share his opinions, feelings, judgments, and personal memories, we are doubly fortunate. Besides immersing ourselves in the novel's plot and characterization, we also get to enjoy the pleasure of the author's company—or more precisely, the company of the persona created by the author.

Notice that I said "novel." It is difficult, though perhaps not impossible, to write a successful short work that employs the omniscient point of view. It takes time to travel everywhere, to learn everything there is to know, to set up house in multiple heads, and to describe it all to the reader. And each time the narrator changes positions, which is what omniscient narrators must constantly do, the reader needs time to adjust to the change. An author using the omniscient viewpoint must be adept at making these transitions. Within the first few pages of *Pride and Prejudice*, Jane Austen accomplishes no fewer than six such switches, alternating vantage points from omniscient narrator to character and back again, then from one character to another, and then finally back to the narrator.

The complexity of the switches inherent in omniscient narration affects the quantity and quality of descriptive passages. We've already said that omniscience provides for ease of exposition. Since a godlike narrator is capable of infinite knowledge, it seems natural that he would want to impart this knowledge to his readers. Exposition appeals more to the mind than to the senses; its playing field is the world of information, ideas, explanation, and analysis. Where most description concerns itself with concrete and sensory details, exposition often involves abstraction. Generally speaking, description *shows*; exposition *tells*.

If your main goal is to describe people, places, or objects in specific and concrete detail, omniscient narration may not be your best viewpoint choice. Omniscience invites telling. After all, there's a lot of narrative ground to cover, and pausing to fully describe a tennis shoe, for example, or the bald spot on the back of a character's head, takes time away from all the other tasks you're called upon to perform as an omniscient narrator. This is not to say that evocative descriptions do not appear in third-person omniscient works. I'm suggesting only that it may be more difficult for you to stop and smell the roses when you're also trying to explain their horticultural origins, comment on their symbolic import, or imagine your way into a rose's thoughts—just a few of the options open to the omniscient narrator.

Another reason the omniscient viewpoint encourages abstraction is because the narrator is capable of dwelling inside his characters' minds. Whereas the objective narrator must describe concretely and specifically the externals of a story, those things that can be witnessed through the senses, the omniscient narrator knows characters, places, and events from the inside out. This internal view makes it easy to bypass concrete details on the road to comment or explanation. Thus in the opening of *Pride and Prejudice*, Jane Austen describes the Bennets not as an outside observer might, with specific physical detail, but rather as a spirit who dwells inside their heads, which is exactly where omniscient narrators dwell.

> Mr. Bennet was so odd a mixture of quick parts, sarcastic humour, reserve, and caprice, that the experience of three and twenty years had been insufficient to make his wife understand his character. Her mind was less difficult to develop. She was a woman of mean understanding, little information, and uncertain temper. When she was discontented she fancied herself nervous. The business of her life was to get her daughters married; its solace was visiting and news.

Austen's description creates no moving pictures for our imaginations and stirs no visceral reactions in our bodies. We are given no smells, sounds, tastes, textures, or sights to experience. Although we learn much about the Bennets, what we learn is what the mind knows rather than what the body experiences. Omniscient narration invites exposition, internalization, and the whole realm of ideas, sometimes at the expense of vivid description.

However, when an omniscient narrator takes the time to describe precisely, concretely, and with significant detail, the results can be stunning. Since many omniscient narrators are articulate, worldly, and literary, their descriptions are often more richly observed and beautifully worded than descriptions by a first-person narrator (who may be intellectually or linguistically limited) or descriptions by an objective narrator bent on revealing "just the facts, ma'am." Here, Charles Dickens takes his time describing the view from Rochester Bridge.

> On the left of the spectator lay the ruined wall, broken in many places, and in some, overhanging the narrow beach below in rude and heavy

masses. Huge knots of sea-weed hung upon the jagged and pointed stones, trembling in every breath of wind; and the green ivy climbed mournfully around the dark and ruined battlements. —from *The Pickwick Papers*

Despite its challenges, the omniscient viewpoint offers many rewards. Like the starship *Enterprise*, an omniscient narrator can boldly go where no man has gone before. He can describe the emotions of green ivy on one page, the smells emanating from Pluto or Neptune on the next, and conclude the chapter with a dead Napoleon's view of Josephine. He can describe scenes hidden from his characters' view, everything that goes on behind all the doors closed in his characters' faces. An omniscient narrator can remember events his characters have forgotten and describe these events in detail—the color and texture of the crib blanket Josephine's mother wrapped around her, the aromas of her first cooked meal. Since he can also move forward in time, an omniscient narrator can even describe the world of Josephine's future—the sights and smells and sounds that will fill her last days.

Third-Person Limited-Omniscient Narrator

Readers like me demand a lot. On one hand, we want to be swept into a character's inner world of dreams, joys, and terrors. We want to smell the cologne he splashes on his face, taste his morning coffee, feel the satin sheets he pulls around him as he climbs back into bed. On the other hand, we don't want to be confined too long. After all, there's a big world out there. What's the weather like? Who won the pennant? For readers who crave both psychological intimacy and worldly verisimilitude, stories told from the limited-omniscient point of view are the answer.

When you choose to write in the limited-omniscient viewpoint, you limit your omniscience in one or more ways. For instance, you might limit your ability to move freely in time and space, to comment on issues arising in the story, or to make judgments. The most common method is to limit your access to characters' inner lives. You can still describe externals—people, places, events—much as an objective observer would, but you inhabit only one character's mind, or perhaps more than one if your story is long enough to sustain your efforts.

As the story progresses, you move between these two worlds—the outer reality, as described in concrete detail by an objective observer, and the inner world of a character's feelings and thoughts. In her short story "Still Life with Fruit," Doris Betts uses the limited-omniscient point of view, alternating between external details objectively reported and subjective musings by her main character, Gwen, who is preparing to give birth in a Catholic hospital.

> The labor room, pale green, was furnished in buffed aluminum. Its single chair was dull metal, straight, uncomfortable. Her clothes had been hung in a green wall locker next to Jesus, including the linen dress with the 24-inch waist she hoped to wear home next week. On her bedside table was a pitcher of water and crushed ice, and a glass with a clear tube in it. She drank water as the sister had ordered. Maybe it went down the sliding ramp where Junior, like some battleship, would be launched to the open sea. He felt to her like a battleship, plated turrets and stacks and projections, each pricking her own organs until they withdrew and gave him room.

The first two sentences of Betts's description include details any observer might notice. The third sentence begins objectively, then moves into Gwen's mind, revealing her wish to wear the dress with the twenty-four-inch waist. The next two sentences switch back into objective reporting, and then we're again inside Gwen's mind, inside her wild imaginings and her physical pain. Betts includes markers—phrases like "she hoped" and "he felt to her like"— to alert us to subtle transitions that move us into Gwen's mind.

Some authors omit these markers, steering us seamlessly between the inner and outer worlds. Some of the subtlest point-of-view switches occur within internal monologues when objective description alternates with subjective description. In internal monologue, the reader overhears the narrator's or character's thoughts, his *stream of consciousness*, a stream that may appear to have little order or coherence. The author seems absent; is anyone steering this boat? If we look closer, we see, yes, someone is steering. Objective description is surfacing, here and there, in the stream. In this section from James Joyce's *Ulysses*, Leopold Bloom is preparing to go to the market for breakfast supplies, but first he goes upstairs to check on his sleeping wife.

> On quietly creaky boots he went up the staircase to the hall, paused by the bedroom door. She might like something tasty. Thin bread and butter she likes in the morning. ...
>
> He said softly in the bare hall: ...
>
> —You don't want anything for breakfast? ...
>
> No. She did not want anything. He heard then a warm heavy sigh, softer, as she turned over and the loose brass quoits on the bedstead jingled. Must get those settled really. Pity. All the way from Gibraltar. Forgotten any little Spanish she knew. Wonder what her father gave for it. Old style. ...
>
> On the doorstep he felt in his hip pocket for the latchkey. Not there. In the trousers I left off. Must get it. Potato I have. Creaky wardrobe. No use disturbing her. She turned over sleepily that time. He pulled the halldoor to after him very quietly, more, till the footleaf dropped gently over the threshold, a limp lid. Looked shut. All right till I come back anyhow.

Some of Joyce's details are reportorial in nature, things an outside observer might note—creaky boots, the jingling quoits, a soft sigh. Others are idiosyncratic, colored with Bloom's emotion, thoughts, and personal history. These two perceptions alternate freely without any mechanical markers provided by the author (except for the switch from "he" to "I"). The passage is like a song alternating between two voices. Both voices describe the scene, but it's the combination of the two that completes the description.

POINT-OF-VIEW DESCRIPTION AS AN ORGANIZING DEVICE

Point of view is an automatic focusing device, a selector of detail. Once situated in a particular point of view, you don't have to worry about including every sensory detail—only the ones your narrator or character would notice. Once you've established the perspective, the eye from which scenes will be observed, you can use that eye to organize and unify your descriptions. And as your character moves physically and psychologically through the story, subtle shifts in his point of view will lead your reader through the terrain of the story.

Jessamyn West opens her story "Love, Death, and the Ladies' Drill Team" with a series of descriptive snapshots. The point of view is third-person limited omniscient, and though the narrator supplies some objective description and information, most of the descriptive snapshots are focused through the eyes of Emily Cooper, the main character. As Emily moves physically through the story, we move with her, experiencing the sights, sounds, and feelings she experiences from each vantage point. When Emily arrives for the drill team practice session, she stands "for a while enjoying the wind—California's warm, dry September wind—before starting up the stairs to Burnham Hall."

As she begins her climb up the stairs, we follow her. Emily's eyes become our eyes, our way of organizing the scenes passing before us.

> Emily was halfway up the stairs when she was hailed from the sidewalk below by Mr. Burnham himself, holding a key aloft. "You one of the Pocohontas girls?" he called.
>
> Emily turned about on the stairs and gazed down at the wide-shouldered old man. The wind was lifting his coattails and tossing his white hair about in tufts, like those of the bunch grass she had known as a girl in the Dakotas.

In these brief paragraphs, West centers us securely within Emily's consciousness. As the story continues, we leave Emily's mind for brief interludes, long enough for the narrator to insert necessary information, but mostly we view the scenes through her eyes. Soon Emily will lean out a window "to watch a tumbleweed, blown into town from one of the surrounding barley fields," and we'll lean out the window with her. Emily is our guide, and we take her hand, looking over our shoulder when she looks over hers, peering down at the sidewalk when she peers down.

Each subtle shift in Emily's perspective is like a trail marker. As readers, we don't have to take a dozen wrong turns, ending up in some blind alley. The author provides a descriptive map for us to follow. West's effective choice of point of view and her subtle shifts of perspective within that point of view create an ordered, organized fictional universe.

EXERCISES

1. Choose a story—one of your own or someone else's—and rewrite the opening paragraphs in a different point of view. Change first person to third, omniscient to objective, objective to first person, etc. Then experiment with other subtle changes. If the story opens with a character's name, remove the name and substitute *he* or *she*; if the characters are known only as *he* or *she*, insert names. Notice how even slight changes in point of view affect the story.

2. Check your prose or poetry draft for point-of-view switches by using a colored highlighter. Whenever the point of view changes, even slightly, mark the transition. Then decide whether the switch is effective or merely troublesome. Using techniques detailed in this chapter, revise any troublesome switches.

3. If you're using the limited-omniscient method in which you have access to only one character's thoughts, check your story to see if you've inadvertently entered a second character's thoughts. If you have, revise the section to remove the internalized phrase, then replace it with an actable action an objective reporter could witness.

4. Using your own natural voice, write the most detailed, sensory, and articulate description of a place or object that you can manage. Then write a description of the same place or object in the words of a first-person narrator who is less articulate than you—a young child, an Alzheimer's patient, an uneducated peasant. What differences do you see between the two descriptions? Did you have to give up any of your own descriptive details to allow your narrator to have his say?

5. Write a physical description in which a first-person main character describes himself so the reader can visualize him. You might want to use a photograph, video, or other graphic representation as your vehicle for relating physical attributes. Your character could also describe himself by relating what others say about him.

6. Write a description of a first-person narrator that reveals his experience of living inside his body and moving physically through the world. Rather than describing how the character looks on the outside, use sensory details to show how it feels to live *inside* his skin. (Refer to the *Kate Vaiden* selection for an example.)

7. Using first-person peripheral narration, describe a place, a person, or an event that your narrator knows little about. Position the narrator on the outside looking in. How does she view her subject? What language does she use to describe something she doesn't really understand? To get started, think of a subject you know little about. Describe it to the reader in your own words, with all the limitations and challenges that partial ignorance requires.

8. Write a description of an object, a person, or a scene that combines objective reporting with internalized thought. (See the "Still Life with Fruit" passage for an example.) Alternate between the two kinds of description, marking your transitions with phrases like "she thought" or "it seemed to him that ... ". Then remove the transitional markers so your description alternates freely between objectively reported statements and highly personal stream of consciousness. (See the *Ulysses* passage.)

9. Describe a scene or an event from the third-person objective viewpoint. Report only what can be known through the five senses; this can include characters' concrete actions or dialogue. You may move in time and space as long as you report only what can be witnessed externally. Do not give your opinion about the event or enter any characters' thoughts.

10. Using the omniscient point of view, describe something that no character in your story could possibly know. You might travel behind the scenes, describing a place your characters could never visit. You might time travel into the distant past or future and describe what you see. You might even enter the consciousness of an animal, a force of nature, or an inanimate object. What does the dog in your story dream of? What is the ocean's memory of your character? What secret is a young girl in India (the girl who will one day become your character's wife) already storing up to keep from him?

CHAPTER EIGHT

The Story Takes Its Place: Descriptions of Setting

When I hear the word *setting*, I immediately think of the physical space in which the events of a story occur, but in truth, place is only one element of setting. The common phrase "the story takes place" refers not only to the *where* of the story but also to the *when*. Setting grounds us, literally, in the literary dream. And descriptions of setting provide the foothold, the physical and temporal vantage point from which to view the events of the story. "You couldn't write a story that happened nowhere," Eudora Welty once told an interviewer. "Time and place make the framework that any story's built on … a fiction writer's honesty begins right there, in being true to those two facts of time and place."

But to describe a setting effectively, in poetry and nonfiction as well as in fiction, we must go beyond merely situating the reader in a particular locale and time period. Every detail that contributes to a sense of time and place is an element of setting. Details of place include the set pieces of a location (its props, furniture, flora and fauna) as well as surrounding elements (the storm hammering outside the door, sunlight ricocheting off the curtains). Time-wise, a story may be said to "take place" not just sometime in the 1850s but, say, on the opening day of summer or the last day of autumn, or more particularly at twilight, high noon, or in the first sleepy moments of morning.

In some literary works, setting serves as little more than a backdrop for elements such as characterization, the sounds and rhythms of language, or plot development. In other works, setting is the most important element, the main character whose personality and eccentricities shape the story's outcome. Between these two extremes lie many variations. Some works, such as *Madame Bovary* and Caleb Carr's novel *The Alienist*, are documentary-like in descriptions of time and place. In other works, settings function symbolically to mirror the events of a story, as in Poe's "The Fall of the House of Usher." Sometimes the setting, including the weather, is a benign, even sympathetic force; other times it acts as an antagonist, challenging the human protagonists in a struggle for survival. Settings can be natural or manmade, realistic or surreal, ancient or modern, beautiful or ugly or anything in between.

Few stories contain only one setting. Even the most static story—one in which the character remains in the same location—often requires us to describe more than one setting. Yes, Zack may remain in his easy chair throughout the story, staring at the television screen. Yet minute by minute the scene is changing. A different soap opera comes on, sunlight through the venetian blind changes from yellow to pink, the spring-loaded sofa cushion that had felt so comfortable three hours ago begins to assert itself. The settings in our stories are constantly shifting. Even if our characters never move an inch, time has its way with their world. And our descriptions must evoke those changes. Too, our characters' thoughts and daydreams may transport them to a different place or time, or we find we need to supply background information about the places and times that have shaped our characters' lives.

In Michael Ondaatje's memoir *Running in the Family*, we sense the effect of time on a narrator's experience of place. Ondaatje, a Canadian writer, was born and raised in Sri Lanka, and as an adult he had made two return trips, in part to explore his family's past. In the following passage, he describes listening to a cassette he'd recorded during his visit.

> Now, and here, Canadian February, I write this in the kitchen and play that section of cassette to hear not just peacocks but all the noises of the night behind them—inaudible then because they were always there, like breath. In this silent room (with its own unheard hum of fridge, fluorescent light) there are these frogs loud as river, gruntings, the whistle of birds brash and sleepy, but in that night so modest behind the peacocks they were unfocussed by the brain—nothing more than darkness, all those sweet loud younger brothers of the night.

Notice that although the present-tense scene itself is static—the narrator sits in a kitchen listening to a recording—the description is active, pulsing with movement, in part because two settings combine in a single moment to create a symphony of past and present experiences. The "[n]ow, and here" of the noises in the Canadian kitchen ("hum of fridge, fluorescent light") mix with the "then" of the Sri Lankan nights ("peacocks," "frogs loud as river, gruntings, the whistle of birds.") In one brief paragraph, the writer not only describes two locales at once but also shows how present-tense surroundings intensify the narrator's memories of places in his past.

A WRITER'S SENSE OF PLACE

For many writers, setting is the primary element that births the creative process. Historical novelists seem drawn to the *when* of the story; mystery writers seem more intrigued by the *where*. Margaret Maron says that once she establishes place, she inserts a character into that place and waits to see what will happen. Other mystery writers look for places where things can go wrong, asserting that danger is closely related to physical location, then set their stories in those places. Maron echoes this sentiment, adding that her own fear of heights often takes her, in her writing, to stairways and cliffs.

"A sense of place" is a popular phrase in literary circles. Good writers, so the theory goes, have a strong sense of place that defines their work. Thus, when we think of Pat Conroy, we think Carolina beaches; when we think of Ivan Doig, we think Montana; when we think of Updike, we think New England. When I first began writing I thought "a sense of place" meant a writer had to live in one place all his life. This assumption, intensified by my experience with a literature professor who claimed I could never be a writer because I lacked a sense of place, almost kept me from pursuing my writing goals. "Where are your roots?" the professor asked. I was a marine brat and had at one time or another claimed allegiance to Texas, Virginia, California, Illinois, and Maryland. I'd spent childhood summers at my grandparents' Indiana farm, but I'd never actually lived there.

And now here I was in a South Carolina university, being questioned by a man whose Southern accent I could never replicate, on the page or elsewhere. I decided I had no roots. If a sense of place was a crucial source of a writer's power, then I guessed I'd never be a Writer (a vocation I once thought of as an uppercase, proper noun).

This didn't mean, however, that I would stop *writing*, a lowercase activity I seemed able to accomplish. After a few years, when I started sending my work to editors, I was amazed that almost every editor commented on my descriptions of settings, my strong "sense of place." It was a riddle so delightful that I didn't wish to solve it.

Many years later, I sat in the lecture hall at the Bread Loaf Writers' Conference listening to Tim O'Brien respond to a question about how the brief time he'd spent in Vietnam had shaped his novels and stories. As O'Brien spoke, I suddenly realized why those editors had commented on my "sense of place." And why the essay I'd written about the South Carolina garage apartment where I'd spent four damp, cockroach-infested *weeks* was more vibrant than my story of four *years* of suburban ennui in California.

"It's not the *amount* of time you spend in a place that matters," O'Brien answered. "It's the *intensity* of the time."

Click: My riddle was solved. When it comes to evoking a sense of place, the intensity of a writer's involvement—based in real-life experience or in the imagination—is more important than the amount of time spent in any one place. Perhaps you've lived in the same town all your life and your window opens to the same herb garden your father worked, on his knees, forty years ago. Or perhaps you've moved numerous times, a marine brat like me, and the window to your father's garden opens only inside your head. Either way, you possess a sense of place. And each time you put pen to paper, describing the smells and sounds and textures of that garden—whether real or imagined, present or past—you plant roots that will feed your stories, essays, and poems.

THE CHALLENGES AND REWARDS OF REAL-LIFE SETTINGS

Real-life settings form the basis of many writers' work. I think of the family apple orchards in Jane Brox's essays, the New England fishing village that animates Frank Gaspar's poems, and the San Francisco streets of Amy Tan's novels. As writers, we naturally focus on the places and times we know well. Our firsthand experience provides us with the sensory details that render a work, in E.M. Forster's words, "spasmodically realistic." And our passionate attachment to the places and times of our lives can infuse our descriptions with emotion no outsider could provide.

Several years ago during an unusually dry spell in my writing life, I drew a map of my grandparents' farm the way I remembered it from childhood—in particular, my twelfth summer. (Remember: Setting equals place plus time.) Then, as if marking sites of buried treasure, I placed an *x* at every location I associated with a particular person or event. I was astounded at the possibilities that rose from the map. By the time I finished drawing the treasure map, I had the beginnings of several poems and a dozen essays. Not every beginning yielded up riches, but many did, and many more remain to be unearthed.

Real-life settings, especially those connected to strong memories and emotions, offer many rewards to the writer. However, if you decide to use a real-life setting rather than a fictional one, you will face several challenges. Descriptions of actual settings, especially those identified by place names and time periods, must be unfailingly accurate. Nonfiction writers must pass the toughest tests for accuracy, but fiction writers and poets who choose real-life settings must also render settings accurately, particularly contemporary ones. If you set your story in an actual place—say, San Francisco or Savannah or Chicago—savvy readers will expect you to know the correct names of streets, restaurants, bars, colleges, and parks, which may require you to research these details. And if your story is set a hundred years ago, or even thirty, you may need to do additional research. Maybe that restaurant you name and describe, the smoky lounge where your two main characters first met, wasn't even built in 1969. Maybe the parking lot at Edgewater and Fourth wasn't a parking lot at all, but a tobacco field. Be assured, someone who reads your story will *know* it was a tobacco field. And though she might not close the cover on your book, she'll at least pause, scratch her head, and reconsider spending time in a setting she no longer believes existed.

Even if we don't identify our settings with recognizable names and time periods, we still face challenges in describing real-life settings effectively, especially settings closely connected to our present-day lives. We may be too close to the bare facts of the description—say, every detail of what our backyard looks like at this time of morning—to select the telling detail that sustains the literary dream (the can't-see-the-forest-for-the-trees dilemma). We may not yet have enough artistic distance to order the description effectively.

And if we're writing about settings in our past, we may have forgotten so many details that our descriptions do not ring true. On the other hand, we may have forgotten just enough. Over time, our memories of a particular place and time may have distilled, our minds culling out unnecessary details so that only the most sensory, telling, and emotionally colored proofs remain.

DESCRIPTIONS OF SETTING IN FANTASY, SCIENCE FICTION, AND MAGIC REALISM

Sensory proofs, which provide what E.M. Forster, in *Aspects of the Novel*, calls "intermittent realism," are necessary ingredients in almost all forms of literature. Even writers who include nonrealistic elements in their work must supply sensory proofs to convince the reader that the events of the story could actually take place within the settings they create. While writers of magic realism generally incorporate extraordinary details within realistic settings, science fiction and fantasy writers often create imaginary settings from the ground up.

Forster uses the metaphor of a carnival sideshow to explain the importance of realistic detail to the fantasy writer. The reader of any novel, he says, must "pay the entrance fee to the exhibition"; that is, he must suspend disbelief in order to enter the fiction. For the reader of fantasy, however, the cost is even higher. Not only must he pay the entrance fee for the main exhibition (the novel), but also, once inside its gates, he must "pay something extra" before he can be admitted into the sideshow (the fantasy).

Thus readers of an epic fantasy such as J.R.R. Tolkien's *The Lord of the Rings* pay a high admission fee to enter the northwestern part of Middle-earth in the year 3001, when Bilbo turns "eleventy-one," and pay extra each time they enter another realm of this highly detailed terrain of the imagination. Not that they mind paying. Tolkien's descriptions of place, time, and characters are rendered with such care that readers willingly suspend any disbelief. And in science fiction works such as Ray Bradbury's story "The Long Rain," we barely pause to question the never-ending rain on Venus, because Bradbury supplies sensory proofs of "intermittent realism."

> It was a hard rain, a perpetual rain, a sweating and steaming rain; it was a mizzle, a downpour, a fountain, a whipping at the eyes, an undertow at the ankles … it hacked at the jungle and cut the trees like scissors and shaved the grass and tunneled the soil and molted the bushes. It shrank

men's hands into the hands of wrinkled apes; it rained a solid glassy rain, and it never stopped.

In works of both science fiction and fantasy, the imaginary environment the author creates is often the most important element, even more important than plot or character. In works of magic realism, settings are important as well, but more important is the collision of the ordinary with the magical or miraculous, and in most cases, the ordinary is established through realistic settings. Toni Morrison's novel *Beloved*, for instance, includes many realistic settings: a Kentucky plantation, a Georgia prison camp, a house in Cincinnati that Morrison even supplies with an address, 124 Bluestone Road. These settings ground the reader in time and place so the magical elements—the ghost of the dead baby, in particular—can stand out against the realistic backdrop.

Another example of realistic setting in magic realism is Rachel Ingalls's novel *Mrs. Caliban*. When I first read the back cover of the book, I thought, *No way, this is not for me. A housewife who has an affair with a six-foot-seven green monster named Larry? Give me a break.* But the novel had been highly recommended by several readers whose tastes I admire, so I gave it a try. After a few pages, I was hooked. Not only was the main character sympathetic, the prose lucid and witty, and the plot intriguing, but to my surprise, Ingalls's setting was so filled with realistic detail that I felt as if I had stepped directly into the story. When Dorothy started hearing strange voices from her kitchen radio, I accepted them as wholeheartedly as Dorothy did. After all, the radio was described as "a large, dark brown old-fashioned set, the kind that looked like a 1930's Gothic cathedral." That was good enough for me.

For twenty-four pages I followed Dorothy through the physical world of the story. Together we rinsed her sweat-soaked leotards and hung them over a very real shower rod, fended off the advances of a supermarket salesgirl in a majorette's uniform who was trying to force a parmesan square down Dorothy's throat, and tied a kitchen scarf over Dorothy's head "to keep her hair from picking up the garlic and onion smells." So on page twenty-five, when the screen door opened and Larry entered the kitchen, I barely blinked.

Oh, I was surprised, of course, as Dorothy was, caught up as we were in hurrying across the checked linoleum, trying to reach the cheese toast before it burned. I was *surprised*. But I wasn't *unconvinced*. I accepted the six-foot-seven green monster because the setting in which he was placed had been delineated with such care.

Whether our writing is centered on the real or the surreal, we must pay a servant-like attention to the settings. Without attention to minute details of time and place—those sights, smells, sounds, and textures of our literary world—the reader will simply not believe that world exists (or might exist, in some other realm). And even if the reader *does* believe, even if he pays admission and enters our story or poem, he will leave as soon as we cease to render that world in all its sensory detail. As writers, we must be vigilant in maintaining the illusion of our literary dream. "Whenever its world of outside appearance grows dim and false to the eye," wrote Eudora Welty, "the novel has expired."

INTRODUCING AND ORGANIZING DESCRIPTIONS OF SETTING

When to introduce a setting, how to organize descriptions, and how to weave descriptions of setting into narrative and expository passages are issues we must consider if setting is to be an integral part of our work. Some writers front-load their works with descriptions of setting, much like stagehands bringing on set pieces at the beginning of a play. Gail Peck uses this technique in her poem "Flood," which opens with a description evoking both place and time.

> That year spring came early
> even for New Orleans, the buds
> unpuckering only to be sheathed in ice,
> then warm again and rain for days,
> the water crawling up our street …

With the front-loading method, setting acts almost as a character, the first character arriving onstage. If you use this method, it's important that your description be lively and evocative enough to hold the reader's attention. Peck's lines engage our imaginative eye. We witness the buds "unpuckering," the slick coverings of ice, and the water "crawling." Because Peck describes the setting as a vivid, active force, we do not become impatient for the human drama to begin. The readers of a novel, settling in for the long haul, will probably be more patient with front-loaded description of setting than will the readers of short fiction or poetry, who expect to be plummeted more quickly into the work's central conflict.

A more common technique than front loading is to introduce your character or narrator first and then describe the setting through the teller's eyes. Joseph Conrad's story "The Secret Sharer" opens with a young captain standing on the deck of his ship before it is about to leave port.

> On my right hand there were lines of fishing-stakes resembling a mysterious system of half-submerged bamboo fences … . To the left a group of barren islets, suggesting ruins of stone walls, towers, and blockhouses, had its foundation set in a blue sea … . And when I turned my head to take a parting glance at the tug which had just left us anchored outside the bar, I saw the straight line of the flat shore joined to the stable sea, edge to edge … . Here and there gleams of a few scattered pieces of silver marked the windings of the river; and on the nearest of them, just within the bar, the tug steaming right into the land became lost to my sight … . My eye followed the light cloud of her smoke, now here, now there, above the plain, according to the devious curves of the stream, but always fainter and farther away, till I lost it at last behind the mitre-shaped hill of the great pagoda.

Notice how Conrad organizes the description. First he positions the captain in a stationary place. Then, through the use of positional markers—"on my right," "to the left," "when I turned," "here and there," "my eye followed" —he guides the reader through an ordered landscape. In this way, Conrad not only describes the panoramic view but also tracks the visual journey of the captain's eyes, creating a sense of movement in a scene that might otherwise feel static. James Wright's poem "Lying in a Hammock at William Duffy's Farm in Pine Island, Minnesota" also employs positional markers, using phrases like "over my head," "to my right," and "down the ravine" to lead the reader on a guided tour of the farm.

Another organizational method is to describe a place that will not hold still for the viewer. The viewer remains stationary while the scene rushes past her eyes. Perhaps she's staring through a train window or watching from the sidelines at a carnival where the attractions—tilt-o-whirls, spinning teacups, Ferris wheels—are in full swing.

An alternative method is to describe a stationary setting that only appears to be moving because the viewer is in motion. While he's skiing down a steep slope or holding fast to a horse's mane, the scene unfolds swiftly, in a blur of colors and shapes. The position of the viewer, which is constantly changing, organizes his view as well as the view of the reader.

You can also organize a description of place by emphasizing one detail, allowing it to stand out from other details by virtue of its color, shape, size, or movement. In the film *Schindler's List*, the red coat on the little girl catches our eye because everything else in the scene is in black and white. James Baldwin uses a similar technique in his novel *Go Tell It on the Mountain* when he describes the street outside the narrator's window. Every detail is heading toward revelation of the visual focal point, the red stocking cap.

> It was the end of winter, and the garbage-filled snow that had been banked along the edges of sidewalks was melting now and filling the gutters. Boys were playing stickball in the damp, cold streets; dressed in heavy woolen sweaters and heavy pants, they danced and shouted .... One of them wore a bright-red stocking cap with a great ball of wool hanging down behind that bounced as he jumped, like a bright omen above his head.

The stocking cap grabs our attention partly because of its color (the only bright swatch in a gray, bleak scene) and partly because of its movement. As in all forms of description, description of setting comes alive when shown in a state of activity.

We've spoken of organizing description through the teller's *eyes*, but details of setting need not be visual. As we've noted earlier, descriptions employing the other four senses often engage the reader more quickly, and more viscerally, than descriptions that rely solely on visual clues. Try describing a place (a school cafeteria, the indoor swimming pool at the Y, a rain forest) using only the sense of smell. Then describe a few visual details. Next, shift your attention to tactile details. What does your hand light upon in this place? Describe the textures you encounter. Then move back to visual details. This particular pattern—moving from smells to sights to textures to sights—is how the following description, taken from *Dodsworth* by Sinclair Lewis, is organized.

> The smell of London is a foggy smell, a sooty smell, a coal-fire smell, yet to certain wanderers it is more exhilarating, more suggestive of greatness and of stirring life, than spring-time hillsides or the chill sweetness of autumnal nights; and that unmistakable smell, which men long for in rotting perfumes along the Orinoco, in the greasy reek of South Chicago, in the hot odor of dusty earth among locust-buzzing Alberta wheatfields, that luring breath of the dark giant among cities, reaches halfway to Southampton to greet the traveler. Sam sniffed at it, uneasily, restlessly, while he considered how strange was the British fashion of having railway compartments instead of an undivided car with a nice long aisle along which you could observe ankles, magazines, Rotary buttons, clerical collars, and all the details that made travel interesting.
>
> And the strangeness of having framed pictures of scenery behind the seats; of having hand straps—the embroidered silk covering so rough to the finger tips, the leather inside so smooth and cool—beside the doors. And the greater strangeness of admitting that these seats were more comfortable than the flinty Pullman chairs of America. And of seeing outside, in the watery February sunshine, not snow-curdled fields but springtime greenness; pollarded willows and thatched roofs and half-timbered facades—
>
> Just like in the pictures! England!

As readers, we enter Lewis's fictional dream with our whole bodies, not just our eyes. Along with Sam, we sniff the London air, walk to our train compartment, touch the embroidered hand straps, settle into a comfortable seat, and open our eyes to the scene outside our window. We settle not only into the place—a British rail car—but also into the time period of the story. Reading Lewis's description, we sink back into the past, an era when coal-fire, Pullman chairs, and Rotary buttons defined the scenery. But Lewis evokes more than a vague time period, the late 1920s. More particularly, it's a February day filled with "watery" sunshine and "pollarded" trees. Through Lewis's sensory proofs and well-organized description, we enter a setting that, though removed from our present-day experience, feels as real as it must have felt to Sam.

RENDERING HISTORICAL SETTINGS

When we write a contemporary story or nonfiction work, especially one set in a recognizable place filled with modern-day props, we trust that our reader will meet us, if not halfway, at least part of the way. We supply a few concrete and telling strokes—of a strip mall, a smartphone, faded jeans, Disneyland—and the reader completes the word painting for us. After all, she's been in enough strip malls to last her a lifetime, she owns a smartphone, she wears faded jeans or knows someone who does, and she's been to Disneyland or has at least seen the brochures.

But when we set our works in an era removed from us, we face the same challenges the writer of nonrealistic fiction faces: trying to render and maintain a "world of outside appearance" that we've not experienced firsthand. Our reader is equally new to this landscape, and we can't assume that she will enter our literary dream as easily as would the reader of a work set in contemporary times.

If our story takes place, say, at the turn of the century, in medieval times, or even, as Jim Crace's novel *The Gift of Stones* does, in the Stone Age, we must go beyond merely researching our subject. We must lead the reader through the world of the story, the way a costumed guide at Williamsburg points to a rusted plow that's outlived its function. Or the way a museum docent calls our attention to the hidden layers of a Rembrandt oil. We must peel back the layers of time to render our setting not only accurately but also concretely, returning again and again to the sensory proofs that ground the reader in our story.

First we position our reader in time and space. We can announce the information directly—for instance, with a sentence that begins "The London of 1620 was ..." or with a chapter title like "San Francisco, 1890." Or we can evoke the setting indirectly through description, action, dialogue, and prose style. In *The Gift of Stones*, Jim Crace uses the indirect method, yet he doesn't take long to ground us in his story. Horseback riders arrive at a village in search of arrowheads and spear stones. A bowman wounds a boy with a spear poisoned with "goat's purge" or "urchin milk" or "silverdew," but rather than finishing off his victim, he goes in search of the arrow because "an arrow can stop a deer, a seal, a hen" and can be bartered for "some honey, say, or skin." After only a few pages, we are situated in a village of stonecutters in a time before written history.

One basic technique for setting the time-stage for a story is to load the stage with set pieces, the furnishings of the era. By *furnishings* I don't mean only chairs, tables, and drapes, but rather all the physical elements—indoor and outdoor, natural and man-made—that make up the historical environment. You may need to conjure up a steam locomotive or an omnibus, a Conestoga wagon or a '37 Ford. Depending on the subject and scope of your story, you might also need to describe the flora, fauna, housing, clothing, food, tools, and other accoutrements of the era you are portraying.

Setting the stage and filling it with set pieces may position your reader in time and space, but it won't keep her there unless you continue, throughout the story, to supply sensory proofs. Thus several pages into his story, after the main character has been fleshed out and dramatic tension established, Crace reminds us of where we are.

> ... the workshops busy with the rhythm of bone and wood and stone, the causeways quiet and empty except for children delivering new flints, the market-place a murmur of transaction as wheat and skin and pots changed sides with axes, spears and knives.

In chapter three we discussed the importance of supplying, in Aristotle's words, "the proper and special name of a thing." Precise naming is especially important when we render historical settings. No one who reads Crace's novel has lived during the Stone Age, and few readers have fashioned primitive implements from stone. Crace has to convince us that the stonecutter's way of life actually existed, at least for the purposes of his story. So he provides the proper and special names of things. The villagers trade not just tools but "borers, burins, sharpeners, harpoons, stone wrist-guards, sickles, fire-flints, sling-stones, scrapers, hand-axes, arrow-heads and tangs and barbs."

But a mere list of set pieces won't convince the reader. Anyone can scan reference books or online sources and supply technical terms; only a good writer can expand these terms into description rich enough to create the literary dream. When one of the artisans, Leaf, is chosen to fashion the blade that will amputate the boy's poisoned arm, Crace describes the process in painstaking detail. We are shown the flint, the anvil, the antler tines, and the wooden mallet. We watch every step of Leaf's preparation, up to and past the moment when:

> ... the blade blank broke loose, spiraled for an instant on the anvil and fell on Leaf's lap. There, on its underside at the point of impact, was the distinctive raised tump of stone, like a tiny bulb or a wrinkle shell. Beyond, in the foothills of the tump, the flint feathered and radiated like a slow tide on a flat beach. It was a good, long blade, still warm from the fire.

In the midst of the description, Crace inserts a disclaimer that begins "There is no need to detail the patience and the expertise with which Leaf etched a pattern of shallow facets ..." and continues with yet another paragraph filled with precise description of Leaf's process. Crace's disclaimer is, of course, ironic.

For without a vivid and believable description, we will not participate in Leaf's dramatic moment, the shaping of the blade that will soon sever a boy's arm.

You may have noticed that Crace's disclaimer begins with a grammatical construction you were cautioned against in our discussion of "filler phrases" in chapter three. Sentences beginning with *there is* or *it was*, you were warned, can deflate the energy of your prose. More often than not, this warning rings true; usually these phrases are no more than fillers. But sometimes they serve important functions. *The Gift of Stones*, though written in vivid, lively prose, is sprinkled with passages like:

> It was his misfortune to be walking …
> It was his seventh year …
> There was a moment when …
> But there was some sense of triumph there …

A writer as skilled as Crace knows what he's doing; these phrases are not fillers. They are necessary ingredients in his descriptions, serving not only to sustain dramatic tension but also to suggest the rhythms of an ancient storyteller's prose. Although the most common way to describe a historical setting is by means of accurate word choice and sensory detail, the style of our prose—whether short and clipped or elegantly long-winded—also plays its part in creating and sustaining the fictional dream.

Or the nonfictional dream. Nonfiction writers must often render historical settings, not only in traditional, historical nonfiction works but also in biographies, cultural and social histories, essays, and even memoirs, especially those that incorporate details of ancestral lineage. Research yields factual details that the writer can use to shape descriptive passages. In the first chapter of his memoir *Family*, Ian Frazier includes a long list of facts, bolstered by sensory proofs, to create a full portrait of the small town of Norwalk, Ohio, at the turn of the twentieth century.

Sometimes the facts themselves, if arranged effectively, are sufficient to describe historical settings. But the nonfiction writer can also combine factual information with "the gift of perhaps" to render time and place. Just because you weren't present at an event—say, your great-aunt's 1904 wedding—doesn't mean you can't write a time and place scene based on the research you've gathered. Build on what you have, whether it's a photograph, letter, newspaper clipping, the weather report from that January day (easily accessible from archival sources), pages from the 1904 Sears catalog, or memories of your conversations with your great-aunt. Create the scene that, based on your research, might have been. As you write, create as full a scene as you would for a fictional story. Describe the sights, sounds, smells, and textures you encounter. Just remember to supply navigational tools for the reader. Phrases such as "I imagine" or "In my mind, the French doors open into a parlor" alert the reader that you are moving into reconstructed or imagined scenes.

COMBINING DESCRIPTIONS OF SETTING WITH NARRATION AND EXPOSITION

In chapter one we discussed how description works alongside narration and exposition to create the world of the story. Although we sometimes have reasons for inserting isolated blocks of description, more often we wish to weave descriptions into the narrative arc or into passages of exposition. Skilled writers are so successful at combining description of settings with other literary elements that we hardly notice the separate threads. But if we look closely, we see how the weaving is accomplished.

One effective method is to use descriptions of setting to introduce, or reintroduce, the characters in our story. In her novel *The Joy Luck Club*, Amy Tan describes the narrator's home street, Waverly Place. Her description begins with the early morning smells that float up from the street and fill Meimei's bedroom, then proceeds spatially, by way of positional markers like "from my bed" and "at the end of our two-block alley," a technique we detailed earlier. Then, in the midst of Tan's tour through Waverly Place—a guided tour from Meimei's house to the end of the alley, then to the sandlot, and back into the alley itself, "crammed with daily mysteries and adventures"— she embeds a section of exposition, which I mark here with italics.

> My brothers and I would peer into the medicinal herb shop, watching old Li dole out onto a stiff sheet of white paper the right amount of insect shells, saffron-colored seeds, and pungent leaves for his ailing customers. *It was said that he once cured a woman dying of an ancestral curse that had eluded the best of American doctors.* Next to the pharmacy was a printer …

As swiftly as Tan slides from description of setting into exposition, she slides back into setting. In this way, her tour continues briskly as she introduces minor characters and reintroduces major ones. At the same time, we learn some of the stories hidden behind the doors on Waverly Place, stories that shape the psychological terrain of the piece.

Tan's description of the alley continues for two more pages, during which she again slides briefly out of the purely descriptive mode to provide bits of exposition and narration, including dialogue, which move the plot along and round out her characters. For instance, after Meimei describes in detail the Ping Yuen Fish Market, she remarks that the sanddabs in the tank had eyes that "lay on one flattened side and reminded me of my mother's story of a careless girl who ran into a crowded street and was crushed by a cab. 'Was smash flat,' reported my mother."

Then Tan moves out of the fish market and to the corner of the alley to Hong Sing's, an authentic Chinese cafe that tourists rarely visit. Once, though, as Meimei recalls, a Caucasian tourist asked her and her friends to pose in front of Hong Sing's so he could take a picture of them. Here's what happened, in Meimei's words.

> He had us move to the side of the picture window so the photo would capture the roasted duck with its head dangling from a juice-covered rope. After he took the picture, I told him he should go into Hong Sing's and eat dinner. When he smiled and asked me what they served, I shouted, "Guts and duck's feet and octopus gizzards!" Then I ran off with my friends,

shrieking with laughter as we scampered across the alley and hid in the entryway grotto of the China Gem Company, my heart pounding with hope that he would chase us.

Look at how much we've learned not only about Waverly Place but also about the characters who people the story. What kind of mother would tell her young daughter the fate of a girl who "was smash flat" by a car? A cruel mother? Or a mother who loved her daughter so much that she wanted to save her from harm? And what do we learn from Meimei's actions? Are her antics toward the tourist merely that—childish antics—or do they reveal conflicting emotions of a child already divided between two cultures? As readers, we're pulled into the mystery of the human drama and we want to know more. More will be revealed, of course. That's the nature of good storytelling. But for now, Meimei is ducking into the entryway of the China Gem Company.

Tan begins the section by describing Waverly Place, and she ends in Waverly Place. Descriptions of setting have grounded the fictional dream and built a framework from which to proceed. But shining between the seams of the framework are splinters of light, bits of narration and exposition that illuminate the story.

USING SETTING TO ILLUMINATE THEME

Eudora Welty seems to *breathe* setting the way most of us breathe air. From this breath, this seemingly effortless evocation of time and place, her stories are born. In "No Place for You, My Love," setting serves not only to ground us in the sensory proofs of the story but also to reveal the characters' emotions, to move the plot along, and even to suggest the story's theme. As early as the story's title, Welty hints at the importance setting will play, and in the first sentence she introduces us to the place, which shares equal billing with the human characters in the drama.

They were strangers to each other, both fairly well strangers to the place …

The place is a New Orleans restaurant where a man and woman meet, through mutual friends, at a luncheon. Both are Northerners, and the man, we soon discover, is married. It's a steamy Sunday afternoon, and as the story progresses the man suggests to the woman that they take a drive south. "South of New Orleans?" she asks. "I didn't know there was any south to *here* …"

His car is a rental car, a detail that adds to the feeling of free-floating alienation. Since neither the city nor the car belongs to either of them, the rules of home do not apply, and their homebound identities seem to dissolve in the humid air. A shyness moves between them, an underlying sexual tension that we sense solely through Welty's description of their surroundings as they walk toward the car.

> … flaked-off, colored houses were spotted like the hides of beasts faded and shy, and were hot as a wall of growth that seemed to breathe flower-like down onto them …

The man and woman drive awhile, mostly in silence. In concrete and sensory detail Welty describes the heat, the mosquitoes, the families walking on the side of the road and fanning themselves with palmetto leaves. She describes the flora and fauna of the place—the terrapins, turtles, and other "little jokes of creation" that "persisted and sometimes perished, the more of them the deeper down the road they went."

We get the feeling that the man and woman are also "little jokes of creation," that they are compelled, through evolutionary fate, to play out their short-lived time together. The farther they drive and the deeper down the road they travel, the more the land reveals its private, vulnerable self. When the land dead-ends into water, they can go no farther without, in effect, becoming amphibious, a feat they accomplish by boarding a ferry. Landscape becomes seascape, and they are in the midst of it.

> Ahead of the boat it was like an exposed vein of ore. The river seemed to swell in the vast middle with the curve of the earth.

After the ferry ride they continue their car journey, for a brief time traveling on a paved road. Soon, however, the paving changes from asphalt to shells. If they are to continue farther south, they must make their way on foot. Which they do, ending their journey in a bar filled with blacks, dogs, and children, one of whom wears "a live lizard on his shirt, clinging like a breast pin—like lapis lazuli." They have gone as far as they can, into the unknown landscape of the South and of their lives together.

They drive back to New Orleans in a wordless, dreamlike state, anchored only by Welty's description: "It was a strange land, amphibious—and whether water-covered or grown with jungle or robbed entirely of water and trees ... it had the same loneliness." In this strange, in-between state the strangers kiss, and the kiss alters, for the moment at least, the landscape surrounding them.

> He had the feeling that they had been riding for a long time across a face— great, wide, and upturned. ... A whole giant body sprawled downward then, on and on, always, constant as a constellation or an angel ...

This moment will not last, of course; such is the nature of moments. As the man and woman drive north, back into their grounded lives, the landscape once again returns to its original state, mirroring the loneliness and alienation of strangers who "had ridden down into a strange land together and were getting safely back—by a slight margin, perhaps, but margin enough ..."

Welty goes beyond merely establishing the setting of her story and providing concrete and sensory proofs to maintain the illusion of time and space. She even goes beyond weaving her descriptions seamlessly into narrative and expository passages. Welty may begin, as she asserts all honest storytellers must, with the bald facts of time and place. But by the end of the story, the *where* becomes more than a place on a map and the *when* more than a slice on a time line. The physical setting is transformed into the landscape of her characters' inner conflicts, a symbol of the heart's journey to find itself.

EXERCISES

1. Make a series of lists.

     - places where you've been in the last twenty-four hours; be very specific
     - places where you habitually find yourself
     - places from your past that are connected to specific events
     - places from your past that are connected with particular people
     - places threatened with extinction—global, local, or only in personal memory
     - places where you feel uncomfortable, where you feel, literally, "out of place"
     - places you've never traveled except in imagination

   Look over your lists. Circle the place that most interests you, then write a description using one of the methods suggested in this chapter or one of the following.

     - Speak to the place as if it were a character, describing what you see when you look at it and how you feel about what you see.
     - Organize your description around a catalog of objects found within that place. Describe each item in concrete detail.
     - Pretend you are looking at the place through a camera lens. Try different angles. Move in for a close-up, pull back for the big view. Describe what you see from each vantage point.

2. Select a place where a character spends time: an office, a bedroom, a swimming pool, a golf course. Then choose three different time periods in your character's story, identifying each period with a phrase that suggests the character's inner landscape at that moment—for example, the morning of her job interview, the night her father died, the day she received the results of the pregnancy test. Describe the setting in terms of how it appears to your character during each of these time periods. Remember, you're describing the same setting, but you're describing it in three different ways, based on your character's inner drama.

3. Move a character to at least three different locations within the same story, three different vantage points from which to view her world. With each move, describe what she sees.

> From the window of her apartment Fran could see ...
> Looking across the breakfast table at her husband, Fran saw ...
> Every night in her dreams Fran saw ...

4. We sometimes refer to a place as having character, meaning that it has been shaped by the hands of time, people, or events. Describe such a place, real or imagined (a beach house, an auto salvage yard, an abandoned school-house, an ancient forest, a barn, a burned-out church), revealing the elements that suggest its history. Pay close attention to physical details. What initials are carved in the wooden school desk? Are weeds crawling through the Edsel's broken window? Choose details that evoke both the human touch and the touch of nature.

5. Describe the same neighborhood as viewed by three different people—for instance, a lifelong resident so accustomed to the scene he barely notices it anymore, a teenager who can't wait to escape the place, and a dewy-eyed honeymooner moving into her first home.

6. Using Amy Tan's description of Waverly Place as a model, describe a neigh-borhood as experienced by a resident walking its streets and reporting on what she sees, hears, smells, and touches. Intersperse descriptive passages with bits of exposition (including dialogue, if you wish) that introduce minor characters, reveal past neighborhood events, and suggest the personality and thoughts of the teller.

7. Take the characters from one of your stories, poems, or essays, and move them into a new setting. Send them into the past or catapult them into the future. Give them a new world in which to live and move. If they've been con-fined within an office building of steel and glass, send them to the country. If all they've known is the ocean, construct a desert in which they can roam. Describe the setting concretely, then position your characters in it. How

does the new setting change the way they look, act, and think? Can you learn anything new about your characters by changing their environment?

8. Describe a natural setting—a woodland, beach, park, mountain—as it appears in each different season or at different times of one particular day. Which details remain the same, and which change? How does the language of your description change depending on the season you evoke or the time of day?

9. Draw a map of a place you remember or one that exists in your imagination. Mark entrances and exits, furniture and props, flora and fauna. Place an x where characters might appear or events transpire. Look for places where things can go wrong. The place might be physically threatening—an icy creek, a steep cliff, a deserted road. Or it might be a setting that invites psychological danger—the principal's office, the monthly weigh-in at the diet center, your mother-in-law's kitchen. Dangerous places suggest trouble, and trouble is one of the keys to compelling narratives. Use the map to seed a new poem, story, or nonfiction piece.

10. After researching a particular historical setting, list at least ten facts you discovered. Expand these facts into fully rendered sensory descriptions, or combine two or more of these facts into one description that situates the reader in this place and time.

11. In his 2013 River Teeth Nonfiction Conference presentation "Knowing Where You Are, Knowing Where You've Been," Robert Root stated, "We don't simply inhabit or pass through place—we carry place inside us; in a sense, place inhabits us." Drawing on this notion, write a description of a place that you carry inside you, a place that inhabits you.

12. Using positional markers such as "on his right," "just ahead of his boat," or "through the ragged grass," move a narrator or character through the landscape of a specific terrain. Let his eyes, feet, and hands guide the reader on the physical journey so the reader feels she is moving as well. Use the passage from Conrad's "The Secret Sharer" as a model.

CHAPTER NINE

Plot and Pace: How Description Shapes the Narrative Line

All good writing is mystery writing. And every successful story, novel, or non-fiction work is a page-turner—or, in the case of a poem, a line-turner. We may begin reading out of curiosity or to pass the time, but we *keep* reading to unravel the mystery. When suspense dissolves, when the mystery is solved, we stop turning pages.

By mystery, I don't mean only "What's going to happen?" Sometimes the outcome is known from the beginning. We don't read about the *Titanic*, for instance, or the Civil War, or Hiroshima, to find out what will happen. We *know* what will happen: The ship will sink, the South will lose, the bomb will be dropped. Mystery extends beyond revelation of uncertain outcomes. It also involves *how* a story is told—how characters develop, how themes and ideas expand, and how the plot unfolds.

The notion of plot used to terrify me; the word alone could send me into a cold sweat. Plot: what the cemetery salesman kept trying to talk me, literally, into.

Plot, I was certain, would bury me. Try as I might, I could see no connection between my descriptions—of characters, settings, and events—and the story's plot. Maybe, I thought, if I can just plan the action, each step of my character's path, if I can just *plot* it all out like points on a grid, I'll be able to write a successful story. My shovel went deep into diagrams, graphs, and outlines until I was in over my head in diabolical plans.

Which leads us to another unfortunate connotation of *plot*: a secret, underhanded scheme to accomplish a hostile or illegal act.

In truth, plot doesn't have to be our final resting place. Nor must it stand coldly apart from our descriptions. In the best stories, as in many essays and poems, plot and description not only coexist; they aid one another. Plot focuses and sharpens descriptions of people, places, and action. In return, description shapes the narrative line by lending immediacy to scene and summary, controlling pace, and modulating narrative tension.

DESCRIPTION IN SCENE, SUMMARY, AND EXPOSITION

Few narratives proceed solely through scene or solely through exposition. Most combine the two methods. A scene is a dramatic rendering, acted out by characters in a particular place at a particular time. When reading a scene, we feel we're witnessing the action firsthand.

Scene is foreground; exposition is background. Exposition provides information the reader needs in order to understand the ongoing story—details of setting, for instance, or characters' backstories, or important facts. Sometimes exposition includes summary description of scenic action. Rather than re-creating the action, summary description sweeps over the larger terrain of accumulated action. A summary is not a close-up but rather a long shot. And where a scene is primarily a *viewing* of an event, a summary is primarily a *telling*.

Jerome Stern, in *Making Shapely Fiction*, suggests that the writer, like a child, should make a scene only when he wants attention. This makes sense. It takes time and energy to write a fully rendered scene, and it takes time and energy to read one. And if everything in the story is vying equally for our up-close, intense scrutiny—which is what scenes demand—we may begin yearning for the relief that summary description provides.

The best writers combine scenic description and summary description or exposition to shape the narrative line. In this passage from James Baldwin's *Go Tell It on the Mountain*, John has just awakened in the room he shares with his brother. It's the morning of his fourteenth birthday, and Baldwin enters the scene directly, supplying specific sensory details.

> He stared at a yellow stain on the ceiling just above his head. Roy was still smothered in the bedclothes, and his breath came and went with a small, whistling sound.

Scenic description comes naturally to most writers. But once we leave the scene and begin to summarize or provide background details, description becomes more of a challenge. Exposition invites abstraction and explanation, and, in its attempt to cover lots of ground in the shortest amount of time, summary sometimes fails to describe the real world or the world of the imagination. As the Baldwin passage continues, John begins thinking about his shortcomings—in particular, what he sees as the sins that blot his life, sins that will keep him from following the straight and narrow path of his forefathers.

> He would not be like his father, or his father's fathers. He would have another life.
>
> For John excelled in school, though not, like Elisha, in mathematics or basketball, and it was said that he had a Great Future. He might become a Great Leader of His People. John was not much interested in his people and still less in leading them anywhere, but the phrase so often repeated rose in his mind like a great brass gate, opening outward for him …

In this passage, Baldwin leaves the scene for a moment. Not the room itself— John is still lying in bed—but Baldwin departs briefly from the scenic method to give us background information. (His summary actually lasts for several long paragraphs.)

Although we are no longer watching the scene unfold, we nevertheless remain involved in the story. We continue to feel the immediacy of the moment, in part because Baldwin, in the midst of summarizing, inserts a sensory description. A gate rises, we are told, in John's mind, and we visualize it—large and brass—as it opens for him.

If during a passage of summary your narrative slows, one way to quicken the pace is to insert a concrete and sensory description. This provides the illusion of scene while still allowing you to supply information. Remember Aristotle's suggestion: Whenever possible, describe your subject in a state of activity. If your subject isn't capable of independent action, you can create the illusion of movement by using active verbs. Baldwin shows the brass gate in action—it rises, then opens.

Sometimes the action in our descriptions is present but hidden, and a slight rewording is all it takes to bring the motion into view. For instance, "Her hair was black and *curly*" can become "Her black hair *curled* in ringlets around her cheeks." Even a static summary passage will appear active and immediate if it includes an active, immediate image.

Another way to achieve immediacy while summarizing is to create the illusion of scenic event. Although a summary is not a dramatic re-creation of an event, it often refers to past or ongoing events. When you write a summary passage that mentions such events, you can't stop to reenter particular moments or to render each detail concretely and specifically; that would require employing the scenic method. You can, however, use descriptive techniques to create the immediacy of scene while still maintaining a lively pace. In the following example, which alternates between scene and summary, Baldwin creates the illusion of scenic events even in the midst of summary.

> Roy stirred again and John pushed him away, listening to the silence. On other mornings he awoke hearing his mother singing in the kitchen, hearing his father in the bedroom behind him grunting and muttering prayers to himself as he put on his clothes; hearing, perhaps, the chatter of Sarah and the squalling of Ruth, and the radios, the clatter of pots and

pans, and the voices of all the folk nearby. This morning not even the cry of a bed-spring disturbed the silence, and John seemed, therefore, to be listening to his own unspeaking doom.

Baldwin's first sentence employs the scenic method; as in the previous example, we're watching John in bed on the morning of his fourteenth birthday. In the second sentence, Baldwin switches to summary, combining information about past mornings into one long sentence filled with sensory details—John's father's grunting, pots and pans clattering.

Notice that Baldwin does not move us into a new scene. Rather he suspends the scene in the bedroom long enough to provide the context, to show how John's emotions on this particular morning have been shaped by his personal history of mornings spent in his parents' house. In one long summary sentence, Baldwin combines information gathered from previous mornings and anchors this information with concrete, sensory description. Finally, in the third sentence, through the transitional phrase "this morning," Baldwin throws us back into the scene.

In only three sentences, Baldwin moves from scenic description to summary and then back to scenic, and we never even feel the bump. His descriptive details create a smooth bridge between the birthday morning and all other mornings. Through sensory description, Baldwin manages to supply important information while retaining a vigorous prose style that keeps the pace of the passage moving briskly.

USING DESCRIPTION TO MODULATE PACE

Readers often maintain that description stops or slows a story's action, and many admit to skimming over descriptive passages in order to see what happens next. (I confess that James Michener's *Hawaii* had this effect on me.) Although sometimes description serves mainly as a transitional device to link scenes of action, description can also create its own vitality. As the gearshift of the narrative vehicle, description can just as easily speed up the action as slow it.

Before we discuss specific ways description can affect the pace of a narrative, let's clarify what we mean by action. Action is not synonymous with activity. Action is motion that pushes the story forward; it's an outward sign of an inward motive. Action serves, as the lyrics of a popular song suggests, to "second that emotion." Activity, on the other hand, is mere random movement. Made-for-TV movies often include lots of activity—cars crashing, buildings exploding, bullets flying—with little or no motivated action. When a viewer or a reader turns off the television or closes the book, complaining that nothing's happening, she's usually referring not to the lack of activity on the screen or page but to the lack of forward movement. The difference between activity and action is the difference between running on a treadmill and running in a race.

If you're concerned with modulating the pace of your story, with speeding up or slowing down your story's action, you first need to clarify your character's motives, either conscious or unconscious. Once you know what your character wants, or what the universe wants for your character, you'll have a better sense of when to vary your story's pace to move the plot along. Tension is created not merely by quickening the pace of a story but by varying that pace to achieve certain results. To maintain suspense, we must alternate between scene and summary, between showing and telling, and between braking and accelerating.

One of the most effective ways to quicken a story's pace is to move from a static description of an object, a place, or a person to an active scene. The classic method for accomplishing this is to have a character interact with a subject that's already been described. Let's say that you've just written three paragraphs describing a wedding dress in a shop window. You've detailed the Belgian lace veil, the beaded bodice, the twelve-foot train, even the row of satin buttons down the sleeves. It's time to move into an action scene, but how do you do this without making the transition obvious?

One method is to initiate an action between your character (let's call her Miranda) and the dress you've just described. Perhaps Miranda is passing by on the sidewalk when the dress in the window catches her attention. Or she walks into the shop and asks the shopkeeper how much the dress costs. You've moved from a static description (of the dress) to an active scene (Miranda in the shop). This method works well to link almost any static description with a scene of action. Describe an elegant table, for instance, complete with crystal goblets, damask tablecloth, monogrammed napkins, and sterling silver tableware, then let the maid pull a cloth from her apron and begin to polish a fork. Or describe a Superman kite lying beside a tree, then watch as a little girl grabs the string and begins to run. You will still be describing, but the nature of your description will have changed from static to active, thus quickening the story's pace.

Throughout this book we've discussed techniques for bringing descriptions to life, including using active rather than passive prose; employing concrete, specific details; and describing our subjects in motion. We've also seen how description can create a sense of immediacy in both scene and summary. All the methods we've discussed can enliven your story's pace. The more effective your descriptions, the more likely readers will be to keep turning pages. Accurate, detailed description, coupled with a lively prose style, is often enough to sustain narrative tension.

Sometimes, however, we control pace best not by speeding up the action but by slowing it down. Filmmakers, aware of this principle, use it to their advantage. Thus, in the clang and clamor of battle—cannons to the left of us, cavalry to the right, swords clashing, thunder rolling—one soldier leans down to recover a fallen flag. The moment seems to last forever. Slowly, slowly his arm bends and his hand begins its languorous ascent, the flag rippling in slow motion. The camera continues its deliberate tracking—up the length of his arm, across his square shoulder, his sinewy neck. Blue veins are pulsing—one beat, two.

At this point, we are clay in the filmmaker's hand. Through his skilled change of pace, he has grabbed our attention. In this suspended moment, this pause in the action, the filmmaker actually increases our desire to know the outcome. He's free to move into the soldier's mind, perhaps into flashback or dream. He's free to dwell a while longer on the physical details of the scene—the soldier's frayed cap, his labored breathing. We will hold still for the details because the filmmaker has slowed the action.

Slow. Withhold. Delay. All techniques for increasing tension.

Perhaps the simplest, most obvious way to slow the pace of a story or an essay is to use short sentences, directives, or fragments. You can also use short paragraphs, thereby creating a visual pause for your reader's eye. (Some writers go a step further by inserting white space between paragraphs or segments.) The previous paragraph takes up only one line, and its one-word fragments require the reader to stop, start, and stop again. In poetry, also, short lines tend to slow the movement. For instance, the opening line to one of my poems—

When you left our new marriage for another woman's bed

—would read quite differently were it broken into smaller bites.

When you left
our new
marriage for another
woman's bed

Breaking the long line not only changes the meaning of the poem by shifting the emphases of certain words; it also forces the reader to slow down, both physically and psychologically.

Another way to slow the pace of prose or poetry is to change the verb tense of the telling. Present tense, although it contributes to a sense of immediacy, can actually prolong a scene. "She is sitting at the window" takes longer to write and to read than "She sat at the window." And even the shortened present-tense version—"She sits at the window"—though it takes as long to read as the past-tense version, gives the impression of prolonged action because it emphasizes the process rather than the completed event. Since a present-tense action is, by definition, an action *in process*, the reader expects to be led through the process and will probably sit still as you describe each step. Using present tense may also slow *you* down as you write, making you more conscious of describing precisely, specifically, and in detail.

In general, it's best to be consistent with the verb tense of your narrative. But sometimes changing verb tense in midstream is effective. Since switching from past tense to present tense usually slows the reader down, it's a good method for focusing attention on a dramatic action—say, a gun being cocked—or for achieving the feeling of suspension that occurs in dreams or reverie. A conscious switch in verb tense also serves a practical purpose: It alerts the reader to a change in focus, time period, or psychological distance.

SPECIAL CHALLENGES OF FLASHBACKS

Flashback is a common technique for modulating the pace of a story. Unfortunately flashback often slows the pace too much, making readers impatient to return to the main story. When this happens it's usually because we haven't established the story's tension effectively beforehand. Although flashback literally looks *back*, into the past, it should serve to push the narrative *forward*. This forward movement might equate with *what happens next*. More often, however, flashback pushes the narrative forward by exploring the *why* and *how* of the main conflict, which the author has already set up.

Flashback is a suspension device, but you can't suspend something that isn't there to begin with. Before a flashback occurs, the main line of the narrative must be threaded tightly. Let's say your main character is a timid, mouse-like bookseller. After a few pages of description—of him, his bookstore, the bag lunch he's brought with him one rainy Thursday—you flash back to his childhood home. Painstakingly you describe the boy's beautiful but distracted mother and her succession of lovers, the leather-bound books that line the shelves of the boy's room, and the yellow chenille bedspread that leaves an imprint on his cheek.

Unfortunately your reader probably doesn't care about the bookseller's childhood—at least, not yet—and she'll quickly become impatient with your flashback descriptions, however original, sensory, and freshly rendered they are. The quality of your description isn't the problem; it's the *timing*. You've inserted a flashback too soon, before the main conflict has been established.

Try backing up a minute and reentering the opening scene: the bookseller in his shop on a rainy Thursday morning. Ask yourself where *that* scene is heading. Maybe a customer—say, a thin, dark-eyed woman in a brown raincoat—is browsing through a medical dictionary. Maybe the bookseller has noticed her before. After all, she comes in every rainy lunch hour, always wearing the same brown coat. He wants to talk to her, maybe even invite her to lunch, but something stops him—what makes him think she would even talk to him, let alone join him for lunch? What on earth could she possibly see in him, and besides, what does he know about women? He's never even been on a date. All these thoughts run through the bookseller's mind as he watches the woman. He takes a step toward her, hesitates, takes another step.

Now is your chance. You've established the tension, the uncertain *what*: Will he speak to the dark-eyed woman? By dwelling a while longer on the main story rather than moving too quickly into flashback, you allow yourself time and space to introduce a problem, maybe two. (The woman is reading a medical dictionary; maybe she's ill.) At this point, having been introduced to the *what*, your reader is primed for the *why* and *how* a flashback can provide: Why is the bookseller so frightened of women? How has he gotten this far without once having a date? Because the main line of the story has been threaded tightly, your flashback description will now be significant to the conflict.

Readers will gladly hold still for descriptions that deepen the essential mystery of a story. But they won't hold still forever. Overlong flashback descriptions are as deadly to a story as are badly timed flashbacks. Generally speaking, the longer the work, the longer the flashback it can support. A novel might sustain a flashback of several pages or more, but a poem may be too brief or tightly focused to allow even one flashback image. It's a question of balance: In most cases, a flashback should not take up more time, space, or energy than the main story. (An easy way to check for balance is to use a highlighter to mark flashback sections. You'll quickly see how much space your flashbacks are consuming.)

If you find that a flashback is taking over your story, or that your flashback descriptions are more intriguing than the descriptions in your primary plotline, reconsider your strategy. It may be that the real story lies within the flashback; the primary story was just a way for you to segue into the flashback. If this is the case, you may need to get rid of the introductory incident and restructure your story so the flashback is your main plotline.

If, however, you find that you've simply gotten carried away with flashback description, you'll need to either cut some of the flashback descriptions or expand the descriptions in your main story. Otherwise the reader will lose his moorings. The main conflict should lie within the primary story. If you stray too far from the main conflict, the reader will become anxious to return to it. He'll start flipping pages, skipping over the descriptions you've labored so hard to craft.

Think of the structural frame of your story as an accordion. When the accordion is collapsed, it represents the framework of your main story; the edges of the accordion represent where your main story's time line begins and ends. Although this time structure need not be long (the main time line of both Virginia Woolf's *Mrs. Dalloway* and James Joyce's *Ulysses* is a single day), it should be carefully delineated and monitored so that the reader does not get lost in the main storyline.

Once you've established the main storyline, you can open the accordion wide to expose its pleated bellows, spaces where you insert flashbacks or other supporting material. Then, as the story proceeds, you open and close the accordion storyline, moving between the main story and the backstories, descriptions, observations, and details that make a story more than merely the sum of its plotted parts.

WHEN THOUGHT IS THE PLOT: TENSION AND DISCOVERY IN NONNARRATIVE WORKS

Although we often think of plot only in terms of stories, plot is an important element in all successful page-turners, including works that proceed by structures other than narrative. As Phillip Lopate writes in his introduction to *The Art of the Personal Essay*, "Even a 'pure' meditation, the track of one's thoughts, has to be shaped, given a kind of plot or urgency, if it is to communicate." How do writers of nonnarrative works create this sense of plot and urgency that keeps readers engaged? How do we proceed when *thought* is the plot?

Lopate's phrase "the track of one's thoughts" suggests one method that successful essayists, in particular, employ. Unlike the lecturer or the textbook writer delivering "just the facts, ma'am," the essayist allows her mind to explore a subject freely, without knowing where the exploration will lead. She is free to digress, elaborate, interrogate, move backward and forward in time and space, and wrestle with her own doubts on her way to discovering something new about her subject. Reading an essay (from the French *essai*: a trial or attempt), we sense the movement of an active mind navigating the world of ideas, events, and experiences. We may even feel we are witnessing these moments of exploration as they occur in real time, as if the essayist is discovering her subject even as the words appear on the page.

In chapter four we discussed a segment from Stephen Kuusisto's memoir *Eavesdropping* as an example of sensory description. Elsewhere in his memoir (in an excerpt published separately as "Night Song") Kuusisto recalls details from his early childhood in Helsinki, or, more accurately, *attempts* to recall them, as we see in the following two separate segments. (The ellipses are the author's own; they do not signal deleted words.)

> And winter wouldn't give up. We traveled into the country and I heard the reindeer bells. Old farm. Runners of a sleigh crossing ice … What else?
>
> There's an old man who sells potatoes from a dory in the harbor. His voice is like sand. He talks to me every day.

Potatoes from the earth, potatoes from the cellar! You can still taste the
summer! You can still taste the summer!

Later I would think of his voice when reading of trolls, under bridges.
What else?
Sound of knife blades in the tinsmith's stall …
The rumble of streetcars …
The clacking of a loom … My mother weaving a rug …

Kuusisto's ellipses suggest the landscape of his present-tense thoughts, as if each detail arrives after a momentary pause. But even more important than the ellipses is the repeated phrase "What else?" We are in effect overhearing the writer talking to himself, ransacking memory for moments that stick. We are witnessing an active mind navigating his subject—in this case, a series of childhood memories.

When you write a nonnarrative work of prose or poetry, consider how description can suggest the movement of your mind as you explore your subject. Let's say you are writing about a visit to your ancestral cemetery. Rather than just describing the scene, include your personal reactions, the questions or reflections that came to you in that moment. If while studying the tombstones you wondered why your great-grandmother was not buried beside her husband, let the reader overhear your thoughts. Weave your questions into the sensory description. Reveal your journey of discovery.

In *Writing the Memoir*, Judith Barrington notes that "the memoirist both tells the story and muses upon it, trying to unravel what it means in the light of her current knowledge." This statement suggests a memoir's double-sided plot: the plot of the past-tense story (the telling) and the present-tense unraveling of that story (the musing). The present-tense entry point, often referred to as the "occasion of the telling," rubs against the past-tense story to create friction. So a helpful question to ask while reflecting upon an experience is not only *Why am I writing this?* but also *Why am I writing this at this particular time? What is the occasion of the telling? Why now? Why here? And how can my descriptions—not only of past-tense events but also present-tense experiences—collide to create a journey of discovery?*

SCATTERING DESCRIPTIVE DETAILS TO UNIFY THE PLOT

In an earlier chapter we discussed how beginning writers often clump descriptive details at the beginning of a story or when a character or setting is first mentioned. Often it's more effective to break these large clumps into smaller bits, sprinkling them throughout the story. This method not only helps you avoid overlong or static descriptions; it also provides continual proofs for your reader.

The notion of sprinkling details throughout a story should not be taken to mean that details can simply be dropped, willy-nilly, along the way. Like episodes in a novel, which must be placed so they amplify the conflict, descriptive details must accumulate, gaining significance each time they are mentioned. Effectively releasing descriptive details a little at a time can strengthen your plotline. Each detail is like a crumb dropped for the reader, creating a trail to follow. In Flannery O'Connor's "Everything That Rises Must Converge," the most important physical detail is the hat worn by Julian's mother. The hat is mentioned many times throughout the story, and each mention nudges the plot along. The first description of the hat, occurring in the third paragraph, is from Julian's point of view.

> It was a hideous hat. A purple velvet flap came down on one side of it and stood up on the other; the rest of it was green and looked like a cushion with the stuffing out. He decided it was less comical than jaunty and pathetic.

The next reference to the hat is not a description of the hat itself but rather a description of an action involving the hat.

> She lifted the hat one more time and set it down slowly on top of her head.

On the next page, the hat is described again, but unlike the first description, this one is brief, only a phrase (which I've noted with italics) embedded seamlessly into a larger narrative passage.

The door closed and he turned to find the dumpy figure, *surmounted by the atrocious hat*, coming toward him.

As readers, we add this phrase to earlier descriptive details. The cumulative description gains momentum, and with each mention of the hat, the conflict between Julian and his mother grows. Although it's not yet clear whether the hat will be the main focus of the conflict, it *is* clear it will play a significant role in the story.

After two more brief references to the hat, O'Connor continues for several hat-free pages. Julian is accompanying his mother to her "reducing" class at the Y, and as they walk to the bus stop, they begin to argue. We learn that Julian hates his small Southern hometown, his mother's racial prejudices, her longing for a past when her grandfather was a wealthy landowner and when "darkies" were "better off" as slaves. Most of all, he hates the way his mother controls him through her childlike helplessness. The next description of the hat demonstrates the anger silently raging inside him.

He looked at her bleakly. She was holding herself very erect under the preposterous hat, wearing it like a banner of her imaginary dignity. There was in him an evil urge to break her spirit.

The adjectives in O'Connor's descriptions have moved from "jaunty and pathetic" to "atrocious" to "preposterous," mirroring the progression of Julian's disgust not just for the hat but for all it represents, the privileged past that his mother refuses to relinquish. The plot thickens as Julian and his mother take seats on a recently integrated bus, joined quickly by the "darkies" whose upward mobility Julian's mother has been railing against. For four or five pages O'Connor doesn't mention the hat; all descriptive attention is focused on the interactions among Julian, his mother, and the blacks with whom they are seated.

The next description of the hat represents a turning point in the plot. O'Connor repeats the same description with which she opened the story; she even uses the same wording.

> ... a hideous hat. A purple velvet flap came down on one side of it and stood up on the other; the rest of it was green and looked like a cushion with the stuffing out.

But this time the hat is on another head, the head of an imposing, strong-willed black woman. Julian notices the hat but does not make the connection until several paragraphs later when his eyes, fixed on "the haughty face" of the woman and the "green and purple hat," widen in surprise and recognition.

> The vision of the two hats, identical, broke upon him with the radiance of a brilliant sunrise. His face was suddenly lit with joy. He could not believe that Fate had thrust upon his mother such a lesson.

As the plot moves toward its tragicomic climax, the hat is mentioned two more times. But the tide of the story has turned. The hat, no longer perched high and proud upon Julian's mother's head, lies defeated in her lap: Everything that rises must converge. By breaking her description of the hat into several small pieces and scattering them throughout the story, O'Connor organizes the plotline, provides the concrete and sensory proofs that anchor us to the world of the story, and tightens the thread of tension between Julian and his mother and, finally, between the old world and the new.

WITHHOLDING DESCRIPTIVE DETAILS TO CREATE TENSION

O'Connor's technique—of scattering descriptive passages throughout the story—relies more on repetition and variation than on slow revelation of detail. We know what the hat looks like the first time it's mentioned; we don't have to wait for the visual image to be made clear. Sometimes, however, a writer consciously withholds descriptive details to tighten a story's tension. This is writing as striptease, the opposite of "what you see is what you get." With the striptease method, what we get is precisely what we *don't* see, what we must wait patiently, or impatiently, to witness. Like the man in William

Sansom's novel *The Loving Eye*, we wait at the window for any sign, however slight, to be revealed.

> One moment the window was empty, a dark square—and the next this strange new woman was standing against the sill.
>
> Her appearance was as sudden as if a blind had been snapped up.
>
> There she stood exactly in the centre of her little theatre of sashes and sill and darkness beyond. One expected her to bow.
>
> He backed away from his own window like a thief.

Looking out his apartment window, the man is surprised, as the reader is, by the sudden appearance of a woman. But Sansom doesn't reveal what she looks like. He delays his description, making us all the more curious, and his use of short paragraphs increases the stop-and-start feeling of the moment. Although the woman appears as if onstage, the man backs away "like a thief." More delay. Even if the woman were to appear again, the man (who is our eye, the camera lens through which we view the scene) may not be there to describe it for us. The suspense mounts.

In the next paragraph, Sansom creates a kind of visual interference, describing in detail the physical barriers rising between the man and woman.

> In between them a wild spring wind drove through the trough of back-gardens, raising sudden birds of white paper, waving the trees, whipping a storm of movement between all the rows of quiet shut windows. But that was outside. In, it was still.

Again, Sansom tightens the tension by the use of halt and delay. Although we feel the internal storm rising within the man, Sansom doesn't satisfy our curiosity. Not yet. Instead he shifts to an external storm, a "wild spring wind" that waves and whips through the landscape.

Although Sansom continues to withhold visual details of the woman, he nevertheless uses description to push the story forward. The man hears sounds from outside—a lumber cart, a blackbird, "the thrash of a beaten mat." The reader overhears the man's heart beating "loud as a clock, faster than the mat" as he crouches among the furniture, vowing not to look out the window again until he receives a sign.

> He thought: Not until that cart has called three times more, I won't move till then ...

As readers, we won't move either. Not until Sansom gives us a sign, releasing the thread of tension he's pulled so tightly. We will hold still for his minute descriptions—of the gardens, a blackbird, even the taffeta swag on the window box—because the descriptions are not only sensory, concrete, and exquisitely rendered but also because they delay the inevitable moment when the woman, in all her complete and described glory, is revealed.

USING DESCRIPTION TO SUGGEST PSYCHOLOGICAL MOTION

Sansom's method—using description to delay the primary action of the story—serves an additional narrative purpose. His descriptions of the external landscape also mirror the internal landscape of the man's feelings; they "second the emotion." Since the passage is written from the limited-omniscient viewpoint, we're allowed access into the man's head. We overhear his thoughts and even hear his heart beating, so when we encounter a description of a storm or a blackbird, we easily make the transition between the outer and inner worlds of the story.

When we write from the objective point of view, however, it's difficult to use description to mirror emotional states. After all, we have no access into characters' minds; we can report only those external details an observer might perceive through his senses. Think of Hemingway, with his cold, objective eye. In most of his stories, the language is spare; he includes no emotional riffs, no detours of philosophical meditations. With Hemingway, what we see is what we get.

Or so it seems on the surface. Yet even Hemingway departs from "just the facts ma'am" to suggest a character's mindscape. In "Hills Like White

Elephants," arguably his most sparse, coolly reported story, the plot proceeds almost entirely by means of external dialogue and action. The two characters in the story—identified only as "the man" and "the girl" (except for one brief mention of the girl's name)—are not described at all in terms of physical attributes. Nor does Hemingway tell us what the man and woman are thinking or feeling as they sit at a table talking. The only clues to the emotional world of the story, the psychological plot beneath the bare action, emerge in Hemingway's descriptions of the neighboring hills. The first description occurs early in the story.

> The hills across the valley of the Ebro were long and white. On this side there was no shade and no trees and the station was between two lines of rails in the sun.

Then, after several lines of dialogue, Hemingway appears to move into the mind of the girl. He doesn't, of course; that would violate his objective point of view. But he suggests her emotional landscape through his next description of the hills, followed by the girl's statement.

> The girl was looking off at the line of hills. They were white in the sun and the country was brown and dry.
> "They look like white elephants," she said.

The colors and textures of the description—white, brown, and dry—echo the aridity and sterility of the moment. Several pages of dialogue ensue, during which we come to understand that the man is trying to talk the girl into aborting their child-to-be. At this point, we are told:

> The girl stood up and walked to the end of the station. Across, on the other side, were fields of grain and trees along the banks of the Ebro. Far away, beyond the river, were mountains. The shadow of a cloud moved across the field of grain and she saw the river through the trees.

Notice how the description has changed. No longer is the scene brown and white and dry. It is green and fecund, ribboned by a distant river.

"And we could have all this," she said.

Looking in one direction, the girl sees one scene; looking in the other direction, she sees quite a different scene. By now it's clear that the choice she makes—the internal, emotional choice of whether to bear the child or abort it—mirrors the external landscape that Hemingway so objectively reports. Although he remains removed from the scene, never entering the girl's mind, the author nevertheless uses description to suggest the girl's feelings, thus propelling the plot beyond merely *what happens next* to the more intriguing questions of *how* it will happen, and *why*.

EXERCISES

1. Read over one of your stories or essays, using two different colored markers to highlight particular passages. With one color, mark the scenes; with the other color, mark the summaries. Is your story composed predominantly of scene or of summary?

   If you've used mostly scenes, and if you feel your reader may tire of dialogue, action, and direct presentation of event, insert brief summaries or other exposition to vary the structure.

   If you've used mostly summary, consider whether you've included enough concrete, sensory details and foreground action to bring the reader into your literary dream. If not, break away from summary to create a scene.

2. Using the passage from *Go Tell It on the Mountain* as a model, insert a sentence or two of exposition in the midst of a scene. Slip the exposition in swiftly, then move directly back into the scene.

3. At a dramatic point in a scene of brisk, even frenetic action, slow the pace. You can do this by using shorter, fragmented sentences or paragraphs, or by switching from past tense to present tense. Once the slow-motion moment has been sustained long enough to rivet the reader's attention, return to the original swift pace.

4. In the middle of a summary, insert a concrete image—a sight, sound, smell, taste, or texture—that creates the illusion of scenic event. For instance, if you're summarizing experiences that have led to a particular moment in a character's life, use sensory language to evoke one or more of these experiences. Let's say you've opened your story with a summary of the jobs Jane has held for the past twenty years. As you summarize, you might mention her "chlorine-soaked summers as a lifeguard" or "the sizzle of grease" as she flipped burgers at the diner. Don't expand the descriptions into fully rendered scenes. Give just enough detail to create the illusion of scene, then continue your summary.

5. If your story or essay lacks suspense because the events unfold too predictably—in chronological order for instance—use scissors to cut your hard-copy draft into discrete scenes. Once the separate scenes are laid out before you, reorder them to amplify the conflict or mystery. Which scene would most likely grab the reader's attention? Which scene might follow this opening scene, revealing just enough to hold the reader's attention?

6. If your story, essay, or poem includes a flashback description, look closely to see if you've inserted it too early. Has your main plotline been delineated, the conflict introduced? If not, insert the flashback later in the text.

7. Break a long description—of an object, a place, or a person—into at least three sections. Plant these sections in different places in the story, as O'Connor does with the hat images in "Everything That Rises Must Converge." Each time your subject is mentioned, vary the details so the description accumulates meaning as the story progresses.

8. After you've described at length a static subject, set the scene in motion by having a character interact with the subject, the way Miranda interacts with the wedding dress in this chapter's example.

9. Using objective narration like that in Hemingway's "Hills Like White Elephants," suggest a character's moods or thoughts strictly by the way you describe a scene, a landscape, or an object in the character's view. Remember, as an objective narrator you can report only what you can witness externally; you cannot enter the character's mind.

10. Try the striptease method of description. Begin with an incomplete description of an object, a person, or a scene—no more than a vague hint of what will later be revealed. (Using pronouns rather than specific nouns is one way to begin.) Depart from the description for a few sentences. When you return, give one or two more hints but do not reveal your subject completely. Delay your revelation by creating visual or other interferences, by switching briefly to another scene, or by using short, elliptical phrases that slow the reader's pace.

11. If you are working on a memoir-based poem or prose work, ask yourself, "Why am I drawn to this subject at this particular time in my life?" Perhaps you recently received a cancer diagnosis, gave birth to your first child, or moved your parents into an assisted-living center. Could your present-tense situation collide with the past-tense story and become the "occasion of the telling"? Perhaps you can weave a present-tense situation into the larger narrative, as Terry Tempest Williams does in her memoir *Refuge: An Unnatural History of Family and Place*.

CHAPTER TEN

The Big Picture

"When all is said and done …" my grandmother would begin. The phrase was her theme song, a way to restore the dropped stitches and chipped dishes, to order the details that cluttered her days. "When all is said and done," she'd continue, "what really matters is …"

You've completed the first or second draft of your story, essay, or poem—maybe even the final draft. Reading over what you've written, you're pleased with your descriptions. They are carefully worded, echoing both the sound and the sense of your subject. They are sensory and concrete, filled with specific details. You've brought your images to life through vivid prose, action-based description, and metaphor. You've fleshed out your characters, created the illusion of time and space, and moved your plot along.

But you're still not sure how it all fits together. When the reader reaches the last line of your poem or the final paragraph of your essay, will he hear that satisfying "click," the sound of a well-engineered lock as the bolt slips into place? Days after he finishes your story—or weeks, or even years, long after he's forgotten individual descriptions—what will remain in the reader's memory?

When all is said and done, we want our descriptions to add up to something. No, not just *add up to*. We want to create something that's more than the sum of its parts. The painting, not just the brushstrokes. The song, not just the notes.

What really matters is, finally, the big picture—what lingers after the small details have vanished. The big picture is affected not only by our descriptions of characters, settings, and events but also by elements of atmosphere, mood, motif, theme, and tone working together to create that "something in the air" or "something underfoot" that the reader intuitively senses.

In this chapter, we'll consider how description evokes the prevailing atmosphere of our story, poem, or essay. Then we'll discuss how the language of descriptions and the attitude and psychic distance of the narrator shape the tone of the work. Finally, we'll examine how description suggests the underlying theme, the deeper subject that lives beneath the story's surface.

SOMETHING IN THE AIR: ATMOSPHERE AND MOOD

My husband believes the whole world should be placed on a dimmer switch. "Lighting is everything," he says, adjusting the shade beside my reading chair. He rips out fluorescent tubes by their ballasts and replaces them with golden incandescent or pink-tinted bulbs that warm our faces to a cherubic glow. Each night as we make our way to bed, we extinguish no fewer than twenty light sources—wall sconces, chandeliers, table lamps, under-counter strip lights, downlights, up lights, votives, tapers—each with its own function yet all working together to contribute to what my husband calls our home's "atmosphere."

I argue that lighting *isn't* everything, that music is important, too, so tonight Michael Feinstein is playing Gershwin, or Ella is crooning, or Jagger is thumping out "Brown Sugar" in the landing above our heads, where my husband has positioned hidden speakers. He's camouflaged the wires, too, threaded them behind walls—because, as he reminds me, beauty is in the eye of the beholder, and you can't behold beauty if you're staring at bare wires.

In literature, atmosphere is the element hidden behind the walls of our story. Atmosphere is closely related to setting, but it goes beyond the bare wires of *when* and *where*. If someone were to ask me, "Where does your life *take place?*" I'd probably provide the most obvious, verifiable answer: "In a townhouse in a Southern city in the early part of the twenty-first century."

Those are the facts of my home's *setting*. But if I were asked to describe my home's atmosphere, facts would not suffice; I would have to use words that evoke moods or feelings. I might begin with a labeling adjective: *cozy*, perhaps, or *restful*, maybe even *elegant* or *romantic* (on those evenings when the lighting is just right and a love song is playing).

An effective description, of course, must go beyond labels. Adjectives like *gloomy, forlorn, cheerful, inviting, sensual*, or *foreboding* may focus our descriptions on a central mood, but they won't help the reader *experience* the atmosphere. "To establish a particular atmosphere, mood, or tone," writes Jerome Stern in *Making Shapely Fiction*, "you must pay attention to your readers' short memory for sensation." Atmosphere, though in part intangible, must be evoked through tangible means.

We've already mentioned the importance of lighting and music. Other elements of atmosphere include details of time, place, and weather; sense impressions; and special effects of language. The opening to Edgar Allan Poe's "The Fall of the House of Usher" showcases all of these elements.

> During the whole of a dull, dark, and soundless day in the autumn of the year, when the clouds hung oppressively low in the heavens, I had been passing alone, on horseback, through a singularly dreary tract of country, and at length found myself, as the shades of evening drew on, within view of the melancholy House of Usher.

This opening sentence—yes, it is one single sentence—could serve as a crash course in how to create atmosphere. First, Poe strings the bare wires of where and when: a country road; an autumn day in a time period when men still rode on horseback to reach their destinations. Then he adds details of lighting and sound: The scene is dark and shadowy; a palpable silence reigns. But this is not a peaceful silence, the kind that might soothe a tired traveler. This is a disturbing silence, described only in terms of what it *lacks*: It is "soundless."

Other details add to the foreboding: clouds hanging low, a lone rider. And beneath it all a subliminal music plays. I imagine an oboe or a cello, its deep tones mournfully forlorn, its rhythms striking like gongs foretelling doom: "dull," "dark," "soundless," "day." Each phrase of the description, like each step of the rider's horse, draws us deeper toward the gloom that awaits us.

Nothing could be further from Poe's doom-filled atmosphere than the atmosphere in the following passage, which demonstrates how another author uses effects of lighting, music, and language to evoke "something in the air." The where and when of the setting are straightforward facts any writer might include: a garden on Long Island Sound; summer nights during the 1920s. But this isn't just any writer. This is F. Scott Fitzgerald, whose combination of lush imagery and musical language evokes an atmosphere that exudes sensuality.

> There was music from my neighbor's house through the summer nights. In his blue gardens men and girls came and went like moths among the whisperings and the champagne and the stars. ...
>
> The last swimmers have come in from the beach now and are dressing upstairs; the cars from New York are parked five deep at the drive, and already the halls and salons and verandas are gaudy with primary colors and hair shorn in strange new ways and shawls beyond the dreams of Castile. The bar is in full swing and floating rounds of cocktails permeate the garden outside until the air is alive with chatter and laughter and casual innuendo and introductions forgotten on the spot and enthusiastic meetings between women who never knew each other's names.
>
> The lights grow brighter as the earth lurches away from the sun and now the orchestra is playing yellow cocktail music and the opera of voices pitches a key higher. Laughter is easier, minute by minute, spilled with prodigality, tipped out at a cheerful word. The groups change more swiftly, swell with new arrivals, dissolve and form in the same breath—already there are wanderers, confident girls who weave here and there among the stouter and more stable, become for a sharp, joyous moment the center of a group and then excited with triumph glide on through the sea-change

of faces and voices and color under the constantly changing light. —from
The Great Gatsby

In chapter five we discussed a writer's "constellation of images," those particular words and images that form his personal vision. Works of prose and poetry also contain these constellations. In the Fitzgerald passage, visual details dot the description like individual stars in a night sky: "garden," "moths," "blue," "yellow," "champagne," "salons," "sun," "verandas." At the most basic level, Fitzgerald's choice of details illustrates Aristotle's "proper and special name of a thing." Each star in the constellation flickers with gaiety, mystery, and romance. But it is the larger pattern they form, the "constellation of images," that creates the atmosphere.

In terms of lighting, Fitzgerald's description is "gaudy with primary colors"; even the cocktail music is yellow. But just as the atmosphere in my townhouse isn't complete without the music drifting from hidden speakers, so the atmosphere of Gatsby's parties cannot be evoked solely through visual clues. Read the first sentences aloud and you'll almost hear the sibilant whispers of partygoers and moth wings. A few lines later, the whispering strengthens and brightens to become the "chatter and laughter and casual innuendo" that finally explode in an "opera of voices" sung in an even brighter, more joyous key.

But as musically suggestive as Fitzgerald's diction might be, his luxurious syntax is the choreographer of the scene. His long, languid rhythms rise and fall, then "with triumph glide on through the sea-change of faces and voices and color under the constantly changing light." His language is as opulent as the women's costumes and as free-flowing as the champagne, continuing breathlessly to the end of the passage.

As readers, we may eventually forget Fitzgerald's colorful and musical descriptions, but we probably won't forget the atmosphere of his fictional dream. Long after the last guest has departed and we've closed the covers on the novel, something—a fragrance, a snatch of song, a feeling—remains in the summer air.

ATTITUDE AND TONE

"Don't use that tone of voice with me," demanded my father before banishing me to the room I shared with my sister. I'd lie on the twin bed, plucking at the chenille spread and trying to figure out what I'd said to make him so angry. Looking back, I now see that it wasn't *what* I said but rather the way I said it—my inflection, the lift of my left eyebrow, the smug smirk. It was *tone* that cinched my doom.

Years later, when I'd finally scraped together enough courage to send one of my stories out into the world, it was returned with a note from the editors. "Your characters are well drawn, their actions believable, and the climax just right. But the tone of the story troubles us. We can't quite put our finger on the tonal problem, but in the end it was serious enough to keep us from publishing the story."

There it was again—*the tonal problem.* This time, though, I couldn't blame it on vocal inflection or body language. The problem lay in the tone of my words as they appeared on the page. As I reread the story I saw what the editors had seen, and I despaired, knowing the challenges that awaited me in the revision process.

Problems with tone are some of the most difficult literary problems to solve. It's one thing to change details of setting, characters, or plot, or to revise a story's prose to make it more lucid. But changing the tone of a story requires reconsidering each sentence, description, and snatch of dialogue. In my case, revising the tone-plagued story meant that I had to interrogate every segment, looking for places where my tone—overly playful? too flippant?—affected the fictional dream. Although tone is not synonymous with attitude, the tone of our descriptions is shaped by our attitude, or the attitude of our narrator. Tone is our personal comment—usually implied rather than stated—toward our subjects, characters, and readers. And one way we reveal our attitude toward our subjects is through word choice.

How Diction Affects Tone

Since tone refers not so much to *what is said* as to *how it is voiced*, tone is concerned less with denotation (the dictionary meanings of a word) than with connotation (the overtones a word acquires over time). In chapter three we discussed how choosing words that call forth a significant image, attitude, and emotion requires moving beyond mere accuracy. Let's say you're describing your neighbor's front yard. Depending on your attitude toward the yard, you could describe it as overgrown, out-of-control, natural, weedy, fertile, flourishing, chaotic, savage, unrestrained, junglelike, or lush. Any of these adjectives could accurately denote the yard's qualities, but each word has a different connotation.

To see how tone affects the vocabulary of your descriptions, choose one subject—an object, a person, or a place—and write three separate descriptions of that subject, based on three different attitudes you might feel toward it. Do not change the basic facts about your subject. If the man you're describing is six feet tall and weighs 130 pounds, don't alter the physical details. Instead alter the words you use to impart those qualities. For instance, you might describe him as slender, skinny, thin, reedlike, Ichabod Crane-ish, lean, lanky, bony, scrawny, narrow, or youthfully fit. Your descriptions could also include details about the character's actions, surroundings, and belongings—all the elements we discussed in the chapter on characterization.

Once you've completed the three descriptions, ask a reader to respond with a word that best suits the tone of each passage, a word like one of these: *admiring, solemn, condescending, awed, nostalgic, satiric, playful, sarcastic, bitter, hostile, apathetic, outraged, friendly, straightforward, evasive, lofty, elevated,* or *strident.* You may be surprised that the attitude you intended to reveal was not the tone your reader "heard" as he read your work. The tone of your descriptions can be altered by factors other than word choice, such as the *sound* of your words, the cadences of your language, and the psychic distance between you and your subject.

What the Dog Hears

Several years ago at the Bread Loaf Writers' Conference, Ellen Bryant Voigt described tone as "what the dog hears" or "what we hear through motel walls." The main point of her lecture was that tone resides predominantly in sound. Since Voigt is a trained musician as well as a poet, when she speaks of tone, I immediately think of music. Musical tone refers to the distinct pitch, volume, color, or duration of a sound. Musicians speak of sweet tones, muddy tones, clear or bell-like tones—even pear-shaped tones.

Singers vary the tone of a musical phrase by prolonging it, shortening it, pitching it higher or lower, making it louder (toning it up) or softer (toning it down), or changing its sound color (breathy, harsh, resonant, liquid). As writers we control the tone of our descriptions not only through the words we choose but by the way we "sing" them. In chapter three we introduced Aristotle's principle of "a musical naming"—that is, choosing individual words and phrases based on their sound qualities. And in our discussion of senses in chapter four, we saw how to employ musical language to evoke the sounds of our descriptions. We can apply these same principles to control the *tone* of our descriptions.

Look back at the three descriptions you wrote that revealed three different attitudes toward the same subject. Notice the sound qualities of your words. Did you use soft, soothing consonants in one description and harsh, cacophonous consonants in another? Did you use deep-toned vowels in one description and high-pitched vowels in another? What about the lengths and rhythms of your phrases? Did one description gallop while the other minced, step by step, toward its end?

In the following descriptions the basic facts of the scene—a woman washing dishes while her children play outside—do not change. But the tones of the descriptions are miles apart.

> She watches through the kitchen window the comings and goings of her
> children as one by one the dinner dishes slide from her hands and into

the steaming dishwater, one plate still holding the memory of potatoes and gravy.

Saucers clatter. Cups clank. Platters rattle. She grabs a plate, scrubs its crusted skin. Dried potato. Gravy. Outside the window her kids scream and scatter.

Although some of the tonal difference between the passages is due to word choice, the sounds of the words and the rhythms of the sentences also shape the mood of the two descriptions.

We've seen how Poe uses sound and rhythm to evoke a sense of gloomy foreboding and how Fitzgerald "plays" his language to suggest the sensual gaiety of a summer party. As you review the descriptions in your stories or poems, don't just *look* at the words, noting their denotations and connotations. *Listen* to their musical pitch, color, and volume, and to the rhythms and durations of your phrases. Since tone resides not only in what you say but also in how you say it, you can't ignore those messages even a dog can understand. Like muffled voices you hear through motel walls, the tones of your descriptions permeate your work's inner boundaries.

Tone and Psychic Distance

In chapter seven we introduced the principle of psychic distance—what John Gardner defines as "the distance that the reader feels between himself and the events in the story"—and we discussed how shifts in psychic distance can erode the fictional dream. It is significant that Gardner refers to what a reader *feels* rather than what a reader intellectualizes. When we feel distanced from a story, as readers or as writers, it's sometimes hard to fully explain our reaction. Why do some stories, essays, or poems pull us close while others keep us at arm's length? And how can we learn to monitor psychic distance in our own work?

Besides altering a work's point of view (a subject we dealt with earlier), the most obvious way to establish and control psychic distance is to alter the physical distance between the subjects we describe and ourselves—or, if we're employing a character-narrator, between the character and the subject being described. In *Rich in Love*, Josephine Humphreys uses physical distance to shape her descriptions while also revealing emotional changes in her narrator, a teenaged girl named Lucille.

Early in the novel, Lucille is helping her father repair the roof on the family home. On the lawn below, Lucille's older sister, Rae, lies on her back sunbathing. As Lucille watches, Rae's new husband approaches, and it soon becomes clear that Rae and Billy are preparing to move, as Lucille's father describes it, into "that honeymoon stage" that "looks possibly explosive." Lucille watches the scene at a psychic distance that mirrors her physical distance. At this point in the story, her new brother-in-law is, to Lucille, just another man, a man whose motives for marrying her sister are suspect. Lucille's description of the scene is almost clinical in its factual reporting.

> Billy's shoes looked like some kind of military boots, heavy-soled and old, stiff as wood. With one toe he nudged her side. Her arm was as fast as a sprung trap, grabbing the boot and twisting it as she rolled her body. Billy was off guard. Rae rolled into the grass with his foot in her hands, and he fell next to her.

Later in the book, Lucille realizes not only that Billy's motives toward her sister are pure but also that he is exactly the kind of man she herself could love. As the physical distance between her and Billy shortens, the psychic distance shortens as well.

> I admit it had once crossed my mind that he had gotten Rae pregnant on purpose in order to marry her. But suddenly I could see that he was not that sort of person. I saw it only now because I had not been close to him before. Now with his face two feet from mine in the moonlight, I saw the planes of his cheeks, the wrinkle between his eyes, telling what kind of person he was: one that can lose himself to another.

If you want the reader to feel intimately related to your subject, try a close-up shot. Describe the character, object, or scene as if it were positioned directly in front of your eyes, close enough to touch. Let the reader see the hand-etched signature on the bottom of the wooden bowl or the white strip on the divorcee's finger where a wedding ring once lay. Let him smell the heaviness of the milking barn after a night of rain and hear the squeak of the farmer's rubber boots. If you want to get even closer, take the reader inside a character's body and let him experience her world—the reeling nausea of Lydia's first morning sickness, the tenderness of her breasts, the metallic taste in her mouth—from the inside out.

Then, when you need to establish distance, to remove the reader from the scene as Shirley Jackson does in "The Lottery," pull back. Describe your object from a great distance. The wooden bowl is no longer a handcrafted, hand-signed original, or if it is, you can't tell from where you are standing. The pregnant woman is no longer Lydia-of-the-tender-breasts; she's one of dozens of other faceless women seated in the waiting room of the county clinic.

As you vary the physical distance between the describer and the subjects being described, you may find that your personal connection with your subjects is altered. Physical closeness often equates with emotional closeness. Consider how it is possible that kind and loving men (like my father, who served in three wars) are capable of dropping bombs on "enemy" villages. One factor is their physical distance from their targets. The scene changes dramatically when they face a villager eye to eye; no longer is the enemy a tiny dot darting beneath the shadow of their planes or a blip on the radar screen. No, this "enemy" has black hair flecked with auburn and a scar over her left eyebrow; she's younger than the wives they left behind.

If you sense that your story calls for a closer, more sympathetic attitude toward the subjects you're describing, try positioning yourself closer to them. The angle of your position is as important as the distance between you and your subject. The psychic distance we feel when Lucille is on the roof, looking down on her sister and brother-in-law, is due in part to her position—a physically superior one. At this point in the story she is wary of Billy's motives, and her stance of judgment matches her bodily stance. But when she stands eye to eye with him, she is on equal footing: one human being to another. Positioning ourselves physically and psychologically on the same plane with our subjects can help us avoid what Gardner refers to as "frigidity" in our writing, one of the "faults of soul" he warns against. Frigidity is coldhearted failure to respond on a deep, human level to the characters and events of our story.

Sometimes, however, our stories require us to view our subjects from an ironic distance. In the passage from the novel *The Bonfire of the Vanities* quoted in chapter six, Tom Wolfe describes his character's wife from a very unflattering angle. Actually, it's not the *wife* we meet but rather her broad backside looming huge in its flannel gown as she crawls to the edge of the bed—hardly the way most of us would wish to be publicly introduced. This description, like others in Wolfe's novel, signals that the author is viewing his characters with irony.

If you find you're so personally involved with your subjects that you're unable to describe them effectively, it may be time to step back and view the big picture. This repositioning will provide a fresh perspective on your subject, suggesting possibilities for humor, irony, or even pathos, qualities that may have been previously missing from your description.

Temporal positioning is another technique for manipulating psychic distance in our writing. Setting a story in a time or place far removed from ours can distance our reader psychologically from the story's events. Although some writers of fantasy or historical fiction manage to pull us close to the human drama, for the most part, the further our story is removed in space and time, the more psychic distance our readers will feel. "Once upon a time," begins James Thurber's *The Princess and the Tin Box*, "in a far country ..."

Reading his first words, we escape to the never-never land of fairy tales—to a time that never was and a place like nothing we've ever known. As the story continues, Thurber maintains his fairy tale distance through simple diction and formal, balanced sentences—no syntactic pyrotechnics here. His rhythms are the timeworn rhythms of the campfire storyteller or the parent lulling a restless child to sleep.

> ... there lived a king whose daughter was the prettiest princess in the world. Her eyes were like the cornflower, her hair was sweeter than the hyacinth, and her throat made the swan look dusty.

Although Thurber's language is simple and straightforward, his similes soar to hyperbole. This is no ordinary daughter. She's a princess! And not just any princess. This princess is so beautiful she puts even the most brilliant natural beauties—cornflower, hyacinth, and swan—to shame. Because Thurber describes her in idealized, unrealistic terms, we sense that this is not a drama we will enter fully. It is, we begin to see, not a drama at all but a fable whose distant tone is sustained by the elements Thurber so skillfully employs: first, the faraway setting of time and place; then the carefully measured prose of the formal storyteller; and finally, the creation of characters who emerge not as living, breathing entities but rather as props to support the fable. Thurber effectively manipulates psychic distance to keep us at arm's length from the story, which is precisely the proper distance a fable requires.

Finding the proper psychic distance for a literary work is one of the most essential tasks a writer performs. And nowhere is this task more crucial than in personal essays or autobiographical works in which the author himself becomes a character on the page. As we mentioned in chapter seven, you might choose to be the main character or a peripheral narrator/character telling someone else's story, but whatever stance you choose, the reader will be affected by the psychic distance from which you view events and characters, including yourself. Most readers—and I include myself here—react negatively to a nonfiction narrator who places himself above other characters, makes himself the hero of the story, or otherwise seems unwilling or unable to achieve the reflective distance necessary to most autobiographical works. As Judith Barrington notes in *Writing the Memoir*, "... I must know that the writer is all right. ... There must be no hidden plea for help—no subtle seeking of sympathy. The writer must have done her work, made her peace with the facts, and be telling the story for the story's sake."

SOMETHING AFOOT: THEME, IDEA, AND DESIGN

Talking about theme always makes me edgy. I never liked writing the "themes" my junior high school teachers assigned, those weekly compositions I plumped and padded—how do you say five hundred words about nothing?—then recopied in standard black ink onto college-ruled sheets. When I entered high school, the beast of theme shape-shifted as I was forced to memorize the four basic themes of literature (man vs. man, man vs. nature, man vs. society, man vs. himself) and to apply them to whatever novel or short story our English class was studying. An avid reader since kindergarten, after three years of deciphering theme I was unable to enter even the most compelling story without hearing the theme-beast huffing menacingly in my ear.

I escaped to college, hoping to fall back into the fictional dream. But the theme-beast was waiting for me at the classroom door. More ferocious than ever, he now sported horns, a tail, and a thick leathery hide. "Using D.H. Lawrence's 'The Horse Dealer's Daughter,'" he hissed, "trace the theme of man's destiny as it relates to love. Cite passages to back up your thesis, but include only those elements of characterization, setting, plot, and imagery that support your discussion of theme."

It took me many years to understand that theme was a naturally occurring element of any successful story or poem and not just a concept English teachers had invented to frustrate me. I came to see how theme shaped the big picture, as did atmosphere and tone, those other literary beasts that had stalked my past. Reading back over my work, I was astounded to discover that even *my* stories and poems had themes that had emerged naturally from my descriptions of characters, settings, and events.

In our earlier discussion we referred to atmosphere as the "something in the air" that contributes to the big picture. Theme can also be defined as "something in the air," though I prefer to think of theme not as the feeling or mood that floats around the edges of the story, but rather as "something afoot," the hidden pattern that lies beneath a story's surface. Theme is the underside of the weaving, the design we may not see until we turn the story over.

We don't have to, of course. Like a beautifully woven shawl, a story, an essay, or a poem can be appreciated simply for its surface beauty and for the warmth it provides. We don't have to turn the story over and admire the warp and woof, the underlying arrangement of color, line, and pattern woven beneath its surface. But if we do, we may discover another design, one as fascinating as the surface design of character, setting, and plot that first caught our eye.

The main theme or idea of a literary work may also reveal itself as an echo, like the musical theme that underscores a motion picture, its tune resurfacing now and again with slight variations. In William Faulkner's *As I Lay Dying*, one of the recurring musical themes is the song of Cash's saw as he builds his mother's coffin. At different points in the book, almost every character describes the sound of the saw, each in his own voice and with his own inimitable rhythms. Jewel describes the sound as "that godamn adze going One lick less. One lick less." Cora says simply, "It sounds like snoring." And Darl's description is heightened by Faulkner's placement of the words on the page.

> I go on to the house, followed by the
>   Chuck. Chuck. Chuck.
> of the adze.

In chapter three we spoke of taking pains to describe the things in your story, of performing the menial tasks that convince the reader that characters, places, objects, and events actually exist within the literary world you create. Sometimes these tasks feel repetitive, for any successful piece of writing is a result of small, cumulative strokes. It's not enough to say something once and be done with it, trusting that the reader will remember the detail and attach meaning to it. Thus Faulkner doesn't stop with one description of the saw, or even with two or three. He weaves one description after another into the fabric of the story so that a pattern begins to emerge. The saw takes on a life of its own, moving from the realm of isolated image to the realm of motif.

Like a repeated scroll in an architectural design or a significant phrase in a musical composition, the noise of the saw contributes to the story's overall design. Sometimes pages go by before Faulkner mentions the saw again; sometimes whole chapters. Between descriptions of the saw the story progresses, and for a while we forget about the coffin Cash is building. Then suddenly there it is again: the sound of the saw in the background, reminding us that, yes, the coffin *will* get finished and yes, the family *will* eventually bury Addie.

A motif often suggests the underlying idea of a story, an essay, or a poem. In chapter nine we discussed O'Connor's use of the hat motif in "Everything That Rises Must Converge." The hat was not the theme of the story; rather, it was the recurring element that not only moved the plot along but also suggested the theme of reversal and loss. An image that appears and reappears in a literary work is like a colored thread in a weaving. It is not the whole design, but it is an organizing element, and if we follow its path we can trace how the larger design is formed.

Sometimes the motif is revealed through chapter titles or other organizational elements. The main ideas and themes of E. Annie Proulx's novel *The Shipping News* are woven chiefly through chapter titles that suggest mariners' knots ("Love Knot," "The Mooring Hitch," "Strangle Knot") and by the descriptions that accompany each term. In the same way, the theme of Terry Tempest Williams's *Refuge: An Unnatural History of Family and Place* is shaped by section headings named for birds ("Whistling Swan," "Red-Shafted Flicker") associated with the Great Salt Lake.

A snake is the visual motif that slides in and out of a story by Ervin D. Krause. "The Snake" is brief, no more than 2,600 words, but Krause's descriptions of the snake comprise about a third of the story, and each description pulls the story's theme a bit tighter. The narrator is an unnamed man plowing a field with a tractor. The other character is his eleven-year-old nephew (also unnamed) who is described as having blue eyes and "finely spun blonde hair and a smooth and still effeminate face"—in short, the picture of innocence.

When the snake first appears in the field's furrow, the man stops the tractor to avoid hitting the snake. After conceding that he'd never much liked snakes, and as a child had even killed them, he goes on to describe this particular snake as "clean and bright and very beautiful." When the snake refuses to move, the man gets off the tractor and follows the snake, intrigued by its beauty,

> ... the brilliant colors on its tubular back, the colors clear and sharp and perfect, in orange and green and brown diamonds the size of a baby's fist down its back, and the diamonds were set one within the other and interlaced with glistening jet-black ...

The man picks up the snake, caressing it with his hand, which "usually tanned and dark" looked "pale beside it." He speaks with reverence to the snake, swearing that "I couldn't kill you. You are much too beautiful." He is amazed at how strikingly the colors of the snake contrast with the black earth and his own pale skin. It's difficult not to notice the suggestion of Eden's paradise in Krause's descriptions: newly turned soil, warm morning, pale hands, a beautiful snake with a forked tongue. Having rescued the snake, the man retreats into blissful innocence, feeling "good and satisfied."

But as we all know, paradise never lasts, and when the snake's "sharp, burning colors" are described as standing out against the soil "like a target," we know the end is near. What surprises us, though, is that it is the smiling blue-eyed boy who bears the "fierce mark of brutality," stomping the snake to death. The man, astounded and angered by the boy's action, reprimands him: "This snake was very beautiful. Didn't you see how beautiful it was?"

Yes, the snake was beautiful. *Was.* What a difference the past-tense verb makes. Eden is no more, as Krause's next description shows.

> The fire of the colors was gone; there was a contorted ugliness now; the colors of its back were dull and gray-looking, torn and smashed in, and

dirty from the boy's shoes. The beautifully-tapered head, so delicate and so cool, had been flattened as if in a vise, and the forked tongue splayed out of the twisted, torn mouth.

Because the ending of the story is so wrenching, an ending every reader should experience for himself, I won't divulge it except to say that the snake, though dead, will continue to shape the story's outcome. And the motif of the snake, sliding in and out of view, will eventually lead us to turn the story over and view its underlying theme: Every person, however young or innocent, old or wise, is capable of evil that can forever reshape landscapes, turning even the palest hands a guilty red.

In the early stages of drafting a work, it's probably best not to focus on issues of theme and overall design. "One world at a time," wrote Thoreau, and most writers would agree. It takes concentration, energy, and imagination simply to describe the world of the story without worrying about what the story looks like underneath. To keep the literary dream alive, we must first train our eye on the people, places, objects, and events of the story, describing what we see. If we proceed backwards, focusing first on the theme of the story or on other structural elements, we risk writing a story no one will want to read. Yes, the underside of the shawl might be intricately woven, but if no one picks it up, if no one throws it over her shoulders, what good is it? The surfaces of our weaving must be durable and beautiful; the story must come first.

THE BIG EAR

If we had a keen vision and feeling of all ordinary human life, it would be like hearing the grass grow and the squirrel's heart beat and we should die of that roar which lies on the other side of silence. —George Eliot, from *Middlemarch*

Throughout this book we've stressed the importance of paying attention to the world around us and training our eyes to see the world in new ways. But attention is also accomplished through the ears; the French *attention* means "to listen." In the title story of Robin Hemley's collection *The Big Ear*, a twelve-year-old boy orders a listening device from a gag catalog (the boy is fond of gag items and employs them often on his unsuspecting victims). When the boy aims the Big Ear in the direction of an object or a person, the sound from the object is amplified. Even situated far from his subject, the boy can eavesdrop on conversations and hear sounds a naked ear could never detect, such as the "dry rattle, then a crumbling sound" of dead leaves being stripped from a branch. The Big Ear can even penetrate windows and walls.

For a long time after I read Hemley's story, I couldn't stop thinking about the boy and his Big Ear. At first I simply enjoyed being in the boy's company, laughing at his brazen antics—what gall! But the more I listened in on the world his Big Ear amplified, the more sympathy I felt for the boy. (One mark of a successful comic story is when you find yourself laughing and crying at the same time.) At one point I wanted to climb into the pages of the book, kiss the boy's forehead the way his babysitter had, and murmur words of comfort. "Yes," I would whisper, "sometimes we hear things we don't want to hear, things a child shouldn't hear, and it changes us for the rest of our lives."

Later, when my reader self left and my writer self appeared (and quick on her heels, my teacher self, God save us all), the Big Ear seemed to lift from the page and float in the space above my head. No longer simply a contraption a boy ordered from a catalog, it had transformed into symbol. As I mentioned earlier, I'm not overly fond of symbols. Too often they're merely grafted onto a story or poem, and the seams show. But when symbols grow naturally from the world of the real—in this case, the concrete and sensory world of which Hemley's story is made—I let them have their say.

Here's what this symbol said: Writers need to grow the Big Ear. We need it to hear the world around us, especially those small sounds that too often get drowned out. With a Big Ear, we can penetrate the walls of our characters' homes, overhear what they're saying not only to their wives and daughters but also to themselves. We can eavesdrop on secrets, the natural and man-made mysteries usually withheld from us.

Aimed in the right direction and focused to a concentrated point, the Big Ear can also silence the noise of the world—the verbal hysteria of radio and television and Internet, the babble of advertisers, even the numbing chatter of what the Chinese call the "monkey mind" inside each of us. If we can silence the chatter, clear our internal airwaves, we will be more able to hear the voice of the poem, story, or essay whispering its secret. As writers, we need to find ways to live within the silence, rather than always filling it up with noise, music, words—even those written words we labor so hard to produce. As Nietzsche wrote, "The author must keep his mouth shut when his work starts to speak."

Yet even when we're able to silence the white noise and to train our attention on our subject—the physical world or the world of the imagination—we may not receive a clear message. At one point in "The Big Ear," the boy thought he heard a man ask, "Are you going to salad control tonight?" As writers, sometimes all we can make out is a tone, a feeling, a mere approximation of sense. It may appear as static, a distant drone, a rumble, or a screech. When questioned about her creative process, Flannery O'Connor answered that no, she never heard voices, only "something that might be a continuing muttering snarl like cats courting under the house."

Occasionally, however, the voice will come through loud and clear. Too clear. Our main character begins speaking in a voice that turns the whole story on its head, canceling out everything that's gone before and sending us back, emptied, to the writing desk. Or our theme, our message, what we thought we knew without a doubt, begins to whisper its secret. It's what we most feared: Truth, with a capital *T.* Mother Truth having her say—surrounded by all the little truths, her lowercase children, biting and scratching and tugging at our sleeves. We had thought we'd slide through this one, an easy in and out, no one gets hurt, then suddenly the story is dusting for prints and they're ours. Description has tricked us into telling the truth not only about our world but also about ourselves.

The Big Ear is a necessary tool for anyone attempting to describe the physical world or the world of the imagination. It helps concentrate our attention, block out distractions, and provide access to the mysteries hidden beneath the surface. But these gifts are not granted free and clear. In exchange, we must pay the price of increased awareness. Like the boy in "The Big Ear," we may overhear what we could have happily done without, something that changes forever the way we navigate our world.

In giving our attention to the thing itself—the sight or smell or taste or sound or texture—we may forget to say what we originally thought we wanted, or needed, to say, some thought or purpose that probably calcified years ago. We become so involved in bringing forth the qualities of the thing itself that we are thrown headlong into the present moment. The roar, the squeak, the corduroy, the itch of it so fully consumes us that we can't stop to think of what it all means—or what our inner censors have warned us not to say. We no longer have to struggle to force breath into our description. Suddenly it gasps and sputters. It begins to breathe on its own.

EXERCISES

1. As an experiment in varying the rhythms and duration of your sentences or poetry lines, write what I call a "grammatical rhyme" modeled on another writer's words. In a grammatical rhyme, you imitate the rhythmic and syntactic structures of a piece while using your own words. Don't worry about reproducing the sense of the passage; pay attention only to the structure of the lines. Here's a brief passage from Richard Selzer's essay "Four Appointments with the Discus Thrower," followed by my imitation of Selzer's syntactic structures.

   > In the evening, I go once more to that ward to make my rounds. The head nurse reports to me that Room 542 is deceased. She has discovered this quite by accident, she says. No, there had been no sound. Nothing. It's a blessing, she says.
   >
   > In my dream, I stumble yet again over the weeds to get to him. The doggy moon barks to me that my boy is gone. "I have sniffed it through my nose," it says. "Yes, there will be no boy. Never. That's the end," it barks.

2. A variation of exercise 1 is to type, or write out in longhand, a passage of prose you admire for its style. One August, mired in my own syntactic rut, I typed several chapters of *War and Peace*. After stretching my literary muscles in this way, I was limbered up enough to try some paragraphs of my own.

3. Write a brief physical description of someone you know. In the first version, use lots of deep vowel tones (long o, long u) and liquid or resonant consonants (r, l, w, y, m, n, ng, z). Then rewrite the description, changing the deep vowels to light vowels (short i, short a). Finally, rewrite it using harsh consonants (k, r, p, hard g, hard c) or sibilants (s, sh, ch). Notice how the tone of the description changes depending on the sound qualities of your language.

4. In chapter two I suggested wearing headphones or earbuds as you walk the same route in your neighborhood several times, varying the style of music on each trip to help you visualize the scene in different ways. This same exercise works to musically "color" the scene and help you vary the tone of

your description. For instance, if you walk past the schoolyard while listening to Louis Gottschalk's "Cakewalk," you'll get a different feeling than you'll get while listening to Edward Elgar's "Pomp and Circumstance"; one composition is comical, almost slapstick in its energy, while the other is dignified and layered with sentimental associations. Like the tones of the musical compositions, the tones of your two descriptions will also be vastly different from each other, affected by the musical score playing beneath the scene.

5. Write an opening paragraph that evokes the atmosphere of a particular scene. Begin with the basics of setting—the where and when. Then add lighting, sound effects, weather, and any sensory detail that will contribute to the mood you want the reader to experience. Refer to the passage from "The Fall of the House of Usher" as an example.

6. Sometimes the weather in our story or poem cooperates *too* fully with the story's events, resulting in a hackneyed description: the wedding morning (of course it's a June morning) blooms sunny and mild; the day of the funeral is cold and gray. Try describing an event with weather details that work *against* the mood or tone most readers expect.

7. If a character in your story is one-dimensional (purely evil, for instance, or too good to be true) change the physical distance or angle from which you describe him. Move in for a close-up on your villain, showing us an endearing personal trait, or describe your hero from far away or from a physical stance that will reveal his all-too-human proportions. Use the same technique for an autobiographical work in which you appear as a character.

8. In chapter nine I suggested that you break a long description into several smaller sections and then sprinkle these sections throughout the story, the way O'Connor sprinkled hat images throughout "Everything That Rises Must Converge." Try the same technique with a sound image—like the sound of the saw in Faulkner's *As I Lay Dying* or the sound of motorcycles in Mary Hood's story "How Far She Went." Start by writing a long description of a sound important to your story—ocean waves, a baby's cry, footsteps, rustling leaves. Then break the description into three or more short passages.

Plant these passages into different parts of the story so the sound image becomes an echo, the recurring musical theme that plays beneath the storyline.

9. In *This Wild Darkness: The Story of My Death*, Harold Brodkey writes, "True stories, autobiographical stories, like some novels, begin long ago, before the acts in the account, before the birth of some of the people in the tale." As an exercise in psychic distance, write an autobiographical piece that begins a month (or a year, or a hundred years) before you were born, or that extends past your death.

10. Experiment with altering psychic distance by rewriting a story, an essay, or a poem using the conventions of a literary genre very different from the original—for instance, as a fairy tale, a science fiction story, a Harlequin Romance, a sports report, a travelogue, a satire, an allegory, or a children's story. Notice how the descriptions change to reflect the genre.

11. As an exercise in thematic design, choose a pattern or template from literature, commerce, art, music, contemporary culture, or from any occupation or discipline that interests you. Then either employ that pattern as the shaping device or incorporate the pattern into your piece in some way. For example, Ellen Morris Prewitt uses the structure of a movie script, complete with various retakes, in her memoir-essay "Snow Melts Either Way"; Nancy Willard uses tarot cards in her essay "The Friendship Tarot"; Susanna Kaysen uses bits of charts, hospital forms, and interoffice memoranda in her memoir *Girl, Interrupted*.

End Notes, Toward a Beginning

This book began with a description of apples in a glass bowl on my table. Those apples are long gone. Some were devoured straight from the bowl. The less perfect ones were stuffed with raisins and stewed. Others were sliced, dusted with sugar and flour and nutmeg, dotted with butter, and folded beneath a fluted crust. A few never made it to mouth or oven. While I wasn't looking, their bodies turned soft and heavily fragrant, bruising from the inside out. I carried them to the garden and laid them on the compost heap.

Now as I prepare to send the book on its way, I reread my words, recalling those two or three descriptions that were delivered into my hand polished and whole. I remember the flawed ones, too, the sentences that simmered forever in their own juices, and the lumpy, sour paragraphs I peeled and sliced, sweetened and seasoned, baked and fried and dried and pureed—how many ways can you spell *apple*?

I'd expected that when the time came to release the words I'd feel proud but sad, reluctant but relieved, the way I always feel sending a book out into the world, the way I felt walking my niece to the bus stop for her first day of school. "Go on," I said, shooing her toward the bus. "You're a big girl. Up the steps, now."

And, yes, I feel all those things, just as I'd expected. What surprises me is not my feelings for the words I'm sending off but rather my eagerness to return to the compost bin. The descriptions I tossed aside, the words that never made it into the book, are already storing up heat. Having been returned to the Eden of their beginnings (*seed*, *core*, *juice*, *skin*), they wait to be resurrected in a new form.

When asked which of his many poems was his favorite, William Stafford replied, "I would exchange everything I've written for the next one." Writing is not about endings. Writing is about how nothing is ever lost—not even the clichés we excise or the mixed metaphors that arrive, like feuding guests, at the same party, and must be shown to the door. The words I tossed into the compost bin—the description of my second-grade teacher Miss Ranney, who wore a silky blonde bun skewered with chopsticks and whose stocking seams were always straight; the joke about the farmer and the cow; the chapter that refused to roll over and die no matter how hard I tried to kill it—wait to be reborn in a new story, poem, or essay. In the beginning was the word. Some things never change.

Index

Abstractions, describing, 55–60, 84–86, 89
Ackerman, Diane, 69, 72
Action, 2, 56–57, 63, 215
  illusion of, 9–10, 215
  in narration, objective, 177–178
  and pace, 217–220
  slowing, 218–219
Adams, Gail Galloway, 76–78
Adjectives, 16, 36, 53, 64, 237
  character, 129–130
  sensory, 69–70, 73, 79
Adverbs, 54, 64
Allegory, 111–112
"Amazons," 137, 151
"American Man at Age Ten, The," 139
Analogy, 111
Animism, 110–111, 120
Aristotle, 8–9, 40–42, 44, 47, 57, 92, 142, 145, 215
As I Lay Dying, 69, 84, 156, 249–250, 257
Atmosphere, 75, 236–239, 257
Attitude, 240–241, 245
Austen, Jane, 179–180
"Autopsy Report," 96–97
Baldwin, James, 198, 214–216
Beauty, describing, 26–28, 35
Beckett, Wendy, Sister, 23
Bergman, Ingmar, 103–104
Berne, Suzanne, 54, 137
Berriault, Gina, 108

Betts, Doris, 182
"Big Ear, The," 252–255
"Blue," 78–79, 90, 102
Bonfire of the Vanities, The, 147, 246
Bowers, Cathy Smith, 110, 116
Bradbury, Ray, 194
"Bread," 41–42
Bright Lights, Big City, 173–174
Brothers and Keepers, 118
Brox, Jane, 41–42, 192
"Camouflaging the Chimera," 171
Capote, Truman, 22, 161–162
Cather, Willa, 168, 170
Character, description, 123–151
  action in, 141–144, 150
  composite, 136
  detail in, 130–131
  direct vs. indirect, 140–141
  exercises, 149–151
  existential problem in, 145–146
  group, 136–137, 151
  inner life in, 140, 144–148, 150, 229–231
  inside-out method of, 167–168
  mirror technique, 167–168
  naming, 125–128, 149
  physical, 129–134
  real-life, 134–136, 151
  sensory, 133–134, 149
  and setting, 137–140, 142, 149–150
  verb usage, 142–143

Chase, Joan, 52, 70–71, 160
Chekhov, Anton, 85
Child's eye, 30–32
Cleaver, Eldridge, 55–57
Cliché, 2, 27–28, 47, 260
    character, 129–130
    escaping, 79, 91, 114
    metaphor, 113–114
Coleridge, Samuel Taylor, 97–98
Color, describing, 45, 64
Conceit, 112
Conrad, Joseph, 48, 197–198, 211
"Cookies, The," 71–72
Crace, Jim, 40, 200–203
Crime in the Neighborhood, A, 137, 151
Detail, 39-41, 57–60, 63, 183–185
Devices, filtering, 50–51
Dickens, Charles, 180
Dillard, Annie, 23–24, 135
Dodsworth, 199–200
Doerr, Harriet, 83–84
Donnée, 20, 35
Dreams, 32–35, 141
Durban, Pam, 52–53
During the Reign of the Queen of Persia, 52, 70–71, 160
Eavesdropping: A Memoir of Blindness and Listening, 72, 223–224
Emotion, 55–57, 63–65
Essays, 86–87, 135–136, 156, 160, 223
"Everything That Rises Must Converge," 225–227, 233, 250, 257
Exposition, 6, 178–181, 213–214
    exercises, 210, 232
    and setting, 204–206, 210
Eye of Madame X, The, 76–78
"Fall of the House of Usher, The," 237–238, 257
Faulkes Chronicles, The, 172
Faulkner, William, 69, 84, 156, 171, 249–250, 257
Figures of speech, 2, 9, 40, 57, 92–95, 109–113
    See also under specific figure of speech
Fitzgerald, F. Scott, 169, 238–239, 243
Flashback, 149, 220–222, 233
Flaubert, Gustave, 131, 139–140, 161

"Flood," 196–197
Forster, E.M., 26, 192, 194
"Four Appointments with the Discus Thrower," 256
Frost, Robert, 110
Gaillard, Frye, 35, 107
Gift of Stones, The, 40, 64, 200–203
Gilmore, Mikal, 141
Gliding eye, 28–30
Go Tell It on the Mountain, 198, 214–216, 232
Great Gatsby, The, 83, 169, 238–239
Greene, Melissa Fay, 147–148
Hampl, Patricia, 53
Haskins, Lola, 109
Hemingway, Ernest, 175, 229–231, 233
Hemley, Robin, 252–253
"Hills Like White Elephants," 175, 229–231, 233
Holy the Firm, 24
Hood, Mary, 70, 79–82
Hopkins, Gerard Manley, 22–24
Housekeeping, 142–143
"How Far She Went," 70, 79–80
Huddle, David, 172
Humphreys, Josephine, 244
Hurd, Barbara, 19
Hurston, Zora Neale, 92–94, 97
Hyperbole, 109, 120, 247
Ideas, describing, 55–57
Imagination, 18–24, 30, 36
    gift of perhaps, the, 19, 139, 150, 204
    and metaphor, 97–98
Ingalls, Rachel, 195
Ingenious Pain, 103, 132, 149
"Inheritance of Tools, The," 45, 65
Ironic distance, 246
Jackson, Shirley, 176, 245
"Jesus Flag, The," 109
Joseph, Allison, 52
Journals, keeping, 33–35, 88
Joy Luck Club, The, 89, 204–206
Joyce, James, 183, 222
Kate Vaiden, 168, 187
Keyes, Daniel, 165
Kitchen, Judith, 78–79, 90, 102

Komunyakaa, Yusef, 171
Kooser, Ted, 101
Krause, Ervin D., 250–251
Kundera, Milan, 145
Kunitz, Stanley, 99
Kupfer, Fern, 19
Kuusisto, Stephen, 72, 223–224
"Lady with the Pet Dog, The," 85
Language, musical, 2, 8, 11–12, 78, 102, 238–239
    See also Word, sound
"Late July 4:40 A.M.," 29–30, 47
Letters on Cézanne, 25–26, 45
Lewis, Sinclair, 199-200
"Long Rain, The," 194–195
Lopate, Phillip, 135, 151, 223
Lorde, Audre, 15–16
"Lottery, The," 176, 245
"Love, Death, and the Ladies' Drill Team,"
    184–185
"Love, The," 110–111
Loving Eye, The, 227–229
Lowry, Beverly, 170
Maclean, Norman, 48
MacLeod, James Lewis, 109
Madame Bovary, 139–140, 161, 189
Madness of a Seduced Woman, The, 146
Markers, positional, 197–198, 204, 211
Maron, Margaret, 190
McAfee, Tom, 165
McInerney, Jay, 173–174
"McKenzie River, The," 43–44, 64
Meditation, 24–25
Memoir, 135–136, 141, 170, 223–224
    exercise, 234
Memory, 20–22, 35
Metaphor, 9, 40, 91–109, 115, 118, 260
    and abstraction, 55–57
    character-inspired, 108
    cliché, 113–114
    and constellation of images, 99–101, 121–
    122, 239
    exercises, 107–108, 119, 121
    extending a, 101–106
    far-fetched, 114, 119

implied, 96–97, 119–120
mixed, 117, 119, 260
original, 97–102
sensory, 77, 82
vs. simile, 95–97
tenor, 94, 96, 112
vehicle, 94, 96, 112
word choice, 117
Metonymy, 111
Miller, Andrew, 103, 132–133
Monet, Claude, 28–29, 101–102
Monologue, internal, 182
Mood, 11, 236–237, 243, 257
Moore, Kathleen Dean, 43–44, 64
Morrison, Toni, 110
Motifs, 101, 225–227, 250–252
Mrs. Caliban, 195–196
Music, 36, 236–239
    See also Language, musical; Word, sound
My Ántonia, 169–170
Nabokov, Vladimir, 83
Naming, character, 125–128, 149
Naming, of things, 41–48
    accuracy, 43–44
    back-door technique, 47–49
    musical, 46–47
    and sensory description, 77
    significance of, 44–46
Narrative line, 10, 213–216, 220
Natural History of the Senses, A, 69, 72–73
Negation, technique of, 47–49
"No Place for You, My Love," 206–208
Nouns, 16, 41, 49
Nye, Naomi Shihab, 71
O'Brien, Tim, 85, 89, 132, 191
Objects, 62–65, 121
Observation, 7, 15–17
O'Connor, Flannery, 59, 225–227, 233, 250,
    254, 257
O'Keeffe, Georgia, 38–39, 42, 58, 83, 121
Ondaatje, Michael, 189
Onomatopoeia, 80, 90
Orlean, Susan, 139
Pace, changing, 10, 216–220, 232
    action, 217–220

flashback, 220–221
  verb tense, 219–220
Paradox, 111, 120–121
Peck, Gail, 196–197
Personification, 109–110, 120
Photographs, 132, 149
Plot, 10, 212–213
  psychological, 229–231
  thought as, 223–224
  unifying, 225–227
Plumly, Stanley, 19
Poe, Edgar Allan, 46, 112, 189, 237–238, 243
Point of view, 10, 152–187
  dramatic, 174
  establishing, 154–157
  exercises, 35, 186–187
  more than one, 156
  scenic, 174
  settling into, 160–161
  shifts, 10, 35, 157–163, 182, 186
Point of view, first person, 153, 155–156, 163–172, 186–187
  main character, 166–169
  peripheral, 167–171
  plural, 171–173
Point of view, second person, 154, 173–174
Point of view, third person, 154–156
  objective, 154, 161–163, 174–183, 187, 229, 233
  omniscient, 154, 178–181, 187
  omniscient, limited, 154–158, 161–163, 181–186
Positioning, temporal, 246
Praying for Sheetrock: A Work of Nonfiction, 147–148, 150
Price, Reynolds, 168, 187
Pride and Prejudice, 179–180
Princess and the Tin Box, The, 246–247
"Prodigy, The," 109
Proofs, 145, 158, 193, 208, 225, 227
  auditory, 82
  descriptive, 131–132
  explained, 10, 59
  sensory, 77, 80, 193–194, 200–201, 203, 206, 208, 227

Prose, active, 49–50
Proust, Marcel, 73–74, 89
Psychic distance, 159, 169, 176, 241
  controlling, 243–248
  exercise, 258
Purpura, Lia, 96–97
Raising the Dead: A Doctor's Encounter with His Own Mortality, 27–28
"Raven, The," 46, 112
Reader, engaging the, 60–62
Refuge: An Unnatural History of Family and Place, 234, 250
Remembrance of Things Past, 73–74
Research, 43–44, 64, 132, 211
  and metaphor, 105–106
Rhodes, Richard, 87
Rhyme, grammatical, 256
Rich in Love, 244–246
Rilke, Rainer Maria, 25–26, 45, 64
Robinson, Marilynne, 142–143
Running in the Family, 189–190
Sanders, Scott Russell, 45, 65
Saner, Reg, 29–30, 47
Sansom, William, 227–229
Scene, 213–216, 232
Scenic event, illusion of, 215–216, 232
Schaeffer, Susan Fromberg, 146
"Secret Sharer, The," 48, 197–198, 211
Selzer, Richard, 27, 137, 256
Sensory description, 2, 7, 9–10, 66–90, 215–216
  atmospheric, 75
  character, 133–134, 149
  exercises, 88–90, 149, 211
  mixed, 74, 89
  muted, 71
  setting, 199–200
  smell, 67–72, 133–134
  sound, 78–82 (*see also* Word, sound)
  synesthesia, 82–84, 89
  taste, 72–75
  touch, 41, 76–78
  verb usage, 53
Sentence, rhythm, 8, 29, 57, 150, 241–243, exercise, 256

Setting, 188–211
  and character, 137–140, 142
  exercises, 209–211
  and exposition, 204–206, 210
  in fantasy, science fiction and magic realism, 194–196
  historical, 200–204
  introducing, 196–197
  organizing, 196–200
  and narration, 204–206
  real-life, 192–193
  sensory description, 199–200
  and theme, 206–208
  See also Atmosphere
Shakespeare, William, 47
"Sidekick," 102
Similes, 9, 92, 109, 115, 118, 247
  exercise, 119–120
  vs. metaphor, 95–97
  sensory, 77
Singer, Peter, 86
"Snake, The," 250–252
Sondheim, Stephen, 123–124
Soul on Ice, 55–57, 64
Statements, direct, 84, 86–87, 90
"Still Life with Fruit," 182, 187
Stones for Ibarra, 83–84
Story of Painting, The, 23
Stream of consciousness, 182–183, 187
Subjects, moving vs. static, 39–41
Suffixes, 55
Summary, 213–216, 232
Suspense, 217, 233
Symbols, 112–113
Synecdoche, 111
Syntax, 7, 46, 49–50, 239
"Tale, The," 21–22
Tan, Amy, 89, 192, 204–206, 210
Tar Baby, 109–110
Tennyson, Alfred, 115
Tension, creating, 10, 217, 219, 227–229, 233
Their Eyes Were Watching God, 93–95
Theme, 11, 248–252, 254, 258
  recurring, 249–250, 257–258
  and setting, 206–208

"Things They Carried, The," 85, 132
Third eye, 22–25
"This Heat," 52–53
"This is My Living Room," 165
Thurber, James, 246–247
"To Fashion a Text," 134–135
Tolkien, J.R.R., 194
Tone, 11, 240–248, 256–257
  and psychic distance, 243–248
Transitions, 11, 187, 216–218
"Tree of Night, A," 161–162
"Tryst, The," 49, 159
Turgenev, Ivan, 49, 159
Ugliness, describing, 25–28, 35
Ulysses, 183, 187, 222
Unbearable Lightness of Being, The, 145
Verb tense, 33–34, 40–41, 45, 51–57, 219–220
Voice, 49–50, 64
Warmth of Other Suns: The Epic Story of America's Great Migration, The, 127–128
"Watching the Animals," 87
Watching TV with the Red Chinese, 85–86
Welty, Eudora, 18, 20, 104–105, 126, 196, 206–208
West, Jessamyn, 184–185
Whisnant, Luke, 85, 89
Wideman, John Edgar, 118
Wilkerson, Isabel, 127–128
Williams, Terry Tempest, 234, 250
Wisenberg, S.L., 19
Wolfe, Tom, 147, 246
Woolf, Virginia, 17, 155
Word
  basket, exercise, 90, 119
  choice, 7–8, 42–48, 117
  connotation, 94, 117, 241
  count, 7, 9
  denotation, 94, 117
  sound, 8, 46–47, 78–82, 242–243
  sound, exercises, 90, 256–257
Writing
  nonnarrative, plot in, 223–224
  polemical, 86–87
Young Men and Fire, 48
Zami: A New Spelling of My Name, 15–16